Notre Dame's Greatest Coaches

NOTRE DAME'S GREATEST COACHES

ROCKNE, LEAHY, PARSEGHIAN, HOLTZ

Moose Krause
AND
Stephen Singular

POCKET BOOKS
New York London Toronto Sydney Tokyo Singapore

Notre Dame:

To Moose's children, Father Ed, Mary, and Philip

Stephen Singular:

To Reid

POCKET BOOKS, a division of Simon & Schuster Inc.
1230 Avenue of the Americas, New York, NY 10020

Krause, Moose.
Notre Dame's greatest coaches / Moose Krause and Stephen Singular.
p. cm.
Includes index.
ISBN: 0-671-86701-6
1. Football—United States—Coaches—Biography. 2. Univerisity of Notre Dame—Football—History. I. Singular, Stephen. II. Title.
GV939.A1K73 1993
796.332'07'70922—dc20
[B] 93-22904
CIP

First Pocket Books hardcover printing September 1993

10 9 8 7 6 5 4 3 2 1

POCKET and colophon are registered trademarks of
Simon & Schuster Inc.

Printed in the U.S.A.

Table of Contents

Introduction

by
Richard A. Rosenthal
Notre Dame Athletic Director

MOOSE KRAUSE

Edward "Moose" Krause was a massive man. He strode toward me, a young man hopeful of being recruited to play basketball at Notre Dame, and I knew the next few minutes would have a significant bearing on the rest of my life. Moose had a dominant presence, but he immediately made everyone with him feel comfortable. He stuck out his hand and gave the impression that he was genuinely glad to have a chance to visit. A lifetime association confirmed that Moose loved everyone and was interested in their thoughts and plans.

Moose was a gifted athlete, arguably Notre Dame's best. He graduated cum laude with a degree in journalism. He was a significant part of the legend of Notre Dame athletics and was the architect of the athletic program. His counsel was sound and actively sought. Moose made friends easily and converted enemies who just couldn't dislike the Moose. Moose believed the role of the athletic director to be that of a champion for the student-athletes. No group was ever better represented or had a stronger advocate. He related with gifted and average athletes equally well. Moose knew all the players on all the teams. His interest and style would permit nothing less. He was talented, tough and committed; however, he was no pushover. One of the players who got a second chance when he ran afoul of University rules was advised by Moose, "If I were you, I'd keep a bag packed." The player later graduated with honors.

As an athlete, Moose was a player's player, and made all those around him better because of his presence. He exhibited the same traits as coach, athletic administrator, father, and friend. Members of the national press repeatedly asked, "What was the basis for Moose's greatness?" While he had many wonderful qualities, any one of which would have distinguished him, his unfailing goodness was, indeed, the principal reason for his greatness. The Moose was human and capable of error—but he was incapable of malice. He had a bent to look at what was good rather than marred, what was right rather than wrong, what could be rather than what was—and because of his attitude he was a happy man.

Legend has it that Moose won a basketball game with a buzzer-beater. The ball deflected to him after he had been knocked to the floor. While lying flat on his back, he flipped in the winning basket. The team was leaving for South Bend the next morning and a paperboy, standing near the front of the parked team bus, yelled "Morning Star." Moose replied, "Morning, son." Those of us who knew him can easily visualize the scene where Saint Peter says, "Morning, Moose," and Moose replies, "Morning, Bishop." We all hope he recruits us one more time.

All of us are fortunate that Moose and Steve Singular collaborated to write this book. I know you'll enjoy it.

KNUTE ROCKNE

Rockne was the beloved father of the Notre Dame athletic tradition and the rich heritage that evolved. His teams generated not only interest in their sport but also in the small university that dared to play the big names in the game. Rockne teams were the lifeline of hope for an immigrant Catholic population that was buoyed in spirit when this upstart, unheard-of-school could win against the best in the land. If Rock's team could succeed, then so could they carve out a life in their newly adopted home. Rock thrived on activity. As a student he played the flute, had the lead in class plays, wrote for the school newspaper and yearbook, fought as a semi-professional boxer, and worked his way through school as a janitor and chemistry lab assistant. He was a third-team all-American end in football, held the school pole vault record, was a finalist in the marbles tournament, and was graduated with a 90.52 average. He was the consummate innovator and yet taught fundamentals with a passion. He was a colossal personality with incredible force and presence, and a man of complete charm. He motivated his teams with a combination of awe-inspiring enthusiasm, a keen sense of purpose, and total respect for opponents.

In 1929, with the Stock Market crashing and the economy going into a tailspin, he conceived the Notre Dame Stadium. Games were played with a few hundred people standing around the sidelines when Rockne built the 60,000 seat Notre Dame Stadium that we know today. Never mind that Notre Dame only had 3,000 students and that the community had a population of less than 80,000, Rockne's concern was that 60,000 seats wouldn't be nearly big enough and had plans to cantilever the stadium to seat 100,000. Visionary or romantic—or both? He won three national championships and more games than any other Notre Dame coach. He insisted on playing the best, a tradition that endures, and his .881 winning percentage is still, after six decades, football's all-time record, college or pro.

His death on March 31, 1931, was inappropriate. It was a contradiction for a forty-three-year-old man with indefatigable energy. It sent an entire nation into mourning. Of the nation's 1,700 newspapers, 1,600 carried Rockne editorials the week of his death. His players, when informed of his death, huddled in small groups in the chapels on the campus and prayed to celebrate his life, prayed for his family, and prayed for themselves—for theirs was an incredible loss. The coach who led them, who taught them, who cared about their future was gone. Sixty years later, in spite of his death, Rockne lives. "Win one for the Gipper" and a legion of other Rockne stories, some true, some exaggerated, are kept alive generation after generation.

Moose Krause, the consummate father figure, loved Rockne and revered the "Rock" as his own father figure. It's appropriate that he's sharing his Rockne experiences with all of us.

FRANK LEAHY

Moose and Frank Leahy coached together and were contemporaries. While personalities differed, they had a common bond in their love for Notre Dame and a mutual respect for the talents of one another.

Frank Leahy was the most intense of our great coaches—all of them men with an intensity quotient off the chart. He had few diversions and no hobbies. He lived 24 hours a day as a football coach. He was a tough fundamentalist and yet still a student of change. He played for Rockne and, like all of Rock's men, idolized him. He had the audacity to drop the Notre Dame box shift in favor of the T formation and only went 7-2 in his first season. Why change? I mean, after all, it was good enough for the Four Horsemen, wasn't it? In 1943, he won the first of four national championships. Seven teams in 14 seasons were undefeated. His players feared him but in every sense revered him. The national championship teams of the forties still meet every year in plenary session. The coach, "The Master," is remembered in story and in heart. He taught them well the meaning of *team*.

Leahy had team meetings from 12:30 to 1:00 each day but always dedicated five of the thirty minutes to the practice of having a team member get up and address the group. So many of his former players excelled in life after football, and all of them credit the training they received from Coach Leahy as the reason for their success.

Leahy drove himself passionately. He believed in winning and character, and saw virtue in both. The "Coach" spent hours discussing the players with his assistant coaches. He was always concerned with which player might misfire and cause a loss in a tight situation. Leahy respected talent and he revered consistency. He didn't believe in most-valuable-player awards, but did believe in most-valuable-people awards. The coach's job was to get the best out of his players. Leahy was good at his job. He was tolerant of a lack of talent and intolerant of not reaching potential.

Leahy genuinely cared about his players, his coaches, and his associates. Even though he was dying, he returned to South Bend from Oregon to be a pall bearer for Jack McAllister, his much-loved but crusty former equipment manager. Mac worked as equipment manager well into his eighties. A fellow pall bearer at Mac's funeral, John Lattner, remembered how Mac was particularly hard on freshmen. Lattner told of his own first day in the equipment room when Mac was so ornery he almost left Notre Dame. In a rare moment of levity, Leahy remarked, "John Lattner, if that had happened, we would have been having this day many years ago."

ARA PARSEGHIAN

Moose Krause believed, if you can't beat 'em, join 'em. Ara Parseghian's Northwestern teams defeated Notre Dame four straight years, and when Notre Dame was searching for a coach Moose sent only one recommendation to Father Joyce—Ara Parseghian. Ara had many interests, and also the amazing capacity to be totally focused during football season. He believed in exhaustive preparation and was a consummate competitor. Only Rockne recorded more coaching victories. During Ara's 11-year head coaching career at Notre Dame, his teams won 95 games and appeared in five major bowl contests. Four times the bowl opponent was undefeated and ranked number one in the country. Bowl games against Texas in 1971 and Alabama in 1973 are among the most-storied wins in Notre Dame football history. Ara had 44 all-Americans who played for him, including three of Notre Dame's great quarterbacks, John Huarte, Joe Theismann, and Tom Clements. Notre Dame won two national championships under Ara and missed a third by 17 seconds in the last game of the year.

Ara joked about the old gentleman, a Notre Dame fan, who attended an early press conference and shouted, "We're with you, Ara, win or tie." He did sense the incredible pressure associated with being the head football coach at Notre Dame. Ara could communicate with his eyes as well as any person alive. He had a keen sense of humor and a commanding presence. His 11 teams produced 10 medical doctors. Ara had offices in the building of the bank I was associated with, and I can remember one morning we both arrived quite early at the parking garage and were walking together to our offices. The night before we had released a very favorable year-end financial report for the bank. Ara quipped, "Congratulations. You're 1-and-0," and then proceeded to say that in business you file an annual report once a year, but in athletics you publish a report each game.

Moose was Ara's athletic director for 11 years and the two of them had a marvelous working relationship. Even though Ara wasn't a Notre Dame graduate, to Moose he was the epitome of a "Notre Dame Man." Eleven years after Ara left the University, history repeated itself. Moose felt the same way about Lou Holtz—not an alumnus, but every ounce a "Notre Dame Man."

Ara's a Hall of Famer, an accomplished speaker, and a guy who's comfortable with everybody. The South Bend Country Club, where Ara plays golf, has honored only three people (all because they were wonderful human beings), and Ara's among them. Miami (of Ohio) University, his alma mater, most appropriately recognized him with an honorary doctor of humanities degree. Ara retired from coaching with the same grace he displayed for 11 years as "the Coach." He still has a plaque on his business office desk—Ara Parseghian, Coach.

LOU HOLTZ

Lou Holtz is, by the nature of his job, a very public figure, totally devoid of privacy, save for the few moments his family can preserve for him. Nevertheless, he is a man totally at peace. He's a contemplative person who thinks through his actions and is not impulsive with major decisions. No one out-works Lou or, for that matter, out-thinks him.

He is a man of absolute integrity. No one is more concerned or committed to his players. His rules are simple but purposeful: rules should be observed or discarded, rules should help not hinder, rules apply equally to all. Simple concepts for a man of purpose and a man of absolute integrity.

Lou loves life, loves competition, and loves to laugh. He enjoys what he does, works hard at doing it, and, therefore, succeeds at assignments. Rockne would have loved him. Lou will win by the code or, if he should lose, he'll "stand by the road and cheer as the winner goes by."

I let Lou know that Penn State has asked Notre Dame to let them out of their contract to play in 1993 and 1994 so that they could more quickly join the Big Ten. He commented, "The Penn State game is good for intercollegiate athletics. However, I understand their situation. Who can we get to replace them?" Florida State, at the time, was ranked number one in the country. "How would you like to play Florida

State?" I said. There was no hesitation. "That would be terrific." Lou believes it's a privilege to play the best, and looks forward to the opportunity.

Lou and I play a lot of golf together. I have learned the hard way that the only time you ever have Holtz beat is to be ahead when the last hole is completed. I'd love to have the money for the number of times I could have won if only I would have halved the last hole. Lou's approach to the problem is if it takes birdie, that's what it takes. How do I produce the desired results?

On the occasion of one of our rounds, Lou's team won the first hole. We halved 2 and 3, and on 4 (a par 3) I hit my tee shot about four feet from the hole. Lou hit next and backed his tee shot from about a foot behind the hole right into the cup. No one said a word—and Lou complained, "That sucker went into the hole. Isn't anyone going to say anything?" The only comment was "Press."

Lou's a special person. It's a privilege to be associated with him and a blessing to have him as a friend.

1 Meeting Mr. Notre Dame

MOOSE KRAUSE PARKED HALF OF HIS LONG BLUE CADILLAC ON the sidewalk in front of Pat's Colonial Pub just outside South Bend, Indiana. He left the other half in the street. Climbing out of the vehicle slowly and with effort, he had the movements befitting a seventy-nine-year-old man whose body had been blocked, tackled, elbowed, and kicked on football fields and basketball courts all across America. He blew a wall of smoke from his big thick cigar, the cloud ascending into the chilly October evening and thinning as it moved higher. He leaned against the Coupe de Ville, caught his breath, and resumed a story about World War II and being stationed on the Solomon Islands in the South Pacific, where he taught the natives to sing the Notre Dame victory march to his soldiers before they went into combat.

"The men loved it," he said in his low rumbling voice, never removing the cigar. "The natives loved it. Everyone loved it except my commanding officer, P. K. Smith, who I don't mind telling you was the meanest SOB in the United States Marine Corps. He didn't think this was very funny. One night he caught me and the natives singing it and I thought he was gonna court-martial me. He called me into his tent and started to yell at me and I said, 'Wait a minute, sir. My men are going on bombing missions all the time, day and night. They're tired and they're scared. They need to relax and laugh about something.' He just looked at me for a while and didn't say anything. Then he told me to get out of there. He never mentioned it again."

Moose exhaled another patch of smoke and looked at his Caddy. "Rock used to park like this around South Bend," he said, referring to Knute Rockne, the legendary Norwegian football coach at Notre Dame during the 1920s. The university was a few miles northwest of Pat's Pub. "No one told him where to leave his car, and no one will bother me either."

He moved toward the tavern gingerly, in a shuffling motion. His knees had no give. He winced with each step. The year before he'd had a hip-replacement operation, and some years before that he'd had a pacemaker inserted in his chest, after a severe heart attack.

"I walk like a duck," he said.

Despite his physical difficulties and advancing age, one thing was certain: no one would dare tell him where to park the Coupe de Ville with the MOOSE K license plates. By now, he was nearly as mythical a figure on the Notre Dame campus as Rockne himself. In 1930, as a freshman at the school, Moose had played for the Norwegian and heard some of the fiery rhetoric that had made him famous.

After Rockne's death from a plane crash in a Kansas wheat field in 1931, Krause played under Coach Hunk Anderson, becoming an all-American tackle (on offense and defense) his junior and senior years. Three times, from 1932 to 1934, he was an all-American basketball center at Notre Dame, and he became the only Fighting Irish athlete ever inducted into both the college football and the basketball Hall of Fame. Today, in the Museum of Science and Industry wing of the Smithsonian

Institution in Washington, D.C., there are film clips of the greatest sports figures of the 1920s and '30s, featuring Ty Cobb batting, Joe Louis boxing, and a very young Moose Krause dribbling a basketball.

Back then, Moose, at six feet three inches and 230 pounds, with muscular shoulders and thick legs, so dominated play under the basket that many people credit him with bringing about one of the game's current rules, the three-second violation, which states that you can be in the area of the court called "the lane" for only three ticks of the clock or your team must give up the ball. The idea was to keep the biggest players from camping under the goal. Moose explains the rule this way: "They wanted me to get my big butt out of the lane."

He played college baseball and was good enough for the Chicago White Sox to give him a tryout, but he could never come to terms with the major league curveball. On his university track team, Moose earned a letter by throwing the discus and the javelin. His senior year he became the only person in the entire 150-year history of Notre Dame (1842–1992) to be awarded a trophy for his sporting achievements by the student body. After his playing career ended, he coached at the school and was then athletic director for more than thirty years, retiring in 1980.

This October marked his sixty-third year of being connected to Notre Dame.

When Moose awakened now on autumn mornings his calves ached and he needed another massage. In recent years, an unexpected gentleness had come to some of his movements, a delicacy for such a hulking man. There was a gentleness in his manner, too, although his deep voice, heavy eyebrows, and pungent cigar could appear intimidating. Sometimes he surprised you with the things he said about people or the questions he asked about love and marriage, or his statements about getting older or his memories of his wife or his remembering on occasion when a hard-nosed Notre Dame football coach broke down and wept. Moose's blue eyes were large and red and occasionally damp. They looked happy at times and at other times deeply sad, but they always gave the impression of having seen an extraordinary amount of life.

Approaching the side door of the pub on this Thursday evening, he spotted his dinner companions and walked toward them on the asphalt, wrapping his sport coat more tightly around him and discharging another wave of smoke.

"Hey!" he called to the small group near the door.

One man broke away and came toward him.

"Aren't you Johnny Lujack?" Moose said, reaching out his hand and taking the other man's. "Johnny Lujack, the famous Notre Dame quarterback and Heisman Trophy winner? The guy who played for George Halas and the Chicago Bears?"

"No," Lujack said, smiling, "but I wish I was. I'd like to meet him. I hear he was really something."

"Nah." Moose pointed the cigar at him. "I saw him play. He wasn't that good."

The men laughed, eager to see one another again and to have the chance to relive the 1940s, when Lujack was a star at Notre Dame and Moose coached there under Frank Leahy. Whenever two people who were associated with Leahy get together, the talk eventually turns away from their own accomplishments and in the direction of this perfectionist football coach and his remarkable success in South Bend. Leahy's first seven teams won four national championships. From 1946 to 1949 they were undefeated.

Many people believe that the golden age of American sports was in the 1920s, when Rockne was at Notre Dame, Babe Ruth was in the New York Yankees lineup, and Jack Dempsey was the heavyweight champ. Other people, and Fighting Irish fans in particular, can make a good case for the 1940s—when Johnny Lujack was quarterbacking their team, Joe DiMaggio was in center field for the Yankees, and Joe Louis held the title. When people speak of Rockne, a tone of awe usually enters their voice and he remains a distant figure, more spirit than flesh. When they talk of Leahy, who died in Oregon in the early 1970s, he suddenly comes alive, standing on the practice field at Notre Dame and fretting about something, speaking with an Irish brogue and glaring at a player because he has done something inexactly. The young man, regardless of whether he's all-American or third-string scrimmage fodder, will keep doing it until Leahy is satisfied.

Notre Dame is known for its football players, but it could also be known for its storytellers. The oral tradition at the school, the handing down from one generation to the next of what happened in the past and who made it happen through hard work and sacrifice, is every bit as rich and colorful as the effort that has been given on its athletic fields. When Moose and his friends gathered, they recalled not only the different decades of Fighting Irish football, but the seasons in those decades and the games in those seasons and the plays in those games, until what transpired on a Saturday afternoon fifty years ago is as vivid as if it were taking place in front of you today.

As a nation, Ireland is renowned for its writers and poets, its talkers and shapers of tales. Some of that must rub off on those who play football in South Bend, who celebrate their past triumphs or complain bitterly about the bad calls they remember receiving half a century after the flag hit the ground.

In the parking lot, introductions were made and the group announced that they were hungry. Everyone went inside, and as Moose stepped over the threshold, he turned to one of his companions and said, "I want you to keep the old women in here away from me. They're everywhere and they all want a date."

Lujack slapped him on the back and they entered the busy restaurant, which was crammed with Notre Dame banners, photos of the school's former football greats, 1992 gridiron schedules, plaques of the team's eleven national championships, and drawings of its seven Heisman Trophy winners (besides Lujack, Angelo Bertelli, John Lattner, Leon Hart, Paul Hornung, John Huarte, and Tim Brown). Memorabilia covered the walls and hung from the ceiling. The tavern was noisy but stately, the way a shrine should be. Moose had taken only a step or two inside when people recognized him and began to applaud. The house lights flickered and music commenced, loudspeakers pouring forth the Notre Dame fight song, the same one Krause had taught to the Solomon Island natives during the war:

Cheer, cheer for old Notre Dame
Wake up the echoes, cheering her name
Send a volley cheer on high
Shake down the thunder from the sky.
What though the odds be great or small
Old Notre Dame will win over all
While her loyal sons are marching
Onward to victory.

The crowd had stopped eating and drinking. People stood and raised their glasses. They pointed at Moose and Lujack. They clapped and whistled and stamped their feet. They mouthed the lyrics that were played in Moose's honor each time he arrived at the pub. When the music stopped, they rushed forward to say hello or to shake his hand or to brush a shoulder or an elbow. Moose smiled at all of them, nodding and waving, never taking the cigar from his teeth and never breaking his measured stride toward his table in the center of the room. From a certain angle he bore a passing resemblance to Charles de Gaulle strolling among the cheering Parisians after the city was liberated in World War II.

"How are ya, Moose?"

"Fine, I'm fine."

"Good to see ya, Moose."

"Good to see you."

"You look great, Moose."

"Yeah, sure."

"How's the golf game?"

"Ahhhh. Not so good anymore."

"You'll get 'em tomorrow."

He reached the table and sat down across from Lujack, who had also been pumping hands with the diners. Johnny gave everyone the same broad, handsome grin, the look of a born crowd pleaser. After leaving Notre Dame in the late forties, he played pro football with the Chicago Bears (George Halas paid him $20,000 a season) and returned to coach two seasons under Leahy at Notre Dame before retiring from the game and going into the car business in Davenport, Iowa. Lujack is an outgoing man with a powerful build and an explosively happy voice. He tells all of his football stories—and there are scores of them—as if he's recounting them for the first time. When he laughs at the punch lines, people laugh along with him because he is so clearly enjoying himself. He reminds you of the good-looking, highly gifted, and very confident football hero who is the star of your high school—except that he is now almost seventy years old.

Sitting across from him was Creighton Miller, an all-American teammate of Lujack's at Notre Dame who eventually became a lawyer in Cleveland; Yankee owner George Steinbrenner is one of his clients. The quiet, balding Miller didn't strike you as an ex–football player, until you studied the breadth of his shoulders or the thick wrists protruding from his sport coat. He is a bit older than Lujack but creates the impression of someone who is still growing inside his clothes. Miller has a dry, funny way of speaking, and most of his humor is aimed at himself.

"Creighton is very modest," Lujack likes to say, "and he should be."

Miller ordered a round of beers for himself and Lujack but none for Moose and the three men huddled amidst the noise and the memorabilia. They spoke of the history of Notre Dame football and its four most successful eras: the Rockne years, from 1918 to 1930; the Leahy years, from 1941 to 1953, with some time out for the war; the Ara Parseghian years, from 1964 to 1974; and finally, the present coaching reign of Lou Holtz, which began in the fall of 1986. Lujack and Miller were part of the earlier periods, but Moose was one of the few threads left to all of the glory days. He'd practiced with Rockne's varsity squad and coached under Leahy. As athletic director he'd hired Parseghian, and in the mid-eighties, although retired, he'd advised the current athletic administration to make Holtz the head man. By then he'd become the athletic director emeritus at Notre Dame.

"That means," he often told people, "that I still work but I don't get paid for it." It meant that he retained a small office in the athletic department where he went each morning to answer mail or phone calls, to write notes of encouragement to Lou Holtz, or to offer a few words of advice to young athletes. At seventy-nine, he remained very involved.

Moose didn't feel about all of the past coaches at Notre Dame as he did about Rockne, Leahy, Parseghian, and Holtz, but he didn't openly criticize anyone. If pushed, he would simply say of one or two others, "They weren't the epitome of what we call Notre Dame men." This didn't imply that they weren't Notre Dame graduates (Holtz and Parseghian went to college elsewhere) or that they weren't Catholic (Rockne became a Catholic after attending Notre Dame but Parseghian never did). The phrase *Notre Dame men* stood for something beyond religious affiliation and educational background, something mysterious and revealed only over time. It had to do with commitment, intensity, an inner drive that cannot be taught, and a desire not simply to be the best but to be better than you were last year.

Lou Holtz said it for all four coaches in a letter he wrote to his squad before the 1988 season, a year in which they went 12-0 and won the national championship: "I expect to see a perfect football team because that's going to be the criteria we use to evaluate it. A loss is absolutely disastrous."

If you start from the premise that all football coaches are a little crazy in their hunger to win—and to master an untamable sport—then the four Notre Dame coaches whom Moose was proudest of are a little crazier than the rest. Crazy in a good way. Crazy in a funny way. Crazy in a way that their players look back on with fondness long after the grueling practices are finished and the shouting over seemingly petty mistakes has faded. Long after they've sworn that the coach has gone berserk with his repetitive drills and attention to detail, long after the locker room speeches have ended and the players have gone on to have children and even grandchildren of their own.

They've never forgotten what was passed along and driven into them decades ago by their football mentors. As time passes, the memories get warmer. It's a strange thing about ex-footballers. Old baseball and basketball players seem to like one another, but old football players and coaches, after battering each other for years, have feelings for the past that can only be described as love.

The gathering at Pat's Pub watched Moose, Lujack, and Miller eat. They stared, nudged their neighbors, and whispered names. Many of them had traveled long distances to South Bend for a football game and everything that surrounds it. The Fighting Irish were playing Stanford the day after tomorrow, and the crowd was jumpstarting the weekend. They'd come to revel in the history and tradition of Notre Dame football, and at this pub history was sitting over at Moose's table eating ribs or liver and onions. Now and then Krause looked up and acknowledged an admirer, usually a middle-aged man (or older) who was dining with his family. Throughout the meal people drifted over for an autograph or to have their picture taken with the men or to say things like, "I saw you play against Army in 1946. I was there and I remember . . ."

All evening long a gentleman at the bar who looked considerably older than Moose had been drinking by himself, sipping whiskey and taking in everything with wide, pale, misty green eyes. He wore an Ivy League cap and a tweed jacket. His hands were so worn they shone. His face was long and flat. It had a small permanent grin. It looked not simply Irish but like a map of Dublin. He was so perfectly suited for this tavern and this night and, despite the considerable liquor in his veins, he'd acted in such a proper manner that you almost thought he'd been flown in from Ireland to enhance the surroundings. He hadn't. He was a local character, seen on the campus during the football season, when the visitors were thick and the air full of celebration.

Throughout the past hour or so he'd been studying Moose and the others at the table, smiling in their direction. He waited until the drinks had been served and the food ordered, waited until the dinner had been eaten and all the snapshots had been taken, waited until the rest of the crowd had thinned. At last he climbed down from his barstool and walked toward Moose timidly, as if he didn't want to disturb anyone but couldn't stop himself from what he had to do.

"Hello," he said, standing at Krause's side and extending his hand.

Moose took it and the two aging sets of fingers were briefly entwined, locked in a grip. The older man's were white and frail, Moose's dark and huge, the hands of someone who had grown up doing heavy labor. Their eyes met and Moose smiled at the man, the same way he smiled at everyone who took the time to come up to him and speak. They exchanged a few words in private, and then the old fellow turned to go back to his seat.

"I hope I didn't bother you," he said.

"Oh, no," Moose replied. "You didn't."

"I'm sorry but I just had to meet Mr. Notre Dame."

"Thanks," Moose said, releasing another cloud of smoke. "Thanks a lot."

The old man sat down at the bar and ordered another drink, raising his glass toward Krause, who was listening to another story about Frank Leahy. The lights in the tavern flickered and the fight song began again, people coming to their feet and belting out the lyrics, looser now, louder than before, Lujack himself singing and also Miller, and even Moose was tapping the edge of the table and humming along.

2 Laying the Foundation

EDWARD WALTER KRAUCIUNAS, THE SECOND SON OF LITHUANIAN immigrants to America, was born on the south side of Chicago in early February of 1913. His neighborhood was known as the Back of the Yards because it was located just behind the thriving Union Stockyards, which gave this part of the city its character and its fragrance ("With all that slaughtering going on," Moose recalls, "it had a dirty smell"). The odors are long since gone, and all that remains of the Yards, which were chartered in 1866, is a stone arch at what once was their entrance. They've been replaced by plain industrial parks made of asphalt and brick.

The resident population is now mostly Hispanic and black. The land is flat and the streets remain as busy today as they were at the turn of the century, when children hawked newspapers on corners and horses clattered along the pavement on their daily milk runs. Houses are jammed together, with only a shaft of light between them. Locust and elm trees shade the sidewalks and cars fill every parking space. Spanish and English mingle up and down the street while distant train whistles blow throughout the day.

Many things have changed in the neighborhood in the past eighty years, but many other things have not. When Edward was a boy, the local joke was that the Yards had a tavern on every block. That was not quite true but close enough to make the point: it was—and remains—a workingman's part of town, full of poverty or near-poverty, the air thick and tangy in the summer, the place cold as iron in the winter, and at times drinking was the only escape.

Walter and Theresa Krauciunas resided at 4614 S. Paulina Street, a two-story flat with a barren facade and tar-paper siding designed to look like brick. They lived on the top floor and ran a butcher shop below. Dobermans lived with them, to protect the business. The family attended church a few streets away at Holy Cross parish (a new sign painted on one of the dilapidated nearby buildings says, "Don't Give Up. Pray. It Works.") The younger son was baptized at Holy Cross and grew up working in the butcher shop.

Edward and his brother, Phil, who was a year older, played sports in nearby Davis Square Park, and on Friday evenings their mother would walk over to the park and give a long blast on a whistle, sometimes more than one. The boys would reluctantly stop their games and talk about them as they followed her home, where they plucked the chickens, packed the meat, and made the Polish sausage their parents sold on Saturday mornings. No one went to bed until the food was prepared and the boys had cleaned up the bloody leftovers of their handiwork.

Edward's mother dreamed of his becoming a classical musician and started him early on the violin. He liked playing the instrument well enough, but going to and from his teacher's house for lessons was dangerous. On the way he had to walk through three different ethnic neighborhoods and none was Lithuanian. The boys who saw him carrying a violin case jeered him, threw snowballs at his head, and called him a sissie.

"First, the Irish kids would beat me up," Moose says. "Then the Italians took a whack at me. And then the Poles. By the time I got home, I knew how to box."

As a youngster he wasn't particularly big or strong, not until he entered high school and suddenly grew to be six feet tall and weighed 175 pounds. He and Phil attended DeLaSalle Institute, which was three and a half miles from their home and right next to old Comiskey Park. They arose at six A.M., ate breakfast, and jumped a trolley to and from DeLaSalle, a long trip on brisk winter mornings and afternoons. By this time Edward had retired his violin—"I was getting tired of fighting"—and taken up the clarinet, while Phil was attempting to become a concert pianist. They practiced daily and their next-door neighbors not only thought they made a god-awful racket, they weren't hesitant to say so. Both boys had a secret desire to try out for the high school football team, but when they mentioned this to their parents, they were told that something had to give: music or sports.

"The choice we made," says Moose, "made our neighbors real happy."

Their coach at DeLaSalle was Norm Barry, who in the course of one season would lead the Institute to a city title and then coach pro football's Chicago Cardinals to a national championship. Later, he become a Cook County circuit court judge. Like most boys, the Krauciunas brothers originally wanted to play quarterback or running back, so they could handle the ball and make touchdowns, but they quickly realized that everyone else had the same ambition. Their chances of making the team, Phil decided, would be greatly enhanced if they were willing to become linemen and learn the difficult business of blocking and tackling. They did just that, and one afternoon in the late 1920s Coach Barry was teaching his high schoolers to throw a block when he saw a towering young fellow lunge at a much smaller boy and fail to hit him, much less take him off his feet.

"You're as big as a moose," Barry yelled at the culprit, "and you can't even knock that little guy down. Try it again!"

Barry not only gave Edward his lifelong nickname, but when the coach had trouble spelling Krauciunas, he shortened it to Krause. In addition to rechristening the young man, he was teaching him how to play football. Moose was larger than most everyone else, he was naturally strong and getting stronger by working in the stockyards in the summertime, and he had the one ingredient every football player needs: an instinctive love of intense physical contact. You can't talk someone into hitting people hard; a person either enjoys doing it or he doesn't. Moose loved it, and six decades after he stopped playing the game, something about watching ferocious blocking and tackling made him feel so good he laughed out loud.

At DeLaSalle he captained the baseball, football, and basketball teams, earned eleven letters, and won all-state honors in football and basketball. His team, the Meteors, won a city basketball championship and two national Catholic prep basketball titles. Despite his athletic success, his future after graduation appeared set. "You're big, you're strong, and you're gonna work in the stockyards," his father had told him more than once. The young man had never considered doing anything else, but in the spring of Moose's senior year, Coach Barry, who had once played with the legendary George Gipp at Notre Dame, took the youngster to South Bend to meet Knute Rockne. Rock's team had won the national championship the previous year, solidifying his reputation as the premier football coach in America.

Moose describes their introduction this way: "I felt like I was in heaven."

Rockne didn't know if the teenager could play, but he was impressed by his size and willing to listen to Barry's recommendation. He offered Moose a scholarship: in exchange for room, board, and tuition, the freshman would have to work as a waiter in the university dining hall.

"I was so lucky," Krause says, gratitude still in his voice. "So lucky. Without Norm Barry I would have ended up in the stockyards just like so many others I grew up with. I couldn't have gotten out, and none of this would have ever happened to me. My family had no money for anything. This was right in the middle of the Depression, for cripe's sake. My ol' man didn't think I would even graduate from high school. He didn't want me going to college, but when I graduated from Notre Dame, he was so proud of me."

Moose lived in a dormitory, as virtually all Notre Dame students still do today, and played on the offensive and defensive lines on the freshman team, which Rockne also coached. The young man made some "walking-around money," as he put it, by coming up with the idea of passing the hat around the dining hall where he worked as a waiter. "For some reason," he says, "people dropped money into it."

One afternoon at football practice Rockne had the freshmen scrimmaging against the varsity in preparation for the biggest event of the year: the upcoming game with Army. A play was run, and Moose charged through the offensive line and slammed into Frank Carideo, the star Irish quarterback, knocking him out cold.

As Carideo lay on the ground, unmoving, Rockne looked around at the scrubs and said, "Who did that? Who hit my quarterback?"

Moose ran off the field and kept running—through the locker room, across the campus, and all the way back to his dorm room, where he closed the door behind him, sat down on his bed and trembled, waiting to be thrown off the team. He was panicked, wondering how he would ever explain to his father that he'd been dismissed from the squad and had lost his scholarship. Before long, one of Rockne's trainers located the big teenager and said that the coach wanted to speak to him. Reluctantly, Krause walked over to Rock's office, trying to think of something to say but not having any luck. He'd have to quit school and go back to the Yards.

Entering the office meekly, he sat down before the great coach, too frightened to speak.

"Are you the young man that knocked out my quarterback?" Rockne said.

Moose nodded. "Yes, sir."

"That's the way to play this game."

"It is?"

"Yes, it is. I think you're gonna make it at Notre Dame."

Rockne shook his hand and Moose sprinted all the way back to his room, thinking he might be able to find a place for himself at the university after all.

It wasn't his only brush with disaster that first year. On another occasion, the freshman had studied diligently for a biology exam, but when the professor handed back his paper, Moose's grade was 30 out of a possible 100. He'd failed miserably. Moose protested that the teacher had made a mistake, and when that did no good, the strapping young man went to the dean of science, who refused even to discuss the matter or look at his test. Krause unceremoniously picked the man up and was about to hurl him across the room, but then changed his mind and set him down. When the rumpled dean had regained his composure, he announced that Moose's Notre Dame career had just ended and he was to be off the campus in two hours.

Shocked and angered, Moose packed his bags and walked over to Rockne's office to say good-bye and to apologize for deserting the team. Rockne told the young man to take a seat and then, in a straightforward manner and with the command of language that made some of his locker room speeches immortal, he explained that uncontrollable things happen in life, but in spite of that a man had to learn to control his emotions and reactions. This was important in the classroom, on the football field, and everywhere else, and it was absolutely necessary if a man was going to learn how to avoid trouble. When the lecture was over, the coach said he would have a word with the offended dean.

Moose didn't just stay on the campus and with the team. After a closer look, it was discovered that he'd scored a 78 on the biology exam, instead of 30, and made more than a passing grade. The teacher was in error. In the years following his confrontation with the science instructor, many people claimed that Moose had a relaxed disposition and was a calming influence on others, especially on some very high-strung football coaches he'd known. He attributed all of it to Rockne.

"He taught me to manage myself," Krause says, "and I never forgot that. You know, things turned out all right with that professor, too. He apologized and we even got to be friends. I played golf with him in later years. Sometimes I beat him and sometimes he beat me."

Moose, like the other freshmen at Notre Dame, was looking forward to three years of playing for the nation's preeminent football coach, but then everything changed. On a wet, dreary morning in late March of 1931, the Fokker F10 that Rockne and seven other men were flying over the Kansas Flint Hills crashed into a hillside, killing everyone on board. The death of Knute Rockne stunned Moose, the Notre Dame campus, the world of football, and the country itself.

Rockne had done more than win a higher percentage (.881) of his games than any other coach in collegiate history—a record that still stands—and more than lead Notre Dame to championships in three different years. He brought a number of new concepts to football and helped turn a Saturday-afternoon diversion, essentially a game for students, into a thriving national institution.

He insisted that his teams play the best opponents, and his squad traveled all over the United States in that pursuit. They played at Soldier Field in Chicago, at the University of Southern California in Los Angeles—a three-day train ride one-way from South Bend—and at Yankee Stadium in New York City. The Army–Notre Dame contests in the Bronx were not only great athletic theater but also introduced the small school from Indiana to the sporting press in the media capital of the nation.

Like many other famous people of the early twentieth century, Rockne had not just one particular gift but two. His first gift was his obvious ability to coach football, and his second was an intuitive understanding of this new force called the mass media, be it newspapers, magazines, moving pictures, or radio. These were not, he grasped before anyone else in the world of college sports, things to avoid or be frightened of, but outlets that could be used in extraordinarily powerful and self-promoting ways. Rockne sensed that the key to most reporters' hearts was to give them a good interview and a few colorful quotes. He always had a surplus around. He also had instant charm. If the cameras were rolling, he came alive and even went so far as to re-create some of his most inspired halftime talks in front of film crews. The resulting clips introduced him to a vast audience.

He knew that the media produced images that were larger than the reality itself, and many people were drawn to those images and even wanted to become part of them. They wanted to see the Fighting Irish team and its articulate, flamboyant leader, they wanted to attend their games, they wanted to read about them and learn more about the players. He was the first coach to suggest that his team's contests be put on the radio, and they were eventually broadcast nationwide; more and more followers of the game were pulled in. Rockne linked football with America's growing publicity machine and in the process expanded both of them.

By traveling from coast to coast with his team, he helped create thousands upon thousands of football fans and especially Notre Dame fans, whose children and grandchildren still support the university. Some of them are alumni, but far more numerous are the so-called "subway alumni"—a term originally applied to those Fighting Irish rooters who lived in Chicago or New York and may have never even visited South Bend. Over the decades these subway alumni have included Catholics in every state; immigrants who came to America looking for opportunity and felt an allegiance to the underdog team from the Midwest; people who liked Knute Rockne; and those who just enjoyed good football.

Without Rockne, it's hard to imagine the evolution of the college game. He laid the foundation for everything that would unfold over the next sixty years on the Notre Dame gridiron.

A few of his players are still alive. They're in their eighties now but their memories of the coach remain vivid, and when they speak of him, they sound like much younger men. They talk about how he tried to motivate them on one occasion by referring to them as "girls." They tell of an afternoon when things were going badly and he walked into the locker room at halftime and directed a scowl at the assembled team, the players sheepishly sitting in front of him, no one making a sound. "Oh, excuse me," he said, "I thought I was in the Notre Dame locker room. I must be somewhere else." First one player yelled back at him and then another, and then they went out and won the game. The old coach, his players say, was a sports psychologist before the term existed.

"I played for Rock in '27, '28, and '29," says Jack Elder, an Olympic sprinter in the hundred-yard dash and one of the fastest runners in Notre Dame history. "The first year I went out for quarterback, but when they told me I'd never make it, I turned in my uniform. I played football for one of the dormitory teams, and Rock used to scout them on Sundays, looking for anybody he could use. He saw me one day and asked me to come back to the team. I did, and in 1929 I intercepted a pass against Army in the last game of the season and ran it back 100 yards. We won the game and the national championship.

"Some people said Rockne was a saint because he performed at least two miracles every year. He never did much yelling at us but could use some dirty words when he had to. We were playing Northwestern once and we beat them and were getting ready to go home. Their students were still up in the stands looking down at us, and they were giving Rockne the bird. So he stared up at them and said, 'You're like a bunch of damn jackasses! You can't beat us so you fart at us!' Then they really let him have it.

"He was always open to new ideas. A sporting goods company had developed a jersey that was supposed to be suitable for warmer weather. Rock agreed to try them out in Atlanta at the Georgia Tech game. During the first half the jerseys became wet and slippery from perspiration. We couldn't hold on to the ball and kept fumbling. Rockne sent one of the managers out for a supply of molasses, and at halftime he had us apply it to our hands and jerseys and underarms. When we were tackled, we gathered up so much grass, debris, and weeds we looked like scarecrows, but we won the game twenty-six to six. Afterwards Rockne gave orders to return the jerseys to the company. He said, 'No thanks,' and added something unprintable.

"When Rockne was killed, I was a sportswriter for the *Chicago Herald and Examiner*. The day before it happened I talked with him for an hour or two in one of our offices. The saddest experience for me was meeting his remains at the railroad station and accompanying them back to Notre Dame. Few men have etched such positive memories in such a short life. He was only forty-three when he died. We used to call him the 'old man.' It wasn't his years that earned him that title. It was his depth."

John McManmon is an ex–football player who became a landscape architect in charge of beautifying the highways of Massachusetts. "I grew up in Lowell, Massachusetts," he says, "and went to Notre Dame because my mother wrote a letter to the school asking them to accept me. They wrote back asking her to send one hundred dollars and she did. I was in South Bend from 1923 to 1926. I didn't think I'd ever make the football team there because Rockne was way over my head, but I played when the Four Horsemen were in the backfield and the Seven Mules were on the line. I was a tackle, one of the Mules.

"Rockne was very articulate and quick and direct. I think he amazed everybody by this ability because you didn't expect it in a football coach. His best speech was in the Rose Bowl in 1924 against Stanford. He liked to talk about history and told us that we had a chance to make history that day, a chance to prove that we were worthy of being remembered many years later. I'd never heard anyone who could say these things and make you believe them and believe in yourself, but he could. We beat Stanford, twenty-seven to ten. When he passed away, the whole nation felt the loss. He preached and practiced so many good things. Rockne himself never thought he was such a big shot. He never realized the full impact he had and he never talked about it.

"I got to play in those games against Army in Yankee Stadium. Rock would tell us this was the place where we should play the best because Army was our biggest opponent. That game made Notre Dame. Jimmy Walker was the mayor of New York and he'd have a parade for our team through the streets of the city. He made a big show of it and he always got an ovation when he rode along with us. Everybody went to New York for that. Everybody came out and cheered. It was the biggest thing there except for New Year's Eve."

Al Grisanti weighed 155 pounds when he attended Notre Dame. He never earned a university monogram (letter) in football, but he has a good explanation for this. "I played for Rockne in 1930," he says. "I was there when Rockne got his first look at Moose. His eyes lit up. He'd never seen anyone so big who could move that fast and that intelligently. I had to scrimmage against Moose, the big bastard. He was scared to death as a freshman, but I took all the abuse. Everyone wondered why I couldn't get anywhere in football—it was because I had to block Moose Krause."

Says Moose, "Rockne would just look at you and say, 'Go, go, go, go!' When you think back on it now, that sounds kind of corny, doesn't it? Back then it worked. Players were different. People were different. The respect they had was different and the coach was special. When Rockne died, no one could believe he was gone. The news went all over. I was in Chicago and I jumped in the car and came down to the funeral in South Bend. It was the biggest one I ever saw. I cried like a baby. Everybody did."

"I came to Notre Dame and met Rockne outside of Washington Hall," says Nordy Hoffman, who was the sergeant at arms in the United States Senate from 1975 to 1981. "It was like meeting God. I shook hands with him and told him I was from Seattle. He said, 'The pink-faced salmon kid. You out for football?' I said, 'No, sir.' He said, 'With hands like that?' I said, 'I never played in high school.' He said, 'You're comin' out for my team. You'll be good because no one has yet taught you anything wrong.' That was 1927. I made the B squad that year and it was a marvelous experience for a kid who never thought he'd play football at Notre Dame.

"Everyone knows about his win-one-for-the-Gipper speech, but he'd also ask you to win for Our Lady or for the school or for your teammates or just for yourself. He was concerned with much more than winning. We were playing against Penn once and Rock told us that we were representing Notre Dame and should dress appropriately in suits and ties for the trip. Two guys who were starters showed up in sweat clothes, and he refused to let them play. We won that game.

"Rockne held dinners at the end of the season and you got to stand up and criticize him. Most coaches wouldn't have done that. I told him, 'There are three ways to die, and carbolic acid is one of them.' It was meant as a joke about poisoning the coach because he was such a hard taskmaster, but I realize now that it wasn't a nice thing to say. He never let me down. Never. He was a great teacher. Shortly before he died, I went into his office and he said, 'I just talked to your father and he thinks you're a little conceited. I told him that we don't have conceited players here. We knock it out of them.' And believe me, he did.

"There was a drugstore in South Bend and it was right across the street from a beer joint. This was during Prohibition. One night myself and two other players were in there drinking, and when we walked out to catch a streetcar, what did we see but Rockne's car parked at the drugstore. We ducked down low in the streetcar so he couldn't see us and we sneaked away. The next day was a Monday and we normally didn't scrimmage on Monday, but he said, 'Put on your pads, gentlemen,' and we went out there and scrimmaged hard. The same thing the next day and the next and the next. At the end of Thursday's practice, he said, 'Gentlemen, I hope all that beer is out of your system.'

"Rock always had a sense of humor. We went down to play Georgia Tech and they were good. Before the game, he told the team that he was sad and not feeling well. Someone asked him what was wrong. He said, 'I've gotta take it easy because my son Jackie is in the hospital and I'm worried that he might not make it.' So we win and when we get back to South Bend, who's at the train station jumping up and down and cheering like hell? Jackie Rockne.

"A few years ago I was coming out of my office in Washington, D.C., and a woman was standing on the sidewalk in front of me, trying to talk to me. I was so busy and feeling so important that I walked right by her and jumped in a cab and rode away. On the ride I started thinking about the woman and about Rockne and about how this was not what he'd taught me. I realized that I was such a jerk. I told the cabdriver to go back to my office and he did. I found the woman and asked her what she'd been trying to tell me. 'I haven't eaten in a week,' she said. I gave her some money and she promised to repay me. I said she already had."

In 1930, Paul "Bucky" O'Connor played in the renowned Notre Dame backfield with Frank Carideo, Marty Brill, Marchie Schwartz, Moon Mullins, and Joe Savoldi, and he was part of one of Rockne's most innovative coaching moves. O'Connor was normally a swift reserve halfback, but before that year's USC game Rockne came up with a ruse: at the practices held in Tucson, Arizona, prior to the team's going into Los Angeles, Rockne had O'Connor wear the jersey of Dan Hanley, an obscure sophomore fullback, and told him to run at half speed, to fumble the ball a lot, and in general to look nervous and incompetent.

Members of the local press were allowed to watch the practices and wrote that young Hanley would be filling in for the injured Mullins and for the expelled Savoldi, who'd lately been bounced from the team for getting married and then divorced. Another Irish running back, O'Connor, they reported, hadn't even made the trip west. Their stories described how Hanley looked slow afoot and wholly unprepared for a game this big; if Notre Dame were to stay undefeated and win the national title, he would have to hold on to the ball. On game day O'Connor wore his regular jersey—number 25—and when he trotted onto the field, the press wasn't sure who he was. He ran for two touchdowns (a third was called back on a penalty) and the Irish won 27–0. Only later did Rockne reveal his secret strategy. When the Irish got back to Chicago, the city held a parade for them. "You'd think Lindbergh had just flown the Atlantic," O'Connor says.

"The thing I remember most about Rockne," he goes on, "was his considerateness for his players. When I first came to Notre Dame, he asked me what I was planning on studying. I said medicine. When I graduated, he'd already lined up five or six medical schools for me and said I could have my choice. I never knew he was doing it. He'd called a man at Yale and asked them to take me, and that was a great, great thing for me. I went to Yale and became a doctor."

Art McManmon is the younger brother of John McManmon, who had played for Rockne from '23 to '26. Art was a tackle on the '29 and '30 Irish squads and a teammate of Frank Leahy's until Leahy got hurt and had to quit the sport. Because his brother had gone before him, Art felt he had something of "a crib sheet" on Rockne when he arrived in South Bend.

"During my years with him, I could see Rock becoming less of a football coach and more of a complete individual," says Art, who lives in West Newton, Massachusetts. "He was such a student of things. In 1929 he examined every phase of the football uniform in order to reduce its weight, and he lowered it by several pounds. He got shoes that were lighter, which helped Jack Elder outrun everyone. Rock came out with the silk jersey, which was hard for our opponents to hold on to. He tightened the thigh pads so they wouldn't flop when you ran. He had us wear ladies' bloomers under our uniforms so we would stay warm.

"He began the two-platoon system. He would start a game with our second-stringers, and their job was not to let the bastards score. He called them the 'shock troops.' Then he would bring in the first string and when the other team saw them coming onto the field, they'd just look defeated. I'm talking about psychology now. He also let a helluva lot of players play so everyone was ready when someone got hurt.

Games were won by these tactics. He was always researching new things and changing his strategy so you could never predict his next move.

"People talk about the great speeches Rockne made, but to me that was the least important thing he did. As you get older, the hero worship stops and you don't want to talk about it. What I remember about him now is that it was '29 and '30 and you couldn't get a job. Rich people were jumping out of windows, but Notre Dame people were going to graduate schools all over America.

"Rockne was known and liked around the country, and he helped so many kids get scholarships at these other universities. He helped Bucky O'Connor get into med school and he helped my brother get into the Harvard School of Architecture and he helped me get into Harvard Business School. I eventually became the president of the Indian Motorcycle Company, out of Springfield, Massachusetts, once the biggest company of its kind. How do you compare the educational assistance Rockne gave me with a locker room speech?

"One time Rock got phlebitis and had to rest himself. They got an old hearse from downtown and put a loudspeaker on top of it and drove it over to the practice field. He lay in the hearse and looked out the windows and conducted the practices from there, coaching us and correcting everything we did through the loudspeaker. That was in 1929, a year we were undefeated and won the championship, just before his last year at Notre Dame. The day he died, the world died. Nothing bigger happened anywhere that day."

3 A Season of Controversy

IF IT'S HARD TO IMAGINE HOW NOTRE DAME FOOTBALL WOULD have evolved without Knute Rockne, it's even harder to imagine how anyone could take that evolution further than Lou Holtz has done. The current coach in South Bend is the epitome of the various strands that Rockne introduced to college football (Holtz grew up listening to the Fighting Irish games that Rockne had requested be broadcast over the radio). A magnet for publicity, excellent at promoting his team, and a gifted speaker, Holtz has another dimension that goes beyond the Rockne charm.

It may be blasphemy to suggest this on the Notre Dame campus, but he has brought together the old religion of Catholicism with the new one of personal power, and the combination is very potent. In a time when motivational techniques and positive thinking have become the bases for massive American industries, Holtz has used them to create great athletic success and much more. His own story of overcoming the odds and achieving his boyhood dreams perfectly matches his philosophy, and he's the walking embodiment of what can be accomplished by deeply believing in one's self.

If Rockne was the first football coach to become a hero to the general public, Holtz has become a kind of guru of the self-help movement. But that's not to imply that he's done it without a few knocks along the way. During the 1992 season, there were bumps aplenty.

Every fall, at least since Holtz had arrived on the campus in 1986, the Notre Dame football team competed for one thing and one thing only: the national championship. Because the school does not belong to a conference, it cannot win a conference title. Going to a bowl game on New Year's Day, even a major bowl, was something that people around South Bend had come to expect, and unless that bowl gave the Irish a chance to finish number one in the country, it always lost some of its luster. When Moose and former Notre Dame players or coaches got together and reminisced, they talked about a lot of things, but they spoke mostly about their team's championship seasons.

The 1992 campaign started out with great promise for the Irish. Four years earlier, Notre Dame had won its first title under Holtz—they'd nearly repeated as champs the following year—and the feeling on campus in early September of '92 was that the team was ready to triumph again. In its preseason issue, the *Blue & Gold Illustrated (B&GI),* which is subtitled "America's Foremost Authority on Fighting Irish Football," carried a front-page headline that read "Making a run at No. 1." In an interview inside the paper, when Holtz was asked about winning another crown, he said, "We don't even talk about it as a team anymore. We know that's what we want to do. We don't have anyone on this team who has won a national title, but we didn't have anybody in '88 who had won either. The positive is that I think the players, the seniors, don't want to leave here without one."

Long before the opening kickoff of Notre Dame's first game,

against Northwestern, much had been made in the national media about the fact that quarterback Rick Mirer, the Irish's most prominent senior, had decided not to leave South Bend after his junior year and go into the National Football League, where many had felt he would be the number one draft choice. He was staying in school his final year to earn his degree and to help the Irish win their twelfth championship, more than any other Division I university, and he was also expected to be a leading contender for the Heisman Trophy.

With Mirer taking the snaps from center, the Irish were, according to most preseason experts, loaded on offense. They had a first-rate quarterback, two excellent running backs in Jerome Bettis and Reggie Brooks, the number one rated tight end in the country (in several publications) in Irv Smith, and a standout flanker in Lake Dawson. They had big talented guards and tackles and, in Joe Moore, one of the best offensive-line coaches in the nation. On paper, where no human being has ever been blocked or caught a touchdown pass, they looked almost unstoppable.

The defense was another matter. In the past four years, it had allowed 135 points in 1988, 173 in '89, 249 in '90, and 261 in '91. In the '92 preseason issue of *B&GI*, Holtz had also said, "The number one concern and number one commitment we have is to our defense. When Notre Dame has had great defenses, it has had great football teams. For us to be an outstanding football team, defense is where it has to start." The Irish had nine returning starters on defense and some highly talented players on that side of the ball—linebacker Demetrius DuBose, defensive end Devon McDonald, cornerback Tommy Carter, and free safety Jeff Burris, among others—but whether they could reverse the points-against trend of recent seasons was an open question.

The early polls figured Notre Dame to be very good—the Associated Press had them ranked third—but not quite great. Miami and Washington, cowinners of the '91 national title, were ranked ahead of them, and many people felt that Florida State and Michigan were at least the equal of the Irish.

Closer to home, of course, the story was different. Football prophets on the Notre Dame campus were using all kinds of logic and voodoo to put forward the notion that this indeed was The Year. Numbers freaks had stayed up late calculating that the third and seventh seasons of a coach's reign were when the best things happened—Holtz had won his first championship in his third year in South Bend and so had Ara Parseghian—and this was Holtz's seventh year on the job. Looking over the Irish schedule, most everyone agreed that the two toughest games would be against Michigan and Penn State, and if the Irish could win those, they could handle the other teams.

Two other things influenced the mixture of recent history, entangled statistics, and blind hope that characterize all fans' belief that this season their boys will go all the way. The first was that it had been nearly half a decade since the Irish had finished on top, and given Holtz's early success and his remarkable ability to generate enthusiasm, Notre Dame fans were hungry for another title. They simply expected it (and with the obvious potential of the offense, expectations had gone even higher). The second thing was that since 1983 the Miami Hurricanes had won or shared in four national championships. No team had ever captured five titles in a period of ten football seasons—the Irish had won four back in the forties—so if the Canes won again this year, some hallowed records were going to fall. In addition to that, Notre Dame rooters thoroughly disliked Miami and vice versa.

As Notre Dame and the Northwestern Wildcats prepared to tee it up at Chicago's Soldier Field on the fifth of September, in the back of every true Irish fan's mind was the vision of his team playing against and soundly thrashing Miami four months later in the biggest bowl of the season, for still another championship.

Notre Dame fans, as fans everywhere are wont to do, were getting a little ahead of themselves. Early in the second half against Northwestern, a perennial Big Ten doormat, the Wildcats were just twenty-five yards away from tying the score. On four separate drives, Northwestern had moved the ball inside Notre Dame's 30-yard line, but each time the Irish defense shut them out. After they'd stopped the Cats once again in the third period, Rick Mirer threw a 70-yard touchdown pass to sophomore flanker Michael Miller, and Notre Dame quickly followed with three more scores. The Irish ran for 391 yards, and tailback Reggie Brooks announced his arrival as an all-American candidate by gaining 157 of them, including a 72-yard touchdown. Notre Dame won 42–7, yet had opened the season with something between a bang and a whimper, and although no one would admit it afterward, all the players and coaches were glad to have Northwestern behind them so they could prepare for the next week's game against fifth-ranked Michigan.

"I understand Michigan will be getting the film of this game," Holtz said. "I'm really concerned, based upon what Michigan did to our offense last year and with the problems we have on defense."

In 1991, the Wolverines had beaten the Irish 24–14, and Elvis Grbac, the Michigan quarterback, had completed 20 of 22 passes and thrown a TD to Heisman Trophy winner Desmond Howard.

When asked about any injuries his team had incurred against Northwestern, Holtz said, "Only to our pride."

Seven days later, the Irish played the Wolverines in South Bend, and the contest added to what could be only be called a year of controversy at Notre Dame (on the September 1 just past, Demetrius DuBose had been suspended for the first two games of the '92 season for accepting a $600 loan and assorted gifts from Grant Courtney, a 1986 Notre Dame graduate; it was the first time an Irish athlete had ever been penalized by the NCAA). For three quarters Michigan looked superior and the Irish trailed 17–7 going into the final period, but Notre Dame quickly marched 65 yards for a touchdown and evened the score at 17–17 with 5:28 remaining, on a Craig Hentrich field goal. To the amazement of virtually everyone watching the game in person or on television, that is how it ended, the first tie at Notre Dame Stadium since 1969.

"I'm really disappointed because I came in here with high expectations to win a football game," said Michigan head coach Gary Moeller. "In no way did I expect to lose and in no way am I happy with a tie."

"It just doesn't seem," said Holtz, "like the game should be over."

If both coaches were dissatisfied with the outcome, some Irish fans and media observers were downright annoyed with the way things had concluded. With 1:05 left in the game, Notre Dame had gotten the ball on their own 11-yard line with one time-out remaining. Holtz called a running play, which failed to get a first down, and then another run, which did accomplish that goal, but it was nullified because the Irish had not had seven men on the line of scrimmage. After the penalty had been walked off, the clock began moving, and the Irish, for reasons that seemed mysterious, did not use their last time-out. Mirer then threw a long pass to Lake Dawson, but he caught it out of bounds for an incompletion. Holtz now called time-out, and on the next play, the last one of the game, Mirer threw another incomplete pass. As the teams walked off the field, a highly unusual thing happened in the stadium. The Irish were booed.

As Holtz was moving toward the locker room, NBC's John Dockery, a former pro-football player who covers the games from the sidelines, approached him and asked why the coach had been so conservative in his play-calling on the last drive. Why hadn't he come out throwing the ball deep in order to get in position for a long field goal? Why hadn't he called time-out after the penalty? Had he been content to play for a tie?

When Holtz replied that he'd started off with a running play to see what kind of pass defense Michigan was in, so that the Irish could throw the ball later, Dockery didn't find this answer acceptable. He asked the same thing again and the situation became awkward, Holtz realizing that either his judgment or his honesty was being questioned. The two men abruptly parted company, and the standing-room-only crowd, along with a huge national television audience, were left to draw their own conclusions. In subsequent days, Holtz gave a more elaborate analysis of his thinking during the final minute of the game—he was worried about Mirer tossing an interception deep in Irish territory and equally concerned about punting from the field position because the two men who handled the long snaps were injured—but perhaps he'd said it best to some reporters not long after the gun had sounded.

"You've got to take so many things into consideration in about twenty-five seconds," he'd said. "You can second-guess all you want, but it's my job to try to make a decision that gives our players the best chance to win. I'm disappointed we didn't win, but we're not going to just throw the sucker away."

This game was immediately compared to the most famous one in Notre Dame's storied football history, the 10–10 tie against Michigan State in 1966. That year the Irish would go undefeated and Ara Parseghian would win his first national championship. Following the Michigan game, people began saying that if the Irish could get through '92 without a loss, perhaps they, too, could go on and win the title with just one blemish on their record. But other people began saying other things, and some of their comments were not family oriented.

If anyone had ever doubted the scope or the seriousness of Notre Dame football, the tie with Michigan should have obliterated those notions for good. On radio talk shows all across the country, the game and Holtz's strategy were hot topics of conversation. Sportswriters everywhere had fodder for at least a week's worth of columns. Irish fans scribbled angry letters to the *B&GI* attacking the coach, some even asking for him to be relieved of his duties, while other Irish supporters wrote letters in his defense. People debated the issue on South Bend street corners and in Chicago bars. They either disliked the way NBC had covered the postgame or they admired John Dockery's work.

The arguments and questions would not go away. Had Notre Dame, the team so well known for last-minute heroics throughout the years and which on this occasion was even playing at home, suddenly lost its courage? Had its coach contracted cold feet and decided to "settle" for a tie? What was the real story behind Holtz's decision? people wanted to know, but even that query was not penetrating enough. What, the post-Freudian gridiron analysts were beginning to wonder, was buried in his unconscious mind during those last sixty-five seconds? Was he afraid the Irish would lose this game as they'd lost one in a remarkably similar situation against Penn State two years earlier? Was he thinking about the 1966 tie that ultimately resulted in a national title for the Irish? Just exactly what was he thinking?

To explain his logic further, Holtz held a local press conference and even went on CNN, the nationwide Cable News Network, to defend his views. The more he talked, the more he revealed the inside of a football coach's mind, which is a very crowded place to be, at least during the season. Describing a few moments near the end of the game, he said, "Michigan had gone out and double-covered and they seemed to be playing quite deep. If we got the first down, the clock would stop. We gave the ball to Reggie Brooks and spread it out again. Now if they played it exactly the same way again, then we had the outcut route, the comeback route, the sideline route. We had all these things. . . .

"If you drop back and run a deep outcut and they blitz five or six people, you're sacked on the two-yard line. The quarterback gets hit from the blind side and the route isn't open. You can say you're going to throw a short one over the middle, but what if they happen to be in a three-five-three prevent? The ball's tipped like it was against Penn State. So you say, 'We want to win the football game,' but it isn't going to be one of those things where you say, 'If we can't win, then they are.' Or, 'We're going to win or they're going to win and nothing else.' "

After listening to all this, one could only conclude that the many commentators who have said that football is not rocket science haven't been paying attention lately. The depth of analysis that followed the Michigan–Notre Dame tie was usually reserved for the national debt, congressional scandals, and the behavior of Madonna. When things quieted down, each team still had 17 points.

* * *

In the third week of the season, at East Lansing, Michigan, the Irish ducked controversy by scoring 21 points in the first quarter against Michigan State and building up a 38–10 half-time lead. Notre Dame scored on its first six possessions, including touchdowns on the initial four drives. Rick Mirer threw for three touchdowns and tied Joe Theismann for the all-time Irish record of TD passes in a career, at 31. The final score was 52–31, and while Holtz was pleased with the outcome, he did not like the fact that his defense had allowed a trio of Spartan touchdowns after Notre Dame had gone ahead 52–10.

"This was," he said with some exasperation, "the longest game I think I've ever been involved in."

The next game, although it was played at home in a downpour, wasn't nearly so long. The Irish fought to a 13–0 half-time lead against Purdue, then quickly scored 35 second-half points behind the running of Reggie Brooks, who had 205 yards on 15 carries for only the eighth 200-yard rushing performance in Notre Dame history. Brooks, a senior tailback, also had touchdown runs of 20, 63, and 80 yards. His first three years in South Bend had been undistinguished, and when asked about this after the game, he said, "Coach Holtz always tells us never to doubt ourselves, and I took it to heart. I never got discouraged. I just kept after it, and my teammates have always believed in me. When I was moved to cornerback in 1990, I knew that tailback was my best position, but I never thought I would have a game like this."

For his part Holtz not only praised the offense but also the defense, which had delivered its first shutout of the season in the 48–0 victory.

"We had a little visit with the defense on Thursday and last night," he said, "and they responded today. They were either going to respond or they were going to murder me."

4 Holtz Disappears, Returns Even Stronger

THE FIRST FOUR GAMES OF THE SEASON WERE A MERE PRELUDE for the drama to come. Everything that had been building in the early weeks of the campaign—the expectations of this team, the minor controversies, the hanging questions about how good they really were—came to a point on Saturday, October 3, when Stanford traveled to South Bend to play the Irish. It was almost as if the whole three-day weekend were staged to reveal just how high a campus can get over an athletic event, just how low it can fall, and just how quickly all this happens.

Football weekends at Notre Dame really commence on Friday although some people arrive on Tuesday or Wednesday or Thursday, unpack their RVs in the parking lot next to the stadium, and let the tailgating begin. Several of the vehicles fly the flag of Ireland and blare folk songs from the mother country. By Friday it's impossible to get a seat on a flight from Chicago to South Bend, impossible to find a room at the Morris Inn, the only hotel on the campus, and if it's Parents' Weekend, as it was for the 1992 Stanford game, it's already becoming difficult to walk across the Notre Dame lawn.

Fans travel to South Bend from every state in the union, and almost all of them wear something holding the Fighting Irish logo—caps, sweaters, shirts, pants, jackets, socks, everything. The clothes indicate whether one is a NOTRE DAME ALUM, a NOTRE DAME STUDENT, or a NOTRE DAME MOM. The most eerie thing seen on campus is a Lou Holtz mask, with cutouts for the eyes and mouth. Eighty-one thousand of these have been sold, the proceeds from which go to a local charity for the mentally ill, and it's downright alarming to see twenty or thirty Holtzes coming at you from every direction, each one of them flashing his big frozen grin.

After seeing the mask for the first time, Holtz said, "Buy it and throw it away. They need the money."

On the Friday morning of a game weekend Moose Krause received visitors at his office or arranged for tickets for his guests. He had a private booth up above the stadium press box, where he watched football with a few close acquaintances or family members. Spike Sullivan, an aging oilman from Oklahoma, had flown in to see Krause and to watch Notre Dame play the Stanford Cardinal (named after the color, not the bird). Buddy Romano, a friend from Chicago, had also arrived in South Bend and would sit with Moose tomorrow afternoon. Several priests would be in the booth as well, and throughout the weekend people would prepare food and give it to Moose before the kickoff: turkey sandwiches, Polish sausage, cut-up vegetables, plates of assorted cookies and other desserts, potato chips and soft drinks. No one would go hungry.

The Notre Dame Quarterback Club luncheon is held at Friday noon before each home game. The luncheon began in

1971, when Ara Parseghian was coach and a handful of fans—twenty-five to thirty men—desired to meet with him on Monday to ask questions about the previous Saturday's game and watch films on the contest. The gathering was intimate and held in the Monogram Room of the Joyce Athletic and Convocation Center on the campus.

Since Holtz's arrival, the club has outgrown its initial meeting place and expanded beyond anyone's imagination. It now has 1,100 card-carrying members, who bring along guests, so the regularly sold-out affairs seat more than 2,500 people, at $11 a head. The event was moved to the concourse area and then to the fieldhouse of the Joyce Center and filled it to the far corners (300 more fans sit behind this and watch the proceedings from the bleachers that surround the hockey rink). Drinks are served at the bar, and you can buy a raffle ticket for a football autographed by Notre Dame's seven Heisman Trophy winners. The walls are hung with blue-and-gold banners of the various Notre Dame alumni clubs around the country. It takes two hundred people to prepare and serve the lunch.

Moose sat in front of the audience, up on the dais with Coach Holtz, athletic director Dick Rosenthal, two players who would give brief talks—junior nose tackle Jim Flanigan and Reggie Brooks—and the week's featured speaker. In days past Moose himself might have stood and delivered a few words, but now he was largely a quiet presence, a reminder of everything that had been accomplished on the athletic fields at Notre Dame and of the spirit behind those achievements. People in the crowd looked up at him and nodded, spoke his name, talked of when they had first met him, and traded a few Moose Krause stories.

When he used to make speeches—he was much in demand as the Irish athletic director—he had a remarkable ability to tell the same jokes over and over again and get a laugh.

"His sense of humor has a lot to do with his good timing," said Joe O'Brien, Notre Dame's senior associate athletic director, who was sitting at a table near the front. "After a few years, people had heard his jokes so often they began giving them numbers. Someone would call out from the audience, 'How about sixteen, Moose? You haven't told us that one yet.' He'd tell it and we'd laugh again."

At the table with O'Brien were two priests from the East Coast, visitors from other parts of the nation, and Beth Holtz, the coach's wife. The luncheon is a friendly gathering, but the previous Friday the club had held its first meeting since the Michigan tie. At the opening of that affair, Holtz had asked his wife to stand at her table, so the crowd would be aware of where she was sitting before they said something terrible about her husband. It was sort of funny.

The meal—green salad, baked chicken, and diced potatoes—was served quickly, and while knives and forks were still in the air, the Notre Dame glee club gave an excellent a cappella rendition of several college fight songs, including the home team's and Stanford's. Coffee was poured, cookies were passed around, and then the guests pushed themselves back from the tables, looked up toward the dais, and the speeches began.

At Notre Dame it's not enough to make good tackles and dodge enemy linebackers. You also have to be able to stand up and entertain a couple thousand strangers right after you've finished eating. Jim Flanigan's talk was relatively smooth, but Reggie Brooks initially looked as if he would rather go hungry and run without blockers than endure this kind of high-pressure performance. After overcoming his nervousness he steadied himself, took a deep breath or two, and gave a good brisk talk, returning to his seat and looking greatly relieved. George Kelly, the special assistant to the athletic director, was this week's featured speaker. He was also brief and enthusiastic.

People enjoyed hearing from all of these men, but it was clear that this weekend, as every weekend, the draw at the luncheon was Lou Holtz. Knute Rockne had once been paid to deliver speeches to Studebaker executives, and Holtz is now given large sums of money to give motivational talks to a variety of audiences all over the country, and Quarterback Club members have been known to remark that they can't believe they get to hear him half a dozen times each autumn at $11 a shot.

"I can't believe it either," says Holtz.

As her husband stood behind the podium, Beth Holtz looked up at him and beamed. Like everyone else present, she seemed anxious to hear what he would say. A few minutes earlier she'd told a luncheon companion that in spite of Holtz's intensity on fall Saturday afternoons, at practices, in his office, and when he speaks to groups, he's calm at home. "He doesn't have it there so much," she said, and anyone who had ever watched Holtz coach football knew what "it" she was referring to.

"It" was the thing that gave him a look of total focus and concentration in the hours leading up to a game. "It" was what caused him to pace the sidelines constantly. "It" was what had once made the frail youngster with the skinny arms, the big glasses, and the slight speech impediment want to play football against much larger and stronger boys. "It" was what had propelled Holtz from a small town in West Virginia to coaching the New York Jets in the National Football League to leading the football program at Notre Dame. No one knew exactly what "it" was, but everyone close to the man knew that Holtz had a lot of it.

He thanked the audience for coming, waved to those sitting over by the hockey rink—they cheered—and began talking about the value of teaching people discipline and teamwork. He still has traces of a speech disorder, which slurs some of his words and causes them to slide together. As he addressed the audience, warming to the task, a most curious thing happened. The slight, unassuming-looking man who only moments before had walked to the podium suddenly disappeared and someone else stepped forward, a different Lou Holtz or a Lou Holtz distilled to his essence, his fire. The words poured out of him, growing louder and faster and more forceful, as if they were coming not only from his mouth but from some hidden source.

He spoke of watching a very late TV show a few nights earlier while preparing for the upcoming game. It was a true story, he said, about a rough group of convicts who were assembled into a football team in prison and matched up against other inmates on the field. The cons had initially hated practicing and considerably resisted those who were trying to coach them, but by the end of the season they'd learned to make sacrifices together, to work as a unit and to respect each other. The show had moved Holtz deeply and his voice trembled as he described it from the podium, leaning closer into the microphone and nearly shouting the words.

To compare a football game to life itself is something that one could easily make fun of, but no one in the audience was chuckling. There was nothing maudlin or sentimental in Holtz's manner—just the belief that if you don't set boundaries and goals and demand something from people in return for giving them attention and resources, they will never be able to find and hold on to their self-esteem.

"Never be afraid to tell people you love them," he said. "Children need to hear this and adults need to hear it and everyone needs to hear it, much more than we realize. Families need this now. Don't ever be afraid to say it to those around you, and don't ever be afraid to cry. We need to connect with each other and tell each other that we care."

It was not exactly like hearing about his strategy to stop Stanford's passing game, and it made you wonder how deeply the boos following the Michigan game had affected him.

His words visibly touched a number of listeners. People had stopped eating to watch him. They'd set down their coffee cups and forks. They'd leaned forward in their chairs. They had the look of those who were in the presence of something powerful but dimly understood. Even his wife was studying him as if she'd never seen him before. Holtz's body had slipped away entirely and his words had taken over, carrying you along with them, into a place that was surprisingly emotional.

Listening to him, you were struck by many things, but mostly by the realization that few people in American public life speak with such force and conviction. We don't expect our politicians to say much because they're afraid of offending someone or appearing vulnerable. The coach up on the podium seemed to be drawing his strength from the very fact that he was vulnerable—to criticism, to his own feelings, and to the feelings of others.

By talking about love, he'd done a strange and unexpected thing. He'd made it sound as if there were many possible answers to highly complicated social problems, and he'd made you feel that you wanted to be part of the solution. Some of the excitement he generated came from the feeling that no one, including perhaps Holtz himself, knew what he was going to say next or where the words had come from. They'd just flowed out of him. He'd said what he felt and said it without apology. Those who believe that leadership qualities are built upon a handsome face, a good physique, and a smooth way of speaking haven't encountered Lou Holtz.

His speech concluded, the coach said that he hoped all of the Stanford visitors attending the luncheon would have a wonderful time this weekend "except for three hours on Saturday afternoon." Then he answered a few questions from the audience, as he does at every Quarterback Club meeting, which gives him a chance to indulge his bent for one-liners. Before the meal had been served, he'd asked people to jot down their inquiries and pass them along to him. While the other men had been making their speeches, he'd done what he always does in such circumstances, sitting with his head down and a pen and scrap of paper in his lap, writing out his thoughts, preparing to respond to the inquiries.

One man wanted to know what Notre Dame's strategy would be against Stanford. Holtz passed over this lightly—no coach would reveal his game plan at lunch in front of the enemy's fans! Another man wondered why he didn't put the Irish players' names on the backs of their uniforms so you could tell who was who on the field. Holtz said he'd think about that, but it was obvious that he wouldn't think long. A woman asked what he was always looking for during a game when he knelt on the sidelines and stared intently into the grass or AstroTurf, depending on where the Fighting Irish were playing that day.

"A hole to crawl into," he said.

Pep rallies start at seven P.M. sharp on Friday evenings and are held in the basketball arena next to the athletic center concourse. Moose no longer attends them, at least physically, but at times his name is invoked. The rally before the Stanford contest was standing room only, and many of those in attendance—about twelve thousand people showed up, which is two thousand more than attend the university—had on their Lou masks.

All Notre Dame games are big, but this one had some added spice. It was Parents' Weekend and it was the first battle against a quality team since the Michigan tie. How would the Irish respond to this challenge? They were undefeated and still had a shot at the national championship, although one now had to have a slide rule to figure out how they could capture the title: If Florida State could beat Miami in their game tomorrow and if Washington were to lose and if undefeated Alabama and Texas A&M were to trip and if someone could knock off Florida State after they took care of Miami and if Michigan were dominated by a Big Ten opponent and if Notre Dame could win the remainder of its games . . . going into the fifth weekend of the season, there was plenty of hope left.

Stanford's head man, Bill Walsh, was making his initial visit to South Bend to coach against Lou Holtz. The year before, Walsh had been an analyst for the Notre Dame games on NBC television and had studied the Irish in depth. Ever since winning his first Super Bowl with the San Francisco 49ers in 1982, and then two more ('85 and '89), Walsh had been tagged a football genius. How would a genius, especially one who'd had all those months to prepare for his opponent, do against a mere mortal such as Holtz?

Well before the pep rally started, the Fighting Irish marching band had come into formation on another part of the campus and begun to step lively toward the arena. On the way the drummers pounded out a heavy, insistent beat—pounded it out again and again—and people who were walking to the rally tended to march in rhythm with the band, whether they wanted to or not. Reaching the arena, the band filed inside and stood at one end of the basketball floor, where it charged headlong into the first of many offerings of the Notre Dame victory march, horns pointed straight at the ceiling and blaring. The crowd rose as if hit by an electric shock and sang with gusto, applauding throughout, thousands upon thousands of hands coming together and echoing around the arena (the song, once planted in your head, seems to have a life of its own and keeps going long after the band stops).

The pom-pom squad performed first and, behind some very heavy rap music, danced itself right into the floor. Band members, mostly the saxophone section, jived along with them, as if they were trying out for the old James Brown Revue. The cheerleaders entered, and to another frenetically loud beat, the males tossed the females into the air like so many autumn leaves, catching them with nonchalance. The leprechaun mascot—a short, red-bearded young man dressed in green knickers, a green vest, a green hat and dark shoes—ran over to the microphone, grabbed it, and said, "All right now! I want all of you to give it up! I want you to give it up big time! I want you to give one hundred and eighty-seven percent tonight and tomorrow afternoon for the best football team in America. I want you to give it and I want you to give it up now!"

The band hit the victory march again, and the football team, which had been stacked in one of the entryways, strolled out onto the basketball court, sitting down on rows of chairs that faced one side of the audience. At the sight of them, the crowd gave it up, pretty much all of it, jamming the aisles and the walls and the metal rafters with wave after wave of noise, shaking the seats and vibrating the floor, the whole arena reverberating with unleashed energy. Cheerleaders flipped over, pom-poms flew, the house shook, and Lou Holtz sat quietly in his seat, crossed his legs, and dropped his head, as if he were in church. He took out a pen and paper, and while madness reigned around him, he made a few notes on whatever was passing through his mind.

When the cacophony had ebbed, the leprechaun introduced one of the players, who muttered a short speech about whipping Stanford, and then the leprechaun presented John MacLeod, the Notre Dame basketball coach, who also talked briefly about tomorrow's game. Another recorded rap song came on full blast, and the cheerleaders loosened their joints to it, every single joint in their bodies. The crooner, a young woman named M. C. Luscious, cried out, "Boom! I got your boyfriend! Boom! I got your man!" She sang the lyrics as if she meant them, and for a while it seemed that everyone had stumbled into an MTV party, but then the leprechaun restored order by asking the crowd to give it up one last time and give it up for good—"for our head coach, Lou Holtz!"

His speech this evening was neither as long nor as intense as the one at the luncheon; he seemed to be focused on the looming contest. He silently wondered, as he always did on Friday evenings before a game, if his team was prepared or overprepared or underprepared. Because his players, along with all the other students at Notre Dame, had been taking their midterm exams this past week, he wondered if the Irish were tired or overwhelmed or unfocused regarding football.

As Holtz stood amidst the screaming throng, he looked smaller than usual, skinnier. He looked isolated, cut off from the festivities and the celebrating, alone with the responsibility of carrying on the winning tradition at Notre Dame. He was not the first man in his position to feel this way, just the most recent. Everyone who had held the job since Rockne, and Rock himself, had known what it was like to have the expectations of hundreds of thousands, perhaps millions, of fans around the nation be a condition of your employment. When Holtz spoke in public, he tended to use a lot of humor, and much of it was directed at himself. After watching him for a while, you sensed that it was a way of protecting himself from all those expectations and of defusing things that could be painful.

When he was finished, the band played the alma mater and the players and coaches put their arms around each other, swaying to the music, producing a hypnotic, powerful effect. Men and women in the audience did the same thing, holding hands and singing along, dabbing at their eyes.

When the band shifted into the victory march one more time, the pom-poms sailed and the event was quickly over, the Irish team walking off the floor and heading to a quiet, spacious room where they would have a prolonged relaxation session, as they always did after the rallies. Then, without their head coach accompanying them, they would ride in buses to a motel in the nearby town of Plymouth, where they could be alone before the game. As they left the basketball floor this evening, neither Holtz nor anyone on the team knew that it would be the last Friday night of this year that they would perform exactly this routine.

Although they were gone, the great crowd lingered in the arena, reluctant to go, still wanting more—more speeches and more dancing and more of the leprechaun—always wanting more from the coach and the players and the school itself. The fans stood and looked at each other or stared down at the floor where the team had just been, leaning toward it in the hope that the event was not yet over. But there would be more tomorrow, plenty more, starting at dawn.

5 Leaving South Bend

BY 1992, MOOSE HAD NOT SPENT SIXTY-TWO UNINTERRUPTED years at Notre Dame. He'd ventured away from the school for a while, but in time he would return to stay, becoming not just a long-term employee of the university but a fixture, a piece of the institution itself. And over the years, the teenager who had once been in awe meeting Knute Rockne would begin to make other young men feel something similar when they met him.

Following Rockne's death, Moose played the next three years at Notre Dame under head coach Heartley "Hunk" Anderson. The early thirties is not the most celebrated athletic period in Fighting Irish history, and Moose, as a defensive and offensive lineman, did not play the most glamorous positions, but he was good enough at executing the trench work of football—blocking and tackling—to be named an all-American his last two seasons.

As one of his coaches put it, "He didn't know the name of everything we were trying to do, but he knew how to do it." His headgear was a flimsy leather helmet with no facemask of any kind, and he wore, by today's standards, minuscule shoulder pads. The hip pads weren't much either. In those days, players were on the field for both offense and defense, and in 1993 Moore played 521 out of a possible 540 minutes. He chose jersey number 69 and for a good reason.

"If I got knocked upside down," he explains, "my number was still the same so people would know it was me."

He broke his nose more than once but never told anyone during a game.

"I was afraid to," he says, "because I thought they'd take me out."

In 1934 he played in the first All-Star game at Chicago's Soldier Field: a group of college all-Americans took on the great Chicago Bears, led by Red Grange and Bronko Nagurski. Moose, who was the captain of his team, broke his jaw on the first down from scrimmage but played fifty-six minutes of the game, which ended in a scoreless tie. After the final gun, he was rushed to a hospital, where he spent the night recuperating and sipping scotch through a straw.

"I tackled Red Grange once, but Nagurski kept running over me," he recalls. "I'd never seen anyone that strong. Everybody was afraid of him, even his own teammates. The guy playing across from me was George Musso, a two-hundred-and-fifty pound lineman, big and tough and mean. After a while he started telling me when Bronko was coming through. 'What do you want me to do about it?' I asked him. 'I don't know,' he said, 'but I'm gettin' the hell out of his way.' "

Although Moose was a two-time all-American football player, many people believe that his best sport was basketball. He set various records for scoring (they've all been broken), and his height and muscle allowed him to overwhelm most of his opponents. He was difficult to move and not averse to using an elbow or his rear end to open up more space. "Most of the basketball players back then were skinny," he says. "After playing football, this game wasn't so hard."

In three years at Notre Dame he scored 547 points, led the Irish to a record of 54 wins and 12 losses, and was voted an all-American center in each of those seasons. His most spectacular moment came at the end of a game against Butler, when he was lying flat on his back but managed to fling a last-second shot toward the goal. It went in, the Irish won the game, and the victory became part of his legend and helped him become the first and only Notre Dame basketball player inducted into the college and pro Hall of Fame in Springfield, Massachusetts.

In 1934 he graduated with a cum laude degree in journalism. Pro basketball was not yet a highly organized sport so that wasn't a career option, but George Halas of the Chicago Bears offered Moose a job at $425 a game. Krause considered it but had been advised by people at Notre Dame and beyond the university that pro football was for roughnecks, a life of hard drinking, carousing, and brute physical combat; the chances of getting seriously hurt were good.

He still enjoyed the game but decided to accept an offer from St. Mary's College in Winona, Minnesota, where he became head of the journalism and physical education departments, served as athletic director, and coached the baseball, basketball, track, golf, tennis, and football teams. He was paid $2,500 a year, plus room, board, and free laundry services. In his spare time he wrote a sports column and hosted a radio show.

"I also drove the school bus," he says.

In his rookie year at St. Mary's, a school of three hundred students, only fourteen young men came out for the football team. The biggest one weighed 150 pounds, which was 80 pounds less than the coach. Moose was afraid of hurting them while demonstrating the art of blocking so he backed off a little, which went against his nature. When giving pep talks on the glories of the college gridiron, he tried to remember the speeches he'd heard from Rockne and attempted to imitate his golden-tongued mentor. His rhetoric wasn't as good as Rock's and neither were his teams, which were regularly trounced. Moose had more success at basketball, and one year his squad won a conference championship.

At St. Mary's he put together a semipro basketball team, a

sideline that would boost his income for years to come. With several players he'd found in the local talent pool, he began to moonlight, joining a floating roundball game, a whistle-stop league. On weekends he took the train to play against teams in Sheboygan, Kalamazoo, Oshkosh, and other towns in the upper Midwest. He made $35 a night and shared 40 percent of the gate with his team members. One opponent was the Duffy Florals, named for a Chicago politician. Another was the Harlem Globetrotters, who were owned by Abe Saperstein. Moose competed against the Trotters not just for show, as with the later Saperstein teams, but to win, and sometimes he did.

"The first game we had with the Globetrotters was in Winona," he says. "We filled up the high school gym. Abe was guaranteed either seventy-five dollars or fifty percent of the gate. The people who were running the game tried to give me two dollars for every dollar they gave him. I told them, 'The hell with that. That isn't right.' They said, 'He won't know the difference.' I made them give Abe fifty percent. He made money and I made money. Years later he told me that he'd been listening at the door that night as we were discussing his percentage. Ever since then we were friends. In 1942, I asked him to come to Notre Dame and play a benefit and he did. He never took a penny for it.

"I got to know the Globetrotters like my brothers. We played against them in Sioux Falls, South Dakota, and in Wisconsin and Michigan and North Dakota. They couldn't sleep in the hotels in these places and had to sleep in their cars. Sometimes we snuck them into our rooms after the games and they were able to sleep there."

In 1935, Moose and his brother, Phil, who was very competitive in several sports, took a group of basketball players to Lithuania. The Krauses had been invited to introduce the game to their parents' homeland and to create a local team for the 1936 Olympics. Both men played on that Olympic squad, and Phil stayed on in the country for several years, coaching the native population and touring Europe with a team until the beginning of World War II. Returning to Chicago, he was married and became a police detective, but his younger brother always maintained that the best athlete in the family was Phil.

By the mid-thirties Moose's parents had closed the butcher shop and opened a grocery store near their home. Walter Krauciunas, who arose every morning at five A.M. and went straight to work, usually took his Dobermans along with him for protection. One morning he went alone, and a few minutes after he unlocked the front door a burglar came in and robbed him at gunpoint. The man shot Walter to death and escaped into the Back of the Yards, never to be caught.

"My ol' man was gone," Moose says, sadness and disbelief in his voice fifty-seven years after the event. "Gone forever. Just like that. They couldn't find the SOB who did it so we never really knew what happened."

In 1934, while Moose was still at Notre Dame, a friend came to him and asked if he could find two hundred young men to attend a sorority convention party that was taking place on the campus. The party featured free food, free drinks, and the opportunity to dance with two hundred young ladies. Moose quickly rounded up the men.

"The hard part," he says, "was getting them all to wear neckties."

At the dance he met Elizabeth Linden, a young woman who'd grown up forty blocks south of his own Chicago neighborhood in a German section of town. She was blond and pretty, with an exceptional smile, and everyone called her Elise. Things started slowly.

"I was trying to get dates with her," Moose says, "but she was engaged to some Irishman. As time went on, Elise went out with me and the other guy went away."

The courtship lasted four years. They were married August 29, 1938, at Chicago's Little Flower Catholic church and then lived at St. Mary's, where Moose was still coaching. In 1939 he was offered a job at Holy Cross College in Worcester, Massachusetts, so he and Elise soon moved east. His new salary was $3,300 and his duties included coaching the linemen on the football team and attempting to revive the school's basketball program. For the next three years he did exactly that, building a respectable team and promoting the game wherever he went. "No one," wrote one of the local columnists in the early forties, "has done as much lately for basketball in New England as Moose Krause."

In Worcester in September of 1940, Elise gave birth to their first child, Edward, Jr. Moose was a father now, taking on more and more responsibilities, and he began thinking of ways to hike his income. Could he hook on with one of the local semipro basketball outfits? The game was already big in the East and getting bigger. There was talk of establishing a regular pro league, but it remained just talk.

Before the National Basketball Association came into being in the midforties, a collection of semipro teams emerged up and down the East Coast, barnstorming from city to city and state to state. Moose made contact with most of them. At one time or another, he played for the Saratoga (N.Y.) Indians, the Pittsfield (Mass.) Golden Bears, the Worcester Narcus Brothers Stationers, the Worcester All-Stars—featuring Solly Nechtem, Earl Brown, Snooks Gallagher, Soup Campbell, and Moose Krause—the Boston Good-Wins, and the New York Celtics.

Moose played against the New York Renaissance, the Brooklyn Americans, the Akron Firestones, the Brooklyn Half-Moons, the New York Giants, the West End House, and the Harlem Yankees. One year the Yankees voted Krause their "best white opponent."

He played in Boston's Mechanics Hall, in the Boston Garden, and in Madison Square Garden in New York. Sometimes he made $50 a game, other times $100 for an evening's work. New England newspapers of that era report that he was usually his team's leading scorer and most colorful figure. Everyone liked reading about a huge fellow named Moose, and he always had a story to tell.

"During one stretch in Boston I was playing against a team that had a great player named Sullivan," he says. "The owner of my team said he'd bump my pay up to two hundred dollars a game whenever we beat Sullivan. I never lost after that. One night I played against a prison team in Kingston, New York. At the opening tip-off I got into the jump-ball circle with an Irish murderer. Nice-lookin' guy with a scary face. The referee threw the ball up, this guy hits me in the mouth with his elbow, and I hit him back. A fight breaks out and all the convicts are tryin' to jump us. They hustled my team out of there and we never went back."

At various times, his teammates included Phil Cavaretta, then a first baseman-outfielder with the Chicago Cubs, and Jim Hegan, who had a major league career with the Cleveland Indians. "They were damn good basketball players," Moose says.

He either traveled alone or Elise drove him from one city to the next, Moose curled up in the backseat taking a nap and little Edward in the front seat with his mother. She drove him to Vermont, Maine, New Hampshire, or anywhere he could find a game. On one occasion Krause was in such demand that he agreed to play the first half of a game for the Narcus Brothers of Worcester and the second half for the Boston Good-Wins. Each side paid him $200 and the Good-Wins won.

Over the decades he forgot the names of most of his opponents but not all of them. "I remember this one team from New York, the Renaissance," he says. "They had a guy named Tarzan Cooper. Big and mean. A real gorilla. That SOB punched me and we got into a fight and rolled around and around on the court and were choking each other. I still got the scratches to prove I was there. They didn't blow the whistle a lot back then. I could push most guys around but not Tarzan. He clobbered me."

Red Smith, a Notre Dame alumus who was widely regarded as the greatest sports columnist ever and ended his career with the *New York Times*, was always said to have a peculiar blind spot when it came to basketball: he just didn't like the game. Moose knew the man personally and can confirm his prejudice.

"Red was a friend of mine," he says. "He saw me playing

basketball in Madison Square Garden once and he wrote, 'I watched the game and all I saw was this big guy knockin' everyone around.' He told me that he'd never seen a game before and never wanted to see one again. A few years later when I was back at Notre Dame, I told him, 'Come out and watch another game.' 'Hell, no,' he said. It just wasn't for him. Red was a drinking buddy of mine and he was a good drinker.

"Grantland Rice [the sportswriter who immortalized one of Rockne's backfields by calling them the Four Horsemen] was a good drinker, too. We all went to Toots Shor's in New York and had fun. Oh, boy, that was something. Tootsie was something. Most of those guys are gone now. Almost all of them. When I think back on them and on all the people I've known and all the places I've been, I realize I've had a very good life, a very lucky life. But I've worked like hell, too.

"I liked the writers back then and always kind of wanted to be one myself, but I never had the time. I was always playing or coaching. Writers were different then. They would come up to you and say, 'What's the story?' and you would tell them. They weren't trying to find out things behind your back. People had a different attitude about sports. They were just happy to be at the game. They were more like I was. They felt grateful to be there."

Moose never played in the National Basketball Association but was one of the people who suggested to Walter Brown that if he created and bankrolled a team called the Celtics, which would play its game in the Boston Garden, they might have a good chance of succeeding. So far the Boston Celtics have won sixteen NBA titles.

Ever since getting married, Moose had turned his earnings over to his wife. Elise paid all the bills, put money in a savings account, and doled it out to her husband whenever he asked for some. This very organized and workable system relieved Moose of having to think about economics, although he never knew how much money they had. The only problem was that after a while he got a little tired of going to his wife and requesting cash. A man needed some pocket money for such things as cigars, gas for the car, small gifts for people, lunch with friends, or a drink now and then. He was too old to be asking for what almost amounted to an allowance. The situation troubled him, but he was determined to find a solution.

"After every basketball game, I used to come home and give Elise all the money I'd made," he says. "Maybe it was one hundred dollars. It just made her so happy to get it. She would smile at me and put her hands together and look very pleased. Maybe it was two hundred dollars.

"It finally occurred to me that no one knew how much I was getting for these games. I decided I would give her half of everything and I would keep half, and she would still get all my regular paychecks. So after a night's game, I'd give her fifty bucks instead of a hundred or a hundred instead of two hundred. Some people might think that was deceitful, but I never did. When you get married, you got to make sure you don't fight about money. That's very hard on people and wrecks a lot of good things. With this new arrangement, she was just as happy as before but now I was happy, too. Everyone was happy."

Moose traveled a lot—as a coach, a semipro athlete, and a recruiter for his college team—and many nights he was on the road while his wife was at home with the baby. He enjoyed moving around, playing basketball, meeting sportswriters, and making new friends in different cities, but he also enjoyed being at home and hoped that one day he would be able to spend more evenings with his wife and family. It appeared that time might be coming when, in early 1942, he received a call from the recently hired football coach at Notre Dame, Frank Leahy, who'd once played on the line for the Fighting Irish.

After college Leahy had coached at several schools before becoming the head man at Boston College, a position he held through the 1940 season. During the thirties, Notre Dame's football program under Elmer Layden, one of the Four Horsemen, had fallen somewhat from the glory days of Rockne, and many people doubted that the Norwegian's coaching achievements could ever be equaled. When Leahy was hired in South Bend, he spent 1941 putting together his own coaching staff and he remembered Moose Krause as an all-American player at the school. He wanted the big man to return to Notre Dame and teach his linemen the fine art of becoming physical—hitting people hard and taking them down.

In the winter of 1942, when Leahy offered Moose a position as an assistant coach, he was delighted and immediately accepted it. He was going home now, back to his alma mater, back to the team he'd always secretly hoped to coach. Everything was just as Moose wanted it, except perhaps for one thing. If he thought he would have more free time or more time for his family working under Leahy, he was badly mistaken. The man was serious about many things—he was serious about everything—but he reserved his greatest seriousness for football.

6 The Man

FRANK LEAHY WAS BORN IN O'NEILL, NEBRASKA, AND GREW UP in Winner, South Dakota. His hometown's name was highly appropriate. It wasn't just that he won at many things but that he was so intent upon winning. He was well proportioned and of average size in every way except for his will. In his youth he was a skillful boxer, with fast hands, an aggressive manner, quick feet, and a hard jaw, the kind of man who finished more fights than he started.

He was also a good football player, good enough to be on Rockne's teams in the late twenties, until he severely injured a knee and could never play again. His inability to put on pads, run onto the field, and butt heads with the opposition no doubt affected his choice of a career. If he couldn't beat you playing the game itself, he could certainly figure out a new strategy that would leave you defeated.

In 1930, after Leahy hurt his knee, he was sent to the Mayo Clinic in Rochester, Minnesota. At that time Rockne was also suffering from a leg ailment and was being treated in the clinic. For two weeks the men lay in side-by-side beds and talked constantly, one subject dominating their discussions: football. Leahy wanted to know everything Rockne had learned about the game and questioned him relentlessly. He wanted to know the technical aspects of the sport and how to motivate young men.

When he got out of the clinic, he began to imitate Rockne in small ways, using certain of his figures of speech, walking the way Rockne walked, making his gestures, and molding himself after the Fighting Irish mentor. In the next decade he honed his own coaching style and motivational techniques at Georgetown, Michigan State, Fordham (where he coached Vince Lombardi), and Boston College, and when Elmer Layden left as the Notre Dame coach to become commissioner of the National Football League, Leahy took over in South Bend.

Leahy's team was undefeated his first year but did not win the national championship. The next year he did something that shocked the world of college football. He may have studied Rockne closely and absorbed much from him, but he was in charge of the Irish now and everyone was about to realize that.

For the 1942 season, he got rid of the famous Rockne Shift offense and replaced it with the T formation, recently popularized by Stanford at the collegiate level and the Chicago Bears in the pros. Trying to improve on Rockne's tactics, went the campus joke of the day, was heresy, akin to a professor going to the Notre Dame administration and asking for permission to divorce. In their opening game, the Irish were tied by Wisconsin—led by Elroy "Crazy Legs" Hirsch—and then lost their home opener to Georgia Tech. Criticism of Leahy was loud and unremitting. He was ridiculed in the papers. Who did he think he was? If something had been good enough for Rockne, why wasn't it good enough for this upstart? How soon would he return to the old offense? Notre Dame beat Stanford the following week, but by then Leahy was back in the Mayo Clinic, diagnosed with "extreme nervous tension."

After his return to South Bend, things gradually improved and the Irish finished the year with seven wins, two losses, and two ties. He did not scuttle the T formation, and the next year Notre Dame used it to win the national championship.

The young coach hadn't learned his Irish brogue from Rockne. That came naturally. When Leahy's former players talk about him, they mimic him in a way that is so consistent it's eerie: his voice must still be rolling around inside of them, just waiting to come out.

Leahy also never picked up Rockne's charm. It was often said of the Norwegian that his team could beat you badly one year but you liked him so much that you looked forward to competing with him the next. It was also said that he could put his players through harsh practices yet they ran into the locker room feeling good about the coach. None of this was said about Leahy. He was so successful against some of Notre Dame's greatest rivals (Army, for instance) that they stopped scheduling the Irish.

As for his players . . . it just took them a lot longer to realize the benefits of having played for him. Twenty or thirty years after his excruciating practices ended, they remembered him with remarkable fondness. They called him The Man. On the surface anyway, the reasons for their shift of feelings appeared to be mysterious.

When Moose started with Leahy in 1942, he primarily taught blocking techniques. He recalls that the practices were harder than most of the games the Irish played and that he was an integral part of the workouts. Leahy often had Moose hit a young man for thirty minutes before practice even started.

"I knocked 'em down," Moose says, "and then knocked 'em down again." Leahy got his coaches involved in the contact to ensure that teammates could not find subtle ways to take it easy on one another during the drills. He also refused to allow his coaches to wear pads; the idea was to show the youngsters how tough the former players were and how soft the team had it now. He wanted his linemen to know that if they could block Moose Krause with some degree of success during the week, Saturday afternoons would be a cakewalk.

"Moose was second-in-command," says Joe Signaigo, who played guard and tackle for Notre Dame in the early forties. "He was always a greater diplomat than Leahy and willing to take the time to show you the right moves. I appreciated that. Leahy would say, 'Let's see this lad block against Moose,' and you couldn't do it. You couldn't move Moose at all, but sometimes he'd do you a favor and let you have a little success. But the next time he'd kill you."

Leahy wouldn't let his coaches wear earmuffs or gloves on the sidelines during games, no matter how cold or wet it became, because he never wanted the players to think his staff couldn't handle a little foul weather. He also practiced the team outside regardless of the elements. A chant grew up around this and can still be heard from his players today: "Rain, hail, snow, or sleet, Leahy's men will always meet."

Every time Moose hears this he laughs, that distinctive chuckle he uses whenever the subject of hard-nosed football comes up. "Frank was a hero to me," he says. "He was a senior at Notre Dame when I was a freshman. He was a boxer and I fought some back then, but he was a lot sharper than I was. He was a tackle in football and so was I. I played against him a few times before he got hurt, and he was always nice to me. He'd call me a kid and then knock me on my ass. He came from a poor family and he always wanted to succeed. When he got injured, it totally stirred him up and I think he decided right then that he was going to be the best football coach in the country.

"I heard so many players cuss Frank when they were playing for him. No one worked people the way Leahy did, and no one made more demands on himself. He lived in Michigan City, outside of South Bend, with his wife and eight children. During the season he wouldn't go home till Sunday and sometimes not then. He'd stay here on the campus all week and sleep in the firehouse. He'd sleep at his desk.

"He was a total student of the game. Every day after practice he'd make the assistant coaches go over every player on the roster. How did he do this afternoon? Is he improving or getting worse? What's his strongest point? His weakest point?

What's his attitude like now? Frank wanted to know everything. He was a good person, but some people—some other football coaches—hated him because he was so successful.

"He had insomnia. At night he would study films of our games in his office and he wanted his coaches there. He just wanted someone to talk about football with him. He was a nuisance. He'd go till nine o'clock, ten o'clock, eleven o'clock, midnight. I'd go home in the evening and eat dinner and then have to come back and watch more film with him. He'd run the same play over and over again until you thought you couldn't watch it anymore. I'd get home real late and Elise always wanted to know where I'd been. I'd say, 'Football practice, honey. Go back to sleep.' She couldn't believe it, and sometimes, I couldn't either.

"He wouldn't let his coaches smoke around him, but one night I wanted to go home so bad I gave all the other guys cigars and we lit them up and started puffing. After a while Frank couldn't take it anymore and he kicked us out. But he never let me do anything like that again."

Leahy was a very proper man with a formal way of speaking. His hair was always parted neatly near the middle of his scalp, and he could look well dressed in sweat clothes. He called people named Johnny "John" and people named Joe "Joseph." After a hard-won victory he might allow himself a drink or two, but at midnight he would remind everyone that tomorrow (Sunday) was a working day that began at six A.M., and when he spoke, the party was over.

"No football teams," he once said, "were ever better prepared, physically or mentally, than our squads at Notre Dame. My goal was to go through ten seasons without a loss."

Leahy had a quality found in many successful coaches in a variety of sports: he kept people off balance by being unpredictable. He could be friendlier than you anticipated or more distant. He could change his mind and allow you to do something that you would have sworn he would never allow. This quality made those around him more alert.

In a concourse tunnel that runs beneath the Morris Inn on the Notre Dame campus is a hallway holding photographs of the university's past. Rockne is there and so is Father Sorin, who founded the school in 1842, and there are pictures of the original buildings and lawns and of the pioneers who built the place.

Every image evokes feelings and memories, but one of the most evocative shows a football game being played in South Bend in the 1940s. It documents not simply another chapter of collegiate athletic history but another time altogether. Leahy is on the sidelines, wearing a dark pinstripe suit, a tie, and shiny dress shoes. Moose, standing next to him, has on a suit and a trench coat. He is sporting, of all things, a black bow tie. Both men are wearing hats and both look absolutely respectable. They could be on their way to a ball.

The players lined up behind them are shorter than Moose and less imposing figures. They wear baggy pants and some still favor the old leather helmets. The team, which is entirely white, appears tough and gritty, with a lot of determined scowls on their faces. Their innocence jumps out at you; the picture seems centuries away from the money and celebrity that have come to be associated with all levels of modern athletics. They look like kids.

One other thing in the photograph holds your attention: the confidence that comes off of Moose and his head coach. Despite appearing a little uncomfortable in his bow tie, Moose is utterly at home on the sidelines, a commanding presence whom everyone literally looks up to. Leahy's chin is cocked at an angle that says, "Go ahead. Just try to hit me. Give it your best shot." The men are in their element, and the image takes you straight back to those Saturday afternoons when America had just won a world war, the country felt good about a lot of things, men wore hats, and football was still a game.

Many of Leahy's players are alive, although the coach passed away in 1973 and was buried in Portland, Oregon, where the Fighting Irish victory march was played at his funeral. After leaving South Bend in the early fifties, he was only briefly associated with football again. He still has the second-highest winning percentage (.855) of any collegiate coach, just behind Rockne, and he won one more national title than his mentor. When Leahy's players and ex-coaches—particularly Moose—talk about him, they generate some of the same good feeling that's in the photograph beneath the Morris Inn, some of the optimism and warmth. They convey a simplicity about the game of football—a simplicity that was bound to change as the decades passed—that is ironic. By bringing so many innovations and such a high level of seriousness to the sport, Leahy himself was one of the people who helped create this change.

There's also a camaraderie between the men who knew and played for Leahy that is perhaps stronger than with any other group of Notre Dame athletes. It might be because most of them did not have pro careers, so their college experience was especially vivid. Or because things really were less complex then and football was easier to enjoy. Or because many of them survived World War II together, which brought them closer. Actually, they survived two wars: the big one overseas and the smaller one with their head coach.

When Leahy's men hold reunions, as they do every year in South Bend during the football season, their wives sit next to them and smile politely or talk among themselves or go shopping with one another, excluded from this kind of old, old male bonding. It's a touching thing to witness. The men have been somewhere many others have not, and that memory lives fiercely inside of them. The glue that holds them together after five decades is Leahy.

Jack Barry, like most of the old players, loves to talk about The Man. The son of Norm Barry, who was Moose's high school football coach, Jack grew up in a tough Chicago neighborhood and thought of himself as a hard-boiled teenager when he arrived in South Bend in 1941, the same year Leahy came back to Notre Dame from Boston College. Barry assumed that the football program would be easy compared to the street life he'd known.

"Frank showed up in February," Jack says. "It had been snowing a lot but he cleaned off the field and said, 'Gentlemen, get your hats on and let's scrimmage.' It was murderous. He had one hundred and twenty players and said he could only use fifty-six of us. No one wanted to get cut or lose his scholarship, so it turned into a bloodbath. I survived and I wasn't very big. It was one fight after another on the field. There were brawls everywhere and I got into a few of them myself. When those practices started, Wally Ziemba was a fat, slow two-hundred-and-sixty-five-pound tackle. When they ended, he was a two-hundred-and-twenty-five-pound center who could move.

"We won every game that year except one, the tie with Army, which was played in the mud at Yankee Stadium. The game was held after a four-inch rainfall all day Friday and Saturday. On one play we tried a reverse that didn't work because our running back slipped and fell down. Dan Topping, the Yankee owner, came into our locker room after the game, and Frank burned his tail for not having the field sodded properly. He really cut loose.

"He was a great motivator. You can do certain things with college players that you probably couldn't do with the pros. Before a game with Arizona he got us all together and said we were going to dedicate this one to the deceased mothers of our players and to his own mother, who was also deceased. He didn't have to open the locker room door after that. We knocked it down and beat Arizona bad.

"We played Carnegie Tech in '41. They'd lost four or five games and were an inferior opponent, but our game with them was close and our fullback failed to score once after being inside their five-yard line. On the train ride home, as we got close to South Bend, it was two on a Sunday afternoon. The senior manager came through the car and said, 'Gentlemen, everyone on the field at three o'clock today.' We got off the train, suited up, and ran the fullback play we hadn't scored on for two straight hours. It was brutal. Leahy went through three or four fullbacks and then he told us, 'Lads, we will never fail to score on that play again.'

"After I left school, Frank asked me to coach his B team and I didn't respond right away. I was getting married at the time. Finally he came to me and wanted an answer. I said I'd do it and he said, 'Practice starts this coming Monday morning at eight A.M.' I said, 'I'm getting married this weekend.' He said, 'Oh, I forgot about that. Practice starts this Tuesday at eight A.M.' And that was my honeymoon."

Joe Signaigo is best remembered for a game against Northwestern in 1941. "I went down with a broken nose and was bleeding profusely," he says. "Blood everywhere. I thought I was gonna die. At Notre Dame only the captain could call time-out and I wasn't the captain, but I called one anyway. I knew it was a mistake. Leahy called me over and I didn't want to get close to him because I was bleeding like a hog and didn't want to get any on his clothes. He looked at me and said, 'What's the problem, lad?' I said, 'I think my nose is broken.' He said, 'Look over there at Moose Krause. He broke his nose three times in one game and he never called time-out. Now get back in there and do some blocking.' I went.

"After the game I saw the doctor and he set my nose and told me not to do anything for at least a week. The trainer came by and told me that Leahy wanted to see me. I went in and said I couldn't practice. 'Why not, lad? What's the matter?' he asked me. 'My nose is broken,' I told him. 'Well,' he said, 'in that case there's nothing more that could happen to it. Get dressed and get out to practice.' "

Bob McBride came to Notre Dame in 1940 as a freshman lineman and left the campus as an assistant coach after the 1953 season. He later spent many years in the trucking business and is now retired in Tucson.

"I have all the regard in the world for Knute Rockne," he says, "but when you compare everything, Leahy was the greatest football coach ever. He won a championship in 1943, and then in '46, '47, and '49. We were undefeated in '48 but didn't win it that year because we had a tie and the press wanted to give it to someone else. In that time, from 1946 through 1949, he didn't lose a single game. Think about that. And Frank always wanted to play the hardest schedule he could because he said it didn't do anyone any good to beat a bum.

"His biggest concern was getting the most out of an individual, and no one ever got more. He was completely dedicated to the team concept. Frank didn't use the first-person singular pronoun. Nothing was 'I.' Everything was 'we' and 'Notre Dame.' He was always sharp mentally, he was the most loyal human being I ever met, and he motivated people by working them extremely hard.

"He had a mind like a sponge. If a high school football coach visited the campus, he would invite him into his office and pick his brain. He would call people all the time—Hunk Anderson, who was Moose's old coach, or Sid Luckman of the Chicago Bears, or anyone else he thought might help him—and ask them questions about football. He was always learning. Add to that that he was a tremendous disciplinarian, and if you couldn't take that, you couldn't play for him.

"Our scrimmages were something. Things would get testy and I saw some good fights, but the players who went at it usually walked off the field arm in arm after practice. Leahy would let the fights go on a little bit. Some coaches wouldn't do that, but he thought that was the best way to cut down on the fighting. When something started, he would say, 'Lads, let's fight, but fight evenly and fair and within the rules.' He always wanted to see who was the toughest man.

"In the spring of '42 we were having long, hard workouts every day. The other students had already gone home for Easter break, and we were really looking forward to going. The day before our vacation he called us in and said, 'Lads, I've just received the greatest piece of news. I spoke with Father Cavanaugh and he's agreed to let us stay at Notre Dame and practice twice a day during the break.' All of the players were crushed, but no one said anything.

"We practiced only once on Good Friday—from about six A.M. to 11 A.M. Afterwards, I dragged myself into the locker room and I was bleeding, exhausted, and beaten. I couldn't move. Another player came in and threw down his helmet and said, 'Now I know exactly how Jesus Christ felt one thousand nine hundred and forty-two years ago today.' "

Angelo Bertelli played at Notre Dame from 1941 to 1943 and became the school's first Heisman Trophy winner his senior year. Because of his strong passing arm and his hometown of Springfield, Massachusetts, he was known as the Springfield Rifle. After college he played with the Los Angeles Dons of the All-American Football Conference in 1946–47 and now lives in Clifton, New Jersey.

"Frank recruited me when he was still at Boston College and I was at Cathedral High School in Springfield," Angelo says. "I never had any trouble with him. I was his quarterback and he was good for me because he liked the passing game and I could throw the ball. He saw to it that if anyone hit his passer during scrimmages, that man paid for it. Jim White was an all-American tackle for us and he'd bloody our own players so no one could get to me. Leahy got very upset if anyone touched my uniform, and I liked that.

"My best game in the 1941 season was against Navy. They were the big power in the East and we won twenty to thirteen to stay undefeated that year. Besides passing and running the team, I played in the defensive backfield. Frank used only one substitute the entire Navy game and it wasn't for me. I played sixty minutes of football that day because he refused to let anyone but his first-stringers on the field.

"The one thing he liked was repetition. I used to kick the extra points. He would have me do this for an hour in practice, so afterwards I could barely lift my leg. Then he would come over and say, 'Oh, what's wrong, Angelo?' I'd say, 'I'm tired.' He'd say, 'Well, lad, then let's try some with the left foot.'

"He was a stickler for every detail. In 1942 he changed from the Rockne Shift to the T formation, which was built around faking and hiding the ball. Once he made this decision there was no rest for me anymore. He had me handing off, spinning around, and concealing the ball all day long. Handing off and spinning around, handing off and spinning around, over and over and over again until I was dizzy. I couldn't wait for Saturday to come so I could stop practicing.

"I was inducted into the Marines in the spring of 1942 on Notre Dame's old Cartier Field, where the team used to play its games. I got to stay in school for a while after that, and I even got to play six games of the 1943 season before I went into the service. One afternoon during the war I was sitting in a Quonset hut on Parris Island listening to Notre Dame play Great Lakes, which had a combination of pro players and college kids. They were a great, great team. It was close, and we finally went ahead fourteen to thirteen. I thought we had an undefeated season locked up, but Great Lakes threw a desperation pass and beat us nineteen to fourteen.

"I came out of the Quonset hut and I was crying. Someone came up and handed me a telegram that said I'd just won the Heisman Trophy for 1943. I think the voters were saying thanks to me for the '41 and '42 seasons when I didn't win it. I was torn with all kinds of emotions. I was in the middle of a war and a very long distance away from my family and friends, away from Notre Dame and the team and football. It was hard to share an award for playing a game with the other men on the island. The whole thing was really something—a day I could never forget. Today when kids come to my house and see that old trophy, they look at me and I'm a big shot for a few minutes.

"When I think back on Leahy, genius is what comes to mind. He was way ahead of his time. The things that we laughed at or mimicked that he was doing back then—the way he would constantly watch films and analyze defenses and his total preparation for the games—are all a standard part of football now. Everyone does that. Frank was so smart. He visited me once when I was on Guam. I took him to the officers' club for dinner and introduced him to twenty people who were sitting at another table. He finished eating and before he left he went back to each of those people, shook their hands, and remembered everyone's first name. We were all amazed."

Bertelli suddenly breaks into laughter, the way many players do when recalling that era. "In 1941 we were playing Northwestern and they had Otto Graham. A very good team. Bernie Crimmins was one of our guards. He was an all-American. It was halftime and Crimmins was lying on a table in the locker room. He was really beaten up and bloody all over—his nose, his face, his ears. He was laid out flat. As we were going out for the second half, Leahy made all of us walk by Bernie and touch him and promise him that we wouldn't let him down. We won the game seven to six. Frank was born to coach at Notre Dame."

After he finished playing for the Irish, Bernie Crimmins coached the offensive and defensive linemen under Leahy from 1946 to 1952.

"Frank would sit up in his tower above the field and watch practice," says Johnny Lujack. "When he saw something he didn't like, he could stare at it for a while and not say anything. One time he did this and then called out, 'Coach Crimmins, those lads you're working with haven't made a Notre Dame block all afternoon. Can you tell me why?' Crimmins didn't answer him. About two minutes later you heard the damnedest collision you'd ever heard and you looked over and saw that Crimmins himself had totally flattened some poor guy with a vicious block. As the guy was trying to come to, Leahy called down from the tower, 'That was very good, Coach Crimmins. That's how we block at Notre Dame.' "

Says Moose, "Leahy wouldn't let any of the professors come to practice. He thought they might be spies for our opponents. If he saw one of them up in a building looking down on the field, he'd send a trainer up there and make him close the blinds. When an airplane flew overhead, he'd stop practice until it was gone. He thought it might be full of scouts."

Creighton Miller, the Irish running back of the early forties, was the son of former Notre Dame player Red Miller and the nephew of one of the Four Horsemen, Don Miller. In 1943, Creighton was in the backfield for Johnny Lujack's first start at quarterback, against Pittsburgh.

"Leahy decided to start John instead of Bertelli because

John was from Pennsylvania," Creighton says. "Before the game John was very nervous, pacing around, but Frank told him to relax. The game starts, we drive the ball down to Pitt's two-yard line, and in the huddle John calls my number. The crowd is cheering, everyone is on their feet. John calls the signals, the line opens a big hole in front of me, but there's one problem—he forgets to hand me the ball. He gets clobbered and comes back to the huddle. I tell him that I'm on his team, my whole family went to Notre Dame, and I'm his friend. He says we're going to run the same play. He does exactly the same thing and gets clobbered again. In the huddle I say, 'What is it? What did I do wrong? Did I tell a Polish joke?' John is Polish. We run the play a third time and he finally gives me the ball and we score. We go over to the sidelines and Leahy asks John how he's feeling. He says, 'My head hurts.' Frank says, 'I don't know why. You haven't been using it.' "

Joe Doyle, of the *South Bend Tribune,* started writing about Notre Dame football in 1949 and still covers it today. "Frank always had the players call me 'Mr. Doyle,' although they had been in school with me and were only a little younger than I was," he says. "If I wrote something he liked, he would say, 'Joseph, you're very perceptive.' Very, very formal.

"I remember one practice when it was getting dark out on the field. There were only a few poles back then with just a couple of lights on each of them. He was kneeling down and peering out there into the darkness. One of the players kept fumbling. Frank watched him do this two or three times and then muttered, "Damn that Floyd Simmons.' A few years earlier Simmons had recommended that the player out there fumbling should come to Notre Dame and Frank had listened to him. He wasn't swearing to anyone, just himself, as he looked at the field. He didn't know anyone else was even there."

Says Bernie Crimmins, "In 1946 we tied Army nothing to nothing at Yankee Stadium. The game was over at four-thirty in the afternoon, but a few of the coaches didn't get out of the locker room until nine-thirty that night. Frank wouldn't let us go. He just sat there and replayed everything over and over again. What had we done wrong? Why didn't we win? Whose fault was it? By the time he was ready to leave, there were no cabs left in that neighborhood. They'd all gone away. We were lost in New York City. We started walking downtown from the stadium and finally ran into a cop. He put in a call and after a while a taxi showed up and took us to our hotel."

Moose also remembers that day. "I told Frank that it wasn't the end of the world. We hadn't even lost the game, but he sat there and cried anyway. Every time we lost he would go into a corner of the locker room and cry. Everyone would try to get the hell out of there so we wouldn't have to watch him. He was just a mess."

"Frank would sleep in his suits in the firehouse," Crimmins says. "Because he didn't go home very often, he'd borrow my clothes. Sometimes, he slept in them. Then he'd wear them around the campus the next day."

"No one abused his training rules back then," says Creighton Miller. "You couldn't, even if you wanted to. He would just kill you the next week during practice. Two practices a day or even three. You survived these things under Frank, and later on you discovered that you needed what he'd done to you, both in the games and after college. At twenty-two years of age you're not savvy and you need discipline."

Dick Rosenthal, an All-American basketball player at Notre Dame in the early fifties and now the university's athletic director, never played for Leahy but has heard some of the stories.

"I was a student on the campus during his last years here, and from time to time I would run into him," Rosenthal says. "One year our basketball team lost two early games and then won the next 18. We played Holy Cross, who was number one, and beat them. Frank saw me after that and said, 'Lad, the students are very proud of you and so am I.' The way he spoke to me that day has stayed with me for forty years. He was just an extremely polite human being.

"People feared him absolutely. One time some underclassmen on the football team decided to go into his office and ask if they could attend a dance. The seniors told them, 'Oh, no. If you do that, you'll never play again.' They went in and he said, 'Go ahead, lads, and have a good time and be sure to behave like perfect gentlemen, like Notre Dame men.' The rest of the team was astounded.

"He was competitive in more than just football. When he discovered that Red Blaik, the Army coach, played golf, he decided he wanted to beat him at it. Frank had never played golf before, but he went out to the driving range and was determined to master the game. The first week he hit so many balls he bloodied his hands."

7 Before the Storm

WHETHER IN THE 1940S OR THE 1990S, AUTUMN SATURDAY mornings in South Bend are spectacular, with their cool blue air, scent of burning leaves, and gently hazy sky. When a breeze rattles the campus elms, they shake down pieces of gold, spinning and glinting all the way to the earth. A light frost sits on the golf course next to the Morris Inn but soon melts away in thin veils of smoke.

As dawn hits the nineteen-foot statue of Our Lady that stands above the university, she glimmers, her face and hands looking utterly serene. The small lake behind the administration office is without ripples, and in the nearby grotto where students and visitors come early to pray, candles have already been lit, standing in rows, flickering and dripping wax, reminding you of the living and the dead, making the morning silence deeper. Then overhead, carillon bells chime the hour, strangely out of tune, ringing across the campus and bringing everything alive.

Notre Dame is a place of old buildings and new ones, a place where sculptures of saints are hidden among the foliage and tree limbs hang over every sidewalk and put shadows on the ground, a place that feels oddly peaceful, but mostly it's a place for rituals.

Saturday mornings are even better when the Fighting Irish are about to play football and are especially vibrant on a Parent's Weekend. Before the Stanford game the festivities started at daybreak, when the parking lots began to fill and voices and music came from automobiles and trucks and RVs, engines raced, and car doors slammed. There was a constant hum in the air that would grow into the sound of a thriving party that would eventually engulf the entire campus. You couldn't go anywhere without hearing the victory march. The Notre Dame band practiced it on a distant field. A man played it near the Morris Inn on a bagpipe. People sang it to themselves. It was on radio and television, but it wasn't the only music competing for your attention. Young men and women opened their dorm windows and let loose an unholy mixture of sixties nostalgia and nineties rap, the songs all getting louder and trying to drown each other out.

By ten A.M. families were zigzagging across the lawns, moving thickly in every direction, parents staring as their offspring pointed out where they attended classes. Everyone wore green or blue or gold, the clothing advertising the Fighting Irish or recalling a past football triumph. One sweatshirt held pictures of Rockne, Leahy, Parseghian, and Holtz. "The tradition continues," it read. More Lou Holtz masks had cropped up everywhere. People strapped them to the front of their heads and to the back. A young woman had on a white shirt whose front read, "Sex Kills." On the back it said, "So come to Notre Dame and live forever."

Adolescents held hands and children rolled in the leaves. Young men threw Frisbees or pigskins, causing bystanders to duck. Half a dozen touch football games were taking place simultaneously on the various quads, accompanied by shouting, cheers, and dancing in imaginary end zones after a score. The sidewalks had become too jammed to walk on and the music was growing more intense. A few extroverts had dragged huge stereo speakers out of their rooms, placed them on the grass, and aimed them at the crowd. When they cranked up the volume on the Young Rascals, alumni began gritting their teeth.

The student body brought out makeshift barbecue grills—fifty-five-gallon oil drums, cut in half and laid on their sides—and started fires in the bellies of the drums. The air became smoky, filled with the odor of burning charcoal. The cooks threw meat on the grills and a massive steak sale was under way, part of another campus charity effort. People lined up for a block to get six ounces of charred beef.

"We take checks and credit cards!" cried one enterprising young man as he leaned over a spitting fire. "But only cash from Stanford fans."

This Saturday, as on every other football Saturday for many years past, Moose arose early and attended the mass held for the players and Lou Holtz in Keenan Hall on the campus. Moose sat near the team but not exactly with them, holding the rosary and praying in silence, not wanting to intrude on their quiet time or preparation for the game. When the service ended, he exchanged a few words with some of the young men and shook their hands, there if anyone needed him.

He acted much as he did when he visited the team's football practices, something he enjoyed as much today as he had four decades earlier. Parking his Cadillac next to the field, he didn't get out but puffed a cigar and stared at the players and coaches, sometimes comparing what Holtz was doing now with what Rockne or Leahy had done in the past. He wouldn't get any closer to the action. When Holtz saw the Cadillac he would nod in its direction, just the slightest movement of his head to indicate that he knew the old coach was present and it was good to have him there.

The mass over, Moose went outside and ran into a small group of people who recognized him and wanted to chat. He was known everywhere on campus and was on a first-name basis with innumerable school employees. He called the waitresses at the University Club "honey" and they called him "Moosie." The people who were responsible for getting him to certain Notre Dame functions on time said it was virtually impossible to hustle him through a crowd; he wasn't any good at brushing off strangers and had a few words for everyone.

Even now Moose seemed surprised and delighted when people wanted to speak with him, as if he still couldn't quite believe he'd made it at Notre Dame. His celebrity went far beyond South Bend. He'd been recognized while on vacation in Switzerland and while fishing in Panama, and once, when he flew to Rome to get away from all the hubbub surrounding the Irish athletic department, his first night in Italy a man approached and asked if he was Ed Krause.

Driving back to his apartment, not far from the campus, he stopped at his wife's grave in the large old cemetery near the Morris Inn. He visited here almost every day. Getting out of the car and walking slowly through the damp grass to her plot, he knelt over it and said a few words before rearranging the fresh flowers he'd brought her earlier in the week. He moved some yellow leaves off this patch of ground, tossed them aside. After a minute or two in silence, he stood and got back in the car, returning to the apartment where he'd lived alone since her death in 1990. At home he made his final preparations for the game, stuffing a few cigars in his pocket and donning a green jacket and a white Ivy League cap.

By eleven, people had started to funnel in the general direction of the stadium. Tailgate parties were at full throttle in the parking lots, and some of the revelers had begun to sing. Small boys and girls on the campus were moving their wares in piercing voices: "Programs! Get your programs here!"

In the recent past Notre Dame had signed a five-year multimillion-dollar contract with NBC, and almost every game on their schedule was now being nationally televised. Huge TV production trucks stood next to the stadium, wires snaking out of the vehicles and people stepping around them. The trucks were brightly colored, like the NBC peacock logo, and impressive looking; something about their size and all the activity they generated showed just how far football had come since the days of Rockne, when he was the first coach in America to ask that his games be broadcast to a nationwide radio audience (Mutual Broadcasting now feeds Irish football to hundreds of radio stations). The NBC trucks told you that the event waiting to unfold this afternoon was connected to parts of the whole world.

By noon the stadium was filling up. Standing atop the old oval structure—up above the press box and up where Moose and a few other dignitaries had their own private booths—you could see people swarming toward the game, moving in waves and streams, a giant swirling river of light and chatter and motion all coming to a single point on the campus. Up here sunlight shook off the red and yellow leaves that surrounded Notre Dame and struck the thousands upon thousands of cars in the parking lots, shimmering in the autumn air. The Fighting Irish marching band was warming up and players from both teams were out on the field, stretching and blocking one another, kicking footballs up through the sky.

8 Touching Bottom

FIFTEEN MINUTES BEFORE KICKOFF MOOSE'S PRIVATE BOOTH WAS nearly full—of people, food, beverages, and boxes of cigars he'd received from admirers. His daughter, Mary, and her husband, Sandy Carrigan, had come from Chicago for the game, while Spike Sullivan, an oilman and old friend of the Krause family, had arrived from Oklahoma. Other visitors from the East Coast were sitting with Moose, and next to them was Bishop Joseph Crowley, the retired auxiliary bishop of the Fort Wayne–South Bend Diocese, who for many years had occupied this spot at home games.

In the booth north of this one were athletic director Dick Rosenthal and his guests, and in the next booth were Tony Roberts and Tom Pagna of the Mutual Broadcasting Network (Roberts's desk was covered with pregame notes). The next booth held the president of Notre Dame, Father Edward (Monk) Malloy, C.S.C., and assorted dignitaries, including Ernest and Julio Gallo, the famous wine merchants from California, and TV talk-show host and Notre Dame alumnus Regis Philbin; and in the next booth was the NBC-TV broadcasting team of Tom Hammond and Cris Collinsworth. Behind the NBC booth was a small tent filled with sandwiches and drinks, where caterers were preparing an elaborate halftime spread.

A portion of a film crew was also on hand. The campus had recently been selected as the shooting site for an upcoming Tri-Star Pictures movie entitled *Rudy*, about a young man named Rudy Ruettiger, who, against all odds, had tried out for Ara Parseghian's football team and wound up playing exactly twenty-seven seconds in Notre Dame's final home game of 1975. Various movie technicians, assistant directors, independent producers, gaffers, and grips were moving from booth to booth to booth and would soon be looking for extras to help re-create Rudy's big moment in front of an artificial crowd. The roof of Notre Dame Stadium was jammed with media types.

Just below the roof was the press box, which by now was full. Reporters from all over the country had come in for the Stanford game and were sitting four deep in long rows, when they weren't getting up and helping themselves to another hot dog and cold soda on the University of Notre Dame. They had pads, pens, tape recorders, telephones, binoculars, and computers, and all of them were kept behind a glass wall that looked out onto the field. They evoked a bevy of horseplayers getting ready for the second race at Aqueduct. Most of them were talking about the game, and the feeling in the air was that something would happen this afternoon that would affect the remainder of the college football year.

The press box and private booths were well equipped with television sets, which were turned on. Many in the press corps and even among the Irish rooters felt that the game they were attending was perhaps the second most important one taking place in America today. Down south, Miami was playing Florida State—the number one team in the nation versus the number three team—in a nationally televised game that had begun well before the kickoff in South Bend. Everyone was watching it.

In recent years Miami had become the archenemy of the

Irish, so each time Florida State did something that hurt the Hurricanes, a wave of excitement and cheering passed through the booths but not, of course, the press box. The oldest rule in sports journalism was in full force this afternoon: no rooting by the reporters. Keep things objective. Don't act as if you care who wins or loses. Don't have personal feelings. Despite all this, everyone present knew that if Miami lost to Florida State, the Irish would find themselves in excellent position for a run at the national championship, provided they kept on winning.

Football coaches constantly preach to their teams not to become complacent during the long season, regardless of who's next on the schedule. Holtz had told the Irish to be ready for a difficult game with Stanford, and he wasn't overly concerned that his team would take the game lightly. The Cardinal had too good of a reputation for that—they were ranked in the top twenty nationally—and too good a coach in Bill Walsh.

Holtz had often said that a football team faces at least three significant crises every year, and that each crisis can make you better. In 1992, the Irish's first crisis had come in the tie with Michigan, but the team had followed that with two easy wins. As the teams down on the field prepared for the kickoff, no one could have known that the second crisis was looming or that what would happen next would dramatically alter Notre Dame's season.

The marching band played the national anthem and everyone stood in Moose's booth. The elderly men took off their caps, looked out onto the gridiron, put their hands over their hearts, and sang along with the melody. Their voices wobbled and they could not stay on key, but that made their effort all the more effective. They sang the old words as if they felt them.

The game began and Moose, whose own private quarters were clearly marked with NO SMOKING signs, fired up a rope and turned his attention to the action below. He was the only smoker present. Nobody said anything, but one of his guests cracked open the window that separated the booth from the fresh air. There were no cigar jokes, although some people stared every time he puffed on the thing.

The Irish started brilliantly, scoring a safety in the first minute. Then they scored a touchdown to make it 9–0 just 2:25 into the game. Moose cheered loudly and gave high fives to everyone in the booth. He looked around and muttered, "The Notre Dame alumni don't care whether we win or lose, as long as we win."

Like all good athletes, he still had great intensity and competitiveness, which poured out of him when he was watching football and Irish football in particular. He could not sit still or remain silent. He fidgeted, shifted in his chair, bobbed his shoulders, and threw a few elbows. When a Stanford player ran downfield, he looked as if he wanted to tackle him. He yelled after every down, continually aired his opinions about the referees or the players, and never stopped mumbling around the barrel of the cigar. A number of great jazz musicians, especially pianists, grunt while they are playing, a completely unconscious thing. Moose was the same way. Each time the ball was put into play, he cut loose.

"Uhhh!" he said. "Let's go out there! Uhhh! Hit somebody! Get that man—now! Uhhhh! Don't tackle like that. That's not what Holtz teaches them in practice. Block him! Uhhhhh!"

Every time Notre Dame performed well, he smiled or laughed, the low, rumbling sound of pure pleasure. Whenever the Irish did something he didn't like, he turned to the person beside him and growled, "Don't just sit there. Do something!" The first time you heard it, you jumped.

His voice, his long, worn face, his beaten-looking knuckles, the large bump on his arm that was the result of an old injury—everything about Moose evoked a time when football was more of a rough-and-tumble sport than a huge business, when coaches hit their players if they were upset with them, when men were not necessarily any tougher than today but tough in a different way. They endured more in silence and didn't expect as much in return for their efforts, except to be able to keep playing. They were discovering a new harsh game, defining it, drawn to its brutish edges and its violence. Sitting next to Moose at a football game, the first thing you learned was that the fiercer the contact, the better he liked it.

When Irish running back Jerome Bettis went down with what looked like a leg injury, one of the elderly men in the booth said, "Get up. Get up and play. You can go to the chiropractor tomorrow. You gotta play today. C'mon. Anyone can play when they're well. It's when you're hurt that it counts."

Moose chuckled.

Bettis got up and played.

The men in the booth applauded him.

The incident brought back something mentioned a few days earlier by Joe O'Brien, the senior associate athletic director at Notre Dame and a 1949 graduate of the university. "Moose goes back to the twenties and thirties," he'd said. "The men from those days who went through the Depression at Notre Dame knew some hard times and they helped each other out. After leaving college, they took chances in business and other fields, and many of them were very successful. They were self-made men. They stuck together and loved each other, and in my mind, they were a special group. Spike Sullivan was one of them. Joe Haggar, of the slacks company, was another. They still come back to Notre Dame and maintain a good association with our athletic department. Why? Because of Moose. He's what holds them together."

As the game progressed, it looked like a rout for the Irish. They moved the ball on the ground, were sharp on defense, and scored again to go ahead 16–0. The television set in the booth revealed that Miami and Florida State were engaged in a close struggle, and this might just be the year that the Seminoles, after many failed attempts against Miami, would finally defeat the Hurricanes. Nothing would have made Moose and his friends happier.

Spike Sullivan, who was quietly enjoying the game, pointed out that Frank Leahy had a grandson on the Irish team: Ryan Leahy, a 284-pound sophomore offensive tackle from Yakima, Washington. Bishop Crowley, red-faced and white-haired and perched on the edge of his seat, pounded on the Formica counter in front of him when he saw something he liked. In the first quarter, he pounded a lot. When one of the guests thanked him for providing such a beautiful day for a football game, he said, "I'm sorry but I can't take credit for that. You must remember, I'm in sales, not management."

When the Irish tried a play that didn't work, one visitor or another would bark at him, "Pray harder, Bishop. You're not praying hard enough."

He grinned and kept his eyes on the field.

A man in the booth asked the bishop if he knew how to make holy water. Turning to the fellow, the bishop gave him the indulgent look that comes from enduring a lifetime of Catholic humor.

"Do you?" the man persisted.

The bishop shook his head.

"Boil the hell out of it."

At halftime, Jim Brock, a representative of the Cotton Bowl, came by and said hello to Moose and his assembled guests. Brock, a short, rotund, effervescent man who calls everyone Hoss and is called Hoss in return, said he was glad to see the Irish playing so well and added that the team might just be in his bowl game come New Year's Day. Moose shook his hand and Brock went smiling toward the next booth.

In hindsight it's always easy to say that you could see the turning point in a sporting event: it was that one play in the first quarter or a single mistake just before halftime. In truth, when a game is unfolding, you never know what is coming next. When Notre Dame went ahead by 16 points, almost every one of the 59,000 people in the stadium thought the home team would remain in control of things. No one could have predicted that Rick Mirer would start to miss his receivers or that the Irish would have five turnovers or that Stanford free safety, John Lynch, would suddenly look like an all-American on play after play or that the Cardinal offense would begin to resemble the San Francisco 49ers when they were winning Super Bowls under Bill Walsh. After the first quarter, Stanford scored 33 straight points and Notre Dame did not score again.

The air slowly went out of Moose's booth. Between the televised comeback by Miami and its eventual win over Florida State and the utter turnaround of events on the field down below, the mood dipped and then crashed. The silence got louder, everyone stared out in disbelief, the food went untouched, and by the fourth quarter it was obvious that no reprieve was coming. There would be no Irish heroics, no fourth-quarter comeback today.

Moose had long since stopped grunting, fidgeting, and trying to tackle the Stanford runners while sitting in his chair. He'd also quit criticizing Mirer for his errant throws and the Irish defense for letting Stanford score all those points. He'd become very quiet. Every now and then someone would compliment the Cardinal on their terrific performance, but people were mostly talking about what they'd done over the summer or the weather or affairs at the university. Nobody wanted to discuss football. On the sidelines Holtz kneeled down, gazing into the natural turf, and on this occasion he really did look as if he were searching for a hole to crawl into.

Earlier in the day, when things were going well for his team, Bishop Crowley had chanted, "Bury 'em, boys, bury 'em." Now he kept repeating, "Peter says to Paul, 'Things are tough all over.' "

That about summed it up. The final score was 33–16, and when the contest ended, the Irish had dropped more than a ball game. With a loss and a tie—both at home—Notre Dame appeared to have relinquished any reasonable hope of getting back into the national championship picture. At least five undefeated teams would now be ranked ahead of them—Miami, Washington, Alabama, Michigan, and Texas A&M—plus a number of other teams with only one loss or tie. The Irish would no doubt lose their place in the top ten, and their upcoming schedule featured tough games against Boston College, Penn State, and USC, all nationally ranked teams.

If Notre Dame fans were not used to losing under Holtz, who had come into 1992 with a 56-17-0 record and a .767

winning percentage at the school, they certainly weren't used to losing in their own stadium. As people filed out of the stands and spread over the lawns in the late-afternoon sunshine, what they were saying and the looks on their faces indicated that their football season had just about come to an end.

"I don't know," Holtz said after the game, "if I've ever been in a game where, personally, I so much wanted our team to play well. But we did not play well. Stanford did a tremendous job and I congratulate them."

In the locker room Bill Walsh at first said he was speechless, but then he said, "I'm so damned excited. I don't have much poise right now. I sort of broke down in front of the team. This game is as big as I've won. I guess after a Super Bowl victory you're euphoric, but this is a wonderful win."

"Winning the national championship is over," Rick Mirer said. "But there are many reasons for us to come back from this loss. Playing for pride is the main reason."

Moose had been invited to a postgame party but decided not to go. "Who the hell wants to socialize after something like that?" he said.

He drove home, ate dinner, and went to bed early, hardly the only person in South Bend with a damper on his evening plans. The campus had the feel of a punctured football. Late Friday night there had been shouts and laughter everywhere, but by ten P.M. on Saturday things were quiet and there was a sense that no one was having much fun. The stadium was completely dark and deserted, except for the cool wind that blew through it and made a soft whistling sound, creaking against the night.

Empty bleachers are eerie in the blackness, but the eeriest sight of all was the huge NBC-TV production trucks, still lined up against the stadium walls but abandoned now and looking very much alone. The activity that had swirled around them had ceased, and for the moment it seemed that everything everywhere had come to a halt and all the people were in hiding.

A few revelers over in the parking lot sang the victory

march and the music came floating toward the stadium, the voices scratchy and out of tune.

Early the next morning two guests at the Morris Inn were standing in the lobby when one of them glanced toward the east and said, "Well, I guess it came up again after all."

Moose attended Sunday-morning mass, then visited his wife's grave, drove home, and watched a replay of the Notre Dame–Stanford game. "It wasn't any better this time," he said, while moving slowly around his kitchen and putting together some lunch.

His apartment was located right next to the St. Joseph River, which runs through the heart of South Bend, and when you stood in his living room and gazed out the window, you got the strange impression that you were floating on top of the water. The rooms were filled with trophies and plaques he'd accumulated over the years, with Notre Dame memorabilia and football literature, with scrapbooks of his accomplishments and pictures of his wife and children. He never mentioned Elise without telling you how attractive she was, how good she'd been to him, and how much he'd enjoyed their lives together.

"My daughter looks just like her," he said. "She's just as beautiful as my wife."

For the past sixteen years he'd lived at this address, most of that time alone, and it had the feel of a bachelor's pad, with the scent of old cigar smoke embedded in the furniture. An assertive host, he not only insisted that you eat with him but then quickly rose from his chair in front of the television and walked toward the kitchen in his shuffling, delicate strides, barely bending his knees each time he took a step. He was surprisingly adept at preparing food and had in no time made a turkey sandwich and begun talking you into having a second one, with pickles on the side, all the while listening to a tape deck play music from the forties.

On fall Sundays he watched both the previous Notre Dame game, analyzing it carefully from his living-room seat, and a pro game featuring the Chicago Bears. He would discuss football in depth anytime and anywhere, and he was much more comfortable talking about sports in general than his own athletic achievements or his personal life.

At unpredictable moments, he would turn to you and ask if you were comfortable or if you were happy or if you were in love. Sitting alone with Moose, you caught a glimmer of how much he'd lived through during the past eight decades—the escape from the Back of the Yards, the rise to glory at Notre Dame, the murder of his father, his military adventures, his fifty-two-year marriage to Elise, the birth of his children, the death of his brother, Phil, in the late seventies, and other honors and tragedies that had come his way in later years.

Even when pushed, he would say little about most of these events, but somehow you could feel them when you were in his living room, watching a game with him and seeing him reach over and light another cigar. You could sense the past in his silence and see the effects of it in his permanently wet eyes. Sometimes, even though it wasn't the case, he looked as if he were weeping.

You knew that he believed much more in quietly enduring hardships than in complaining about them, and you could also sense, after being around him for a while, that his experience of life was essentially complete and there was nothing left for him to prove, nothing much that he wanted to do since the death of his wife, but you had to know Moose a little better to understand what this really meant.

Football games still interested him, as did watching his team compete, and he could not view the Irish on the TV screen without offering his advice. During a time-out, when he was asked about his favorite brand of cigars, he said, "I'll smoke anything."

When asked why he liked the stogies so much, he said, "They're all I've got left. I can't drink. I can't eat most foods. The doctors have told me that. I don't have sex anymore. But I can still smoke."

For a few moments the room was filled with sadness, but when he spotted an Irish player making a good tackle on television, he laughed and leaned forward in his chair, rolled his hand into a fist, threw it into the air, and shouted, "That's the way to do it! That's how we play football at Notre Dame."

He laughed again, that vital rugged sound, and took a long drag on the heater, blowing smoke across the room and falling back against the cushion.

"I'll talk to Lou tomorrow," he said. "I'll tell him we've lost games before and come back. I'll tell him about Leahy losing a game and crying. I've been here long enough to know the season isn't over yet. Lou will bounce back. You're damn right he will."

9 Getting Busy

AS MUCH AS MOOSE LOVED FOOTBALL AND AS SERIOUSLY AS he took it, he knew it was only a game. Over the years, he'd been far too close to real human misery to confuse the sport with other kinds of suffering.

In February of 1944, Moose had joined the Marine Corps and became an air-combat intelligence officer for a bombing squadron. Before going abroad, he told Leahy, who did not have plans to enter the military, that he was making a mistake. When the fighting ended, Moose said, the returning players were going to ask their coach what he'd done to defeat Germany and Japan, and if his answer was nothing, he would not command as much respect as before.

And once these young men had been overseas, Moose went on, they would come home as different people, older and more experienced, more like men than college boys, and if their coach did not understand what they'd been through and seen in combat, he would have trouble communicating with them. Leahy listened, and before long he, too, had signed up. A joke still heard around Notre Dame grew out of this decision: people said that Frank Leahy got away from the strain of coaching Irish football by going off to war.

Moose was leaving behind two sports in South Bend. The Irish's head basketball coach, George Keogan, had died in February of 1943, and even while Krause continued to coach for Leahy, he'd also been given Keogan's job. He'd played basketball under the man in the thirties and was now committed to carrying on his successful record on the court. Moose was also grateful to Keogan for helping him develop one of his trademarks.

"When I was growing up," Moose says, "my old man would never allow me or my brother to drink or smoke. Never, ever, do it, he told us, and if you ever do decide to do it, come to me and I'll help you. Back then, it was during Prohibition and he was making his own booze. So Phil and I went to him and he poured us a drink and gave us a cigar. I puffed the cigar and swallowed the whole glass of whiskey. So did my brother. I got sick and threw up and never drank again until I graduated from Notre Dame. I didn't like the cigar either.

"One night after graduation George Keogan took me to a banquet at the YWCA. He introduced me to all these women and he offered me a cigar. I started smoking it and everyone seemed to like that. I got up to make a speech, and while I was talking, I held the cigar like I knew what I was doing. It felt good in my hand. I made a toast and said, 'Here's to the ladies. The best years of my life I've spent with another man's wife—my mother.' I got a laugh. Keogan looked at me and was surprised. He didn't think I could be funny. I didn't either. He said, 'Hey, that's pretty good.' After that I kept on smoking."

For his active military duty, Moose was stationed on the Solomon Islands in the southwestern Pacific. From there he studied the movements of two hundred thousand Japanese who were in the area, and he told American pilots where to drop their bombs on the enemy and its ammunition. It was here that he was nearly court-martialed by his commanding officer for teaching the natives how to sing the Fighting Irish victory march. Moose wasn't in combat but often stayed up all night with the men who were about to fly their missions, telling them jokes and football stories, trying to allay their anxiety and fear. He doesn't talk much about the war, and almost everything he says about it has some connection to Notre Dame.

"I was always recruiting new fans," he says. "By the end of the war I'd converted most of the men I came in contact with. I did it by bringing in films of the games we won but not the ones we lost."

During lulls in the fighting, he set up basketball or football games on the island to take the men's minds off their work. Once peace was declared, Moose, like most other soldiers, couldn't wait to come home.

In January of 1946 he was discharged as a first lieutenant and quickly resumed his varied duties in South Bend. He was still coaching the basketball team, still working fourteen-hour days during the football season, and still responsible in the off-season for recruiting high school gridiron stars all over the country. That meant getting in his car (the Notre Dame administration was very much against flying since the death of Rockne) and driving to the East Coast, where he spoke with young football players and their parents in Massachusetts, New Jersey, Pennsylvania, and several other states.

This was before recruiters used film, so he could not return to South Bend with movies of the prospects. He not only had to describe the young men's characters to Leahy and talk about their ability to make their grades at Notre Dame, he had to be able to outline their physical skills in precise ways, their strengths and weaknesses and potential.

"If you didn't know how to spot talent," Moose says, "you had problems with Frank."

Moose not only knew football, he knew how to go into people's homes and tell them that although attending Notre Dame would not be easy and that all student athletes would be expected to graduate from the school, it would be excellent preparation for the rest of their lives.

Strangers tended to trust him. It might have been because of his size or his gravelly voice, an instrument made for talking about football, or because of his success and reputation in several different sports. It might have been his face, which was open and honest and in some mysterious way really did resemble the sincere expression of a moose, or because he meant just what he said. People liked him and even tolerated his cigars (big stogies are a superb way of testing whether or not folks enjoy your company). Whatever the reason, he got a lot of good players to come to South Bend.

In 1946 his second child, Mary Elise, was born, and Moose and his wife now occupied a modest but comfortable home just off the campus. If there was a golden era in his professional and personal life, it was the period following the war. Everyone in his family was healthy, the football program was entering its longest stretch of unbroken success, and the Krause home was alive with activity and celebration. Elise entertained every football weekend, opening her doors to other coaches, to their wives and children, to the Fighting Irish players, to the faculty and alumni, to students who were far from home or came from other countries, and to those who visited South Bend for a game.

One woman from the East Coast, a total stranger named Ella Maddox, followed Edward junior home one Friday afternoon and wound up staying with the family for several weeks so she could see another home game. She came back the next year and spent most of the season.

Moose kept his football trophies and other awards downstairs, where people would gather to talk about the upcoming game or to relive their gridiron memories. Cigar in one hand, a drink in the other, leaning back in his favorite chair and listening to tales of Rockne or Leahy, he was utterly at home. Kids played at his feet, young women guests were pregnant, the house was filled with laughter, and if he was overwhelmed with work, trying to meet his duties as a coach in two major sports, he was exactly where he desired to be.

From the forties onward he would be approached many times with job offers from other schools or professional football teams. He had friends in Chicago and Philadelphia and New York; he had friends everywhere. He was already showing skills as a natural fund-raiser, and when football people noticed this, they believed he would be good for their organization. He turned down all offers, even when there were opportunities to make considerably more money than he was earning at the university. He was loyal to Notre Dame, but it went beyond that: he was becoming a South Bend institution himself.

A fragment of writing survives from the forties. The author is Elise Krause, and she gives a sense of what it was like to be married to Moose in those years, raising young children and living in the midst of their busy household: "By the end of the season, I feel like a Marine suffering from battle fatigue and truly I am very happy when it ends. Ed too is a different person. During the season he must play the games in his sleep at night as he jumps, twitches, turns, calls out and tosses all over his bed. In the morning, I doubt he feels he has hit the pillow. The happiness enjoyed after victories is wonderful and even though the losses are hard to take, we coaches' wives do get a lot closer to our husbands with their victories and even more so with their defeats."

Frank Leahy had spent the war in the Navy stationed on several Pacific islands. After coming home, he was, most people agree, a slightly different coach. He wasn't easier on his teams or coaches and he wasn't any less of a perfectionist. He didn't work shorter hours or approach the game in a more relaxed manner, and he was still capable of telling the press—as he did during the unbeaten streak from 1946 to 1949—that he was afraid his team wouldn't make a first down in the upcoming season. The change in him was subtle and best reflected in the way his postwar players remember him. Their recollections are not as distant as those of the earlier players. As Leahy got older and more successful, he, like Lou Holtz four decades later, began to reveal a more human side to others, but no one ever forgot who was in charge.

"Frank loved telling the press how bad Notre Dame was

going to be," says Moose. "He said it so often that people started calling him Crying Frank. Then he would go out and beat the hell out of people. It made some other coaches mad and it made some of them not like Notre Dame. There's still some resentment around the country for that. The more Frank coached, the more confident he became, but he never wanted anyone around him to feel overconfident.

"One time I told a reporter that I thought we had a pretty good team, and he wrote that I'd said we were going to go undefeated. Leahy jumped all over me, asking me how could I ever do such a thing and who did I think I was? I told him that I'd never said anything like that to the papers and never would. It took him a while to get over it."

Joe Doyle was beginning his sportswriting career in South Bend as Leahy was approaching the end of his football days. "I think that by the late forties, when he told you how awful Notre Dame would be in the upcoming season, you had a sense that he was putting you on a little," Doyle says. "In the early forties, he really meant those things when he said them. He feared everything. He always wanted an edge and was always looking for new ways to motivate his players. Frank knew that you couldn't play football without having confidence and believing in yourself. If you're fishing for Moby Dick, you've got to take along the tartar sauce."

"We were playing the Iowa Seahawks one year," says Johnny Lujack. "They had some pro players and we were the underdogs. We got on a bus and Leahy took us out to a cemetery to say a prayer over Rockne's grave. I pray faster than some people and I finished before the rest of them. I looked around and saw George Keogan's grave, so I walked over to it and knelt down and started to pray for him. When Leahy saw me, he said, 'Come away from there, lad. Visit that man during the basketball season.'

"Another time we were playing Wisconsin and the score was tied at a critical moment in the game. Bob Neff was our left tackle and he missed an important block on their safety. Pete Ashbaugh, a star in our defensive backfield, was standing on the sidelines, and when he saw what Neff had done, he called out to him, 'You son of a bitch! Hit that man!'

"Leahy came over to Pete and was frowning, very upset. He looked right at him and said, 'Oh, lad, as long as you're representing Our Lady, you will never again use such a display of profanity. And if you do, you will turn in your uniform. Do you understand?' 'I certainly do,' Ashbaugh said. About three plays later, the same thing happened with Neff, and Ashbaugh didn't make a sound. Leahy found Pete and said, 'I do apologize, lad. Robert Neff is a son of a bitch.' "

Lujack mimics his old coach's brogue better than anyone else and laughs every time he does it. "The week after this happened with Ashbaugh," he says, "Frank had the team watch films of this one play where Neff had missed his block. He kept running it and rerunning it. After showing it the fourth or fifth time he said to Neff, 'I'm going to run this once more, Robert, and if you don't block that man this time, I don't know what I'm going to do with you.' Neff was so ashamed he went home, packed up his things, and was going to leave Notre Dame. Bill Earley talked him out of it, and the next year Neff was an honorable-mention All-American.

"Frank always made the players get up and talk to the whole team. You never knew when he was going to ask you to do this, but you knew it was coming. You could say anything you wanted and you had to talk for five minutes. That really helped me later on when I had to speak in public."

When Leahy's men talk about the forties, the name mentioned most often is Zygmont Czarobski. Ziggy came from Chicago, stood six feet tall, weighed 213 pounds (or somewhere in the neighborhood), and according to the *Fighting Irish Football Encyclopedia,* he was the "leading orator, raconteur and jokester of the Leahy years and a professional Irish personality after that. Leahy may have been impossible to take without Ziggy in the wings." Everyone from those days has a Ziggy story or two, but he was more than the team clown. He was a starting tackle on three national championship rosters ('43, '46, and '47) and became an all-American lineman.

Moose speaks about Ziggy with more affection than he does when talking about anyone else: the two men use to block the hell out of each other in practice, when Krause was a coach and Czarobski a player. The walls of Moose's small Notre Dame office are reserved for his favorite coaches—Rockne, Leahy, Terry Brennan, Parseghian, and Holtz—but there is only one Irish player up there: Zygmont himself. Ziggy was the life of the team and of the reunions Leahy's players held in later years.

"One time Frank saw him taking a shower before a game," says Bernie Crimmins. "Leahy studied him for a minute and was totally perplexed. 'Why are you doing that now, lad?' he asked. Ziggy shrugged and said, 'It's too crowded after the game.' "

"Czarobski always had a hard time with his weight," says Bob McBride. "He liked to eat more than he liked to practice. One year Leahy told him that if he weighed an ounce over two twenty, he wouldn't get a uniform. He came in and weighed two twenty-two. We only had a couple of hours to get him down to playing weight, so we took him up to the handball court, put him in a rubber suit, and worked him until he was ready to drop. When he got on the scales, he weighed two seventeen."

"Ziggy would get up to two forty or two forty-five and Frank would always be watching him around the scales," says Joe Signaigo. "He figured out a way to jiggle the scales so they weighed him light. He was always sneaking something past the coach."

"We were getting ready for Purdue one year and having a long hard practice," says Moose. "Ziggy was at one end of the field and Leahy was at the other. Ziggy got hungry and began to chant, 'We wanna eat! We wanna eat!' Frank heard this and looked around, like he couldn't believe his ears. Nobody was crazy enough to do something like that at one of his workouts. He must have been hearing things.

"A few minutes later he heard it again. This time Ziggy had several of the guys saying it: 'We wanna eat! We wanna eat! We wanna eat!' Frank turned and started to run up the field toward them. There was anger in his eyes. You could see the old boxer in him. He looked ready to fight. People got out of his way and everyone stopped what they were doing to watch. Ziggy saw him coming, but he was still leading the chant: 'We wanna eat! We wanna eat! We wanna eat!' When Frank got there, the other players got real quiet, but Ziggy looked at him and said, 'We wanna eat—Purdue!' Leahy just turned and walked away."

"Ziggy wasn't the best student Notre Dame ever had," says Lujack. "He used to tell people that he was in school for two terms—Roosevelt's and Truman's. One year he and I played for the East in an East–West game in San Francisco. He was going out every night and the rest of us were right behind him. The night before the game, our coach, who was Andy Kerr from Colgate, had a bed check and the only two guys he found sleeping were from Yale.

"During the game, the West scored and Ziggy stood in the middle of the field and said to their team, 'Gentlemen, that was a fine drive.' Then he led our team in a cheer for them—'Rah, rah, West. Rah, rah, West.' Ziggy was Polish and I was Polish so I understood his sense of humor, but Coach Kerr wasn't Polish and didn't understand any of it. He didn't know what the hell was going on. You should have seen the expression on his face when we came off the field. After the cheer, we beat them forty to nine. I was the MVP of that game, but Ziggy should have been."

"Ziggy came before me at Notre Dame, but I heard a story about him that I always remembered," says John Lattner, who played for Leahy from 1951 to 1953. "The team was going through a terrible practice, wasn't accomplishing anything, so Frank called them together and said, 'Oh, lads, our workouts are truly horrible. We're not hitting and we're not doing anything right. We're going to go back to the start and work on the basics.' He picked up a ball and said, 'This, gentlemen, is a football. It has twelve pounds of air in it.' Ziggy interrupted him and said, 'Wait, Coach, you're goin' too fast.' They all laughed and then went out and knocked the hell out of each other.

"Ziggy died in the early eighties. I went to his funeral. Father John Smyth was doing the service, and in the middle of it a gust of wind came up and blew away his notes. He wound up his speech quickly by saying we should all have a good time remembering Ziggy. Everyone stormed out and had a party and left Ziggy at the altar. Forgot all about him."

Running back Creighton Miller was another of Leahy's players who might have been considered, in today's sports lingo, as something of "a project." He hadn't come to Notre Dame on a scholarship so, unlike most of the other young men on the team, he wouldn't lose his financial support if he didn't play football. That gave him a little more flexibility.

"Creighton was kind of a wild kid," says Moose. "He'd play football for a while and then he'd want to quit. He'd break a few rules and do a lot of things other players didn't do, but Frank would always get him back on the team."

"Everyone was afraid of Leahy, including me," Miller says. "He used to send guys down to the movie houses in South Bend to look for me. I'd be hiding in there when they walked in, and I'd slink down lower in my seat and never respond when they called out my name. After a while, they usually left.

"After a couple of years Frank tried to give me a scholarship because he thought it would give him more control over me, but I never accepted one. I'd get so tired in his practices that I thought I was going to pass out. One day I sat down on the field and he had the whole team come over and look at me. Then he insulted me by calling me Fluffduff.

"He took me into his office and called me Fluffduff again. I said, 'I like that name.' He stared at me and said, 'You're not supposed to like it, lad. It's supposed to inspire you to play harder.' I said, 'Well, I really do like it.' That confused him. He was like a Marine sergeant and you don't love those guys, at least not until you've won the battles. He and I eventually became friends and I ended up respecting him a lot.

"My problem was that I had high blood pressure and had trouble passing the physical to play college football. I don't think Frank believed this about me. He thought I was just lazy. I went into the service and only lasted four days at Fort Dix because of this situation. They tested me and the numbers proved that I really did have high blood pressure. When I came back to Notre Dame, Frank said to me, 'Your discharge means something. What is it?' I said. 'It means I have very high blood pressure and I don't want you to run me into the ground.' He never bothered me again."

Says sportswriter Joe Doyle, "Moose was lying in bed with a bad cold in the winter of 1946. He was very sick. The phone rang at one A.M. and his wife picked it up. When Moose asked her who it was, Elise said she thought the young man's name was Leon Hart and he was down at the South Bend train station. Leahy had invited him out to visit the campus and he'd just arrived in town.

"Moose had been recruiting Hart for weeks, and when he heard the name, he jumped out of bed and ran for the door in his pajamas. His wife said, 'Where are you going?' and he said, 'To the train station, honey. I've got to pick him up.' She said, 'You'll die out there.' He said, 'It doesn't matter. If I don't get Hart on the team, Leahy will kill me anyway.' "

Hart, who hailed from Turtle Creek, Pennsylvania, which is right outside Pittsburgh, became an end for the Irish and one of the all-time great Notre Dame blockers. He played in South Bend from 1946 to 1949 and was not only the third Irish player but the second lineman in the nation to win the Heisman Trophy. He was never in a losing game in college and scored an average of once every five times he touched the ball. He played eight years with the Detroit Lions and was on three NFL championship teams. The first train ride Hart ever took from Turtle Creek to South Bend cost $12 and he was seventeen years old.

"I called Moose that night when I arrived because I knew it was too late to call Leahy," he says. "When his wife told him who was on the phone, I could hear him yelling in the background. Then I could hear him banging and crashing into things as he came to the phone. He drove out to get me in his overcoat and bedclothes. He took me over to the football stadium, where there were some beds in the training room for all the guys who were returning from the army. Moose put me in there and left. I got undressed and got in bed, and at two or three in the morning this big rough-looking character started shaking me. He said, 'Get the hell out of my bed.' I moved real fast.

"That was my introduction to Notre Dame. It was probably the worst-recruiting school of all time. You had to really want to go there. The next morning I got out of bed and was wandering around looking for some breakfast. I went over to the athletic department and found a secretary who was nice enough to give me a pass for a meal. I didn't know what was going on and I was kind of discouraged about being there, but I thought if anyone cared enough to get out of bed at one A.M. with pneumonia and come get me, maybe I better stay there and play football.

"After the war a lot of players returned to Notre Dame. In 1946, there were twenty-one men who wanted to play end and I was trying to make the team at that position. One of them was Zeke O'Connor, who was eventually switched to tackle. In the Rockne style of football, players went one-on-one with the coaches in practice. Moose was working over the tackles one day and Zeke came out of a crouch and threw an elbow and hit him right in the face. Moose turned a lot of different colors and then knocked the stuffing out of O'Connor and left him lying on the ground.

"A few years later Coach Bob McBride tried to do that to me and I just about killed him. Leahy came running over and watched this and didn't try to stop it. I never forgave him for that. I wasn't the kind of player who needed that sort of motivation.

"When I was a freshman, we'd been practicing one day for about three hours and Leahy just wouldn't give up. George Connor, one of our star tackles, was taking it easy and the old man noticed it. He came over to me and told me to unwind, so I did. I hit Connor and drove him at Leahy's feet. Frank looked down at him and said, 'Oh, George Connor, look what that freshman did to you, lad.' It woke George right up.

"Leahy was the greatest man I ever met. He had far more influence on your life than you ever believed or realized until much later. Nothing is beyond your reach, he taught us, if you put yourself to it and use loyalty, hard work, dedication, and degradation. Those were the four things he believed in most. Get down on the ground and dig for it. Get dirty. As hard as he made you work, you knew he was working twice as hard. And he expected the same thing from his coaches.

"Leahy's locker-room speeches were not only good, they were much better than Moose's when he had to fill in and coach us. The tougher the game, the harder the speech Frank gave us. The easier the game, the longer the speech. Against Army in 1946, all he said was, 'All right, boys. Army's out there waiting for you.' Against Indiana, he talked forever."

In 1946, George Connor won the Outland Trophy as the outstanding lineman in the country. The following season he was named captain of the Irish team.

"In 1947," he says, "I got to deal with Leahy in terms of how he dealt with our players. In the second to the last game of the year, against Tulane, our running back Terry Brennan tore up a knee and was in a cast. We were going to Los Angeles two weeks later to play USC and Brennan's name wasn't on the list to make the trip. I went over to Frank's office and said I had to talk to him. 'Sit down, lad,' he said, and I did. I said, 'If Terry isn't going, no one is going.' He looked at me and I didn't know what was coming. With him you never knew. 'Is that right?' he said. I said, 'Yes, it is.' I got up and left. An hour later, Brennan was on the list. We went out there and won the national championship. Leahy just never liked having people injured.

"One time in the locker room before a game he said, 'I'd rather have my son lose his right arm than for us to lose this game.' The next week he'd say, 'I'd rather have my son lose his left arm than for us to get beat today.' By the end of the season, we had that kid totally dismembered.

"Frank got sick once and Moose had to give us a pregame

pep talk. He was wearing a cowboy hat and smoking a cigar and pacing around the locker room. He started in on how sick Leahy was and how he hadn't even been able to shave for a week. One of our halfbacks, Bob Livingstone, called out, 'Let's buy him some razor blades!' He and Leahy didn't get along too well. Moose ignored the remark and kept talking about how we had to win this one for the coach. He built it up and built it up, smoking and pacing, and finally he told us to get out there and tear them apart. Somebody looked at him and said, 'You forgot to name the starting lineup.' Moose roared back, 'You're all starting!'

"After we left Notre Dame, we discovered that Leahy was really a very naive person. He'd come into Chicago and talk to some of us about our lives. He always seemed surprised at how grown up we were and at the things we were doing as men. It was like we were still the age we'd been at Notre Dame. He was so involved in coaching that he wasn't very worldly. All he ever thought about was the game."

John Lattner, the halfback who played for Leahy in the early fifties and won the Heisman Trophy in 1953, was involved in one of the most famous of all the stories about the coach.

"When I was a junior and we were playing Purdue, I fumbled five times," Lattner says. "That was a record I set and I don't think it's ever been broken. Going back to South Bend on the train, I asked our assistant coach Bill Earley if I could go home and see my sick brother instead of remaining with the team after we'd arrived home. I wanted to get away from everyone for a while. Leahy didn't like this idea but he let me do it.

"On Monday he had a chalk talk, and his first statement was 'Oh, my God, lads, do you realize there's a traitor among you—an enemy who disgraced you and everyone else who loves Notre Dame in front of fifty-nine thousand people last Saturday?' He didn't mention my name, but he didn't have to. I felt terrible inside.

"He gave me a forty-five-minute lecture on my fumbling. When I tried to leave, he told me to come back and he said,

'I can't understand how you could do this. Do you have any trouble with girls?' 'No, I don't,' I said. He told me that he'd heard that I used to go to the racetrack, and he asked if I'd bet on the game against Notre Dame. I said, no, I hadn't done that.

"He asked me to do him a favor. He said, 'Go to confession, lad, and confess those five mortal sins you committed last Saturday.' He wanted to eradicate fumbling out of my system forever. Then he told me to carry a football around all week to my classes. And I did, because I was afraid that he'd toss me off the team if I didn't. After that, I never fumbled very much.

"You don't care how hard you work as long as you win, and Frank won. He was a great guy. One of the biggest things I learned from him is that you don't give up. You either learn how to do it the old way or you find a new way. I'm in the sales business now and it's nothing for me to have people say no to me. I just keep going."

Says Moose, "Frank worked so hard he got sick a lot. Three times I had to take over and coach the team. We beat USC, Washington, and Tulane. I'm the only undefeated football coach in Notre Dame history. In one of those games, we were leading USC twenty-six to nothing and I told our quarterback, George Ratterman, 'No matter what you do, keep the ball on the ground and don't throw it.' We get down to their goal line and he throws an interception and their guy runs it back for a touchdown. He comes over to the sideline and I go out to kill him. He says, 'Sorry, Coach. He was the only one open.' "

As the forties gave way to the fifties, the Notre Dame teams were not only less triumphant than in the recent past, the head coach's health began to crack. Those around Leahy could see him aging, although in 1953 he was only forty-five years old, just two years older than Rockne when he'd died. Leahy's posture became stooped, he walked in shorter steps along the sidelines, his face sagged into a permanent frown, and he looked decades older than he was.

In his last years in South Bend people began to say that the three hardest jobs in America were being president of the United States, mayor of New York City, and head coach of the Fighting Irish. As with other men in his profession, Leahy had become a victim of his own extraordinary success. Fans now expected remarkable winning streaks and clusters of national championships, and he expected himself to be able to deliver those things. When he didn't, his past success was little comfort.

On October 24, 1953, he collapsed in the Irish dressing room at the halftime of the Georgia Tech game, which was being played in South Bend. The cause was pancreatitis—a severe inflammation of the pancreas gland—and the original prognosis was that he might die. Father Edmund Joyce, C.S.C., was brought into the locker room, and he administered last rites over the coach. There were Notre Dame players in the dressing room that day who wondered if their coach was feigning the illness as a motivational tool. He'd tried other things that were nearly as dramatic, but this was no ploy.

When the team came out for the second half, Moose was up in the press box where he'd once been stationed as an assistant coach. He couldn't find Leahy on the field. "I didn't know what the hell had happened," he says. "When I saw he was gone, I went down and told Joe McArdle to coach the rest of the game."

Joe Doyle never talks about Leahy without breaking into a grin. "Eddie Erdelatz coached at Navy and they were coming to play Notre Dame the next week after Frank collapsed," he says. "He had to miss Navy and Erdelatz was angry about it. He told me before the game, 'Goddammit, I want him to be here. When I met him four years ago, I thought he would be very friendly to me, but he was stiff and standoffish. The next time I met him I decided to be distant with him, but he was very friendly to me. Just like my best buddy. The next time I was friendly to him and he was stiff again. Acted like he didn't know me. This time around I was just gonna wait for him to make the first move and not do anything. And now the SOB won't even show up!'

"That was the way Frank worked people. He would have a couple of drinks with you and then turn completely different so you didn't quite know who he was."

Leahy recovered from his illness and worked the remainder of the 1953 season, but he knew that if he didn't want to die on the sidelines, he was finished at Notre Dame. When he retired, he'd coached four Heisman Trophy winners—Bertelli, Lujack, Hart, and Lattner—and had recruited a fifth, Paul Hornung. Winning percentage aside, his teams' overall performance was perhaps a shade better than Rockne's. Leahy had had six undefeated seasons (to Rock's five), four national titles (to Rock's three), thirty-nine consecutive games without a loss (to Rock's twenty), and a final record of 87-11-9 to Rock's 105-12-5.

After leaving South Bend, Leahy moved to Oregon and lived another twenty years, working in public relations for several different businesses.

"Frank's funeral was in Portland," says John Lattner. "We were wheeling him to where the hearse was waiting to take him to the cemetery, and they were playing the victory march. We decided to carry him instead. Of the eight men who were holding up the casket, six had already had heart attacks. Only George Connor and I hadn't. The casket got heavier and heavier as we got closer to the hearse. We were panting and sweating. I turned to Connor and said, 'Oh, George, Leahy always said that the last ten yards were the hardest.' "

Moose was at the funeral. "All his players were there," he says, "and they all stood up and said what an SOB he was because he worked them so hard. I was the last one to speak. I said, 'Yeah, he was an SOB. You worked hard on Monday, Tuesday, Wednesday, Thursday, and Friday, but you celebrated on Saturday after the game.' And the men cheered."

"One night years after I'd left Notre Dame, I came back for a visit," says Johnny Lujack. "Creighton and I and Frank went to dinner at Eddie's Restaurant. We'd had a few cocktails and were reminiscing. He was no longer a coach and we were out of football and we were all relaxed.

"It got late, about two in the morning, and as we left Eddie's, Frank suggested that we drive by the campus. We were coming up the boulevard that goes right by the golden dome with Our Lady on top of it, and he told me to stop. I pulled over and we all looked up. The moonlight was hitting the dome and it was very quiet outside. No one spoke for a while. Then Frank said, 'Gents, there might be the greatest sight the world has ever known. It's a shame that everyone can't see it.' Creighton and I just looked at each other. There wasn't anything you could say."

10 The Revival

In 1949, as the Leahy era was beginning to wane, Moose stopped coaching football to take another job, becoming the head of the Notre Dame athletic department, a post he would hold for the next thirty-two years. His basketball coaching days were also finished. His record on the court was 98 wins and 48 losses, and one of his most memorable victories came against the Baron, Kentucky's legendary Adolph Rupp, although Moose admits he had help in that game from the Notre Dame band. The trumpet section had stationed itself right behind Rupp's bench and made a point of blasting out its melodies and harmonies whenever the Baron called a time-out and attempted to instruct his players.

"Rupp couldn't hear a damn thing," Krause says, "and neither could his team."

When offered the chance to become athletic director, Moose didn't hesitate for long. His third child, Philip, would arrive in 1950. Moose had seen enough of the road and knew that jobs as athletic directors were more stable than coaching positions. Not only was he ready to settle into an office routine, he was also growing weary of banging heads and shoulders with young linemen who were getting bigger and stronger every year.

"Coaches don't do that kind of stuff anymore," he says. "And if they do, at least they get to wear pads, but Frank wouldn't hear of it."

While he was athletic director, many new sports at Notre Dame achieved varsity status—lacrosse, soccer, hockey, swimming, field hockey, and volleyball—plus five women's sports, including basketball, field hockey, fencing, tennis, and volleyball. His reputation as AD is best summed up by the remark of an Irish alum from the sixties: "If St. Peter ever needs a break from his work at the pearly gates, the man to spell him is Moose Krause. The only thing harder than figuring out who gets into heaven is trying to disperse the money at the Notre Dame athletic department without making everyone mad. That was his job for three decades."

In his early days as AD, Moose helped the football program in ways that weren't completely obvious. If there were schools that had grown tired of playing the Irish because Leahy had defeated them so often and so badly, there were also schools that Moose could now call up and schedule (or reschedule) because he had a good personal relationship with their athletic directors. People enjoyed doing him favors. As one sportswriter put it back then: "Moose'll talk 'em into playing the Irish and Frank'll beat 'em up."

When Phil Krause thinks back on growing up in the 1950s and '60s, during the first decade or so of his father's tenure as the Notre Dame AD, he remembers the grand pregame and postgame parties at his home, and he recollects going into Moose's crowded office on the Saturday mornings before home football games. His dad, looking bigger than life itself, would be seated in a huge chair behind a huge desk, smoking a long cigar and wearing a Notre Dame cap or a cowboy hat, blowing smoke and waving his hands as he regaled the high school coaches and their gridiron stars, who'd been brought to South Bend to see the tradition and ceremony that surrounded the game of football, filling them with tales of the Irish's storied past.

"When the kids walked in and met Dad, their eyes would get wide and their mouths would all open," Phil says. "They would gawk when he told them about all the football heroes and coaches he'd known. Here was one of Rockne's old players asking an eighteen-year-old to become part of the history of the school, and he might have Johnny Lujack or Paul Hornung standing there with him. The kids would say, 'My God! Look at him!' It was all part of the recruiting process at Notre Dame and it worked. The school wasn't the easiest sell because of the academic requirements, but this helped a lot.

"Dad was always proud of the football record, but his biggest achievement as athletic director was overseeing a program in which ninety-eight to ninety-nine percent of the players graduated and did it without violating the rules. He was always totally against paying college players anything—cars or clothes or whatever. In his mind, you were lucky to be getting a college education at Notre Dame. That was enough."

The first decade of Moose's tenure as AD was not the best period for the Irish football team. (It's almost accurate to say that Notre Dame has flourished in the even-numbered decades and had difficulty in the odd-numbered ones. If the twenties and forties were unqualified successes, the thirties and fifties were not. The last several decades have had mixed results.) Part of the problem in the fifties, which Moose acknowledged in later years, was that Notre Dame had tried to keep the head coaching job strictly in the university family.

After Leahy retired in 1953, he was replaced by twenty-five-year-old Terry Brennan, a good all-purpose halfback for the Irish from 1945 to 1948. Following his graduation from college, the young man coached Mt. Carmel High School to three consecutive city championships in Chicago before returning to South Bend as a freshman coach and then to take over from Leahy. In his first two years, Brennan was 17-3, but he was 15-15 the next three years and departed as head coach four days before Christmas of 1958. His last season, the student body hung him in effigy on three separate occasions.

Joe Kuharich, a South Bend native who'd played for the Irish in the 1930s, was hired next. In 1955 he'd been the NFL's coach of the year with the Washington Redskins, but when he tried to bring a pro-style passing offense to Notre Dame, it didn't work. Between 1959 and 1962, his record was 17-23—the only losing football coach in the history of the school.

For the 1963 season, Hugh Devore, who'd played on the Irish line next to Moose in the 1930s, was brought in as an interim coach, until the university administration could find someone they were comfortable offering a longer contract. Under Devore the team went 2-7. In 1963, for the fourth straight year they were beaten by a school that would never have been competitive with them in earlier days: Northwestern. Moose had watched this development—and this quartet of losses—not so much with annoyance as with curiosity about the opposing head coach. Who was the man who kept beating Krause's beloved football team?

His name was Ara Parseghian and he'd already expressed interest in coming to South Bend. He'd watched the demise of Kuharich and the lack of success by Devore and then contacted the Notre Dame administration about being hired as the next coach, although he felt that as a non-Catholic and non-alumnus, his chances were slim.

Moose wanted him, and after using his gifts of persuasion on the university officials, he got his way.

"The priests here are wonderful people," Moose has said on more than one occasion, "but they don't know much about football."

Because he had not attended Notre Dame and his only experience with the Irish football program was on the other sideline, Parseghian's introduction to the new job was something of a jolt. His selection had been announced and he traveled to the campus to sign a contract, and to meet the Notre Dame press for the first time. Negotiations with Father Joyce were underway upstairs in the Morris Inn and the press waited downstairs for a news conference.

When Parseghian and Father Joyce could not immediately

agree on terms, Parseghian decided to return to Northwestern. He suddenly appeared in the lobby carrying his bag and read a brief statement that said, "Because of a premature announcement, terms of a contract have not been worked out and any decision about the job will have to wait."

Parseghian walked out the door and it wasn't until a few days later that the contract problems were solved.

Nearly thirty years later, when asked why he abruptly left the Morris Inn on that occasion, he refuses to answer that question, declaring that he doesn't want to say anything that would embarrass the university. There are proud men and there are proud men. It takes about fifteen seconds in his presence to realize that Parseghian is one of the proudest and most competitive people you will ever encounter. Approaching seventy, he may have lost a little of his edge. One can only imagine how tightly he was wound in 1963.

"When Ara got here," Moose says, "he was so overwhelmed by everything that he had to get away. After he left the Morris Inn, I got in my car and followed him. When I caught up with him, I said, 'Look, you belong here and you're gonna be all right.' He was so concerned because he wasn't a Catholic. I said, 'Rockne wasn't a Catholic, don't worry about it.' He wanted to come here so badly but he was frightened. After this happened at the Morris Inn, I later took him to a Notre Dame basketball game, and we went out on the court at halftime and I introduced him to the crowd. All the students stood up and began cheering, 'Ara! Ara! We want Ara!' He was so happy then he was on a cloud.

"I was always straight with him. I told him when he started the job, 'You're gonna have trouble here because some people hate Notre Dame. You know it and I know it and you're gonna have to live with it.' In 1964 our first game was against Wisconsin. He was staying at a hotel with the team, and the night before the game people were calling him from all over the country and sending telegrams, wishing him good luck. He couldn't believe it. He had no idea how many people follow Notre Dame. He couldn't get any sleep. I told him to check into another room and we wouldn't tell anyone where he was. He was fine after that."

Parseghian knew that he hadn't been hired just to lead Notre Dame back to a winning record. Fifteen years had passed since Leahy had taken the Irish to a national title, and the alumni and student body were anxious for a return to glory. That was the new coach's job and no one could have gone about it with more dedication. Serious football people, including coaches and players who fancied themselves familiar with organized minds when it came to the gridiron, had never seen one like this. But he was more than organized. He was also shrewd.

"The hold Ara got on people was something that needed to happen after what had come before," says Joe Doyle. "The Notre Dame team in 1964 really wasn't that good. We had John Huarte and Jack Snow and they got better as the season went along and Huarte ended up winning the Heisman Trophy, but what was more important was how Ara got the student body reinvolved in the football program.

"In the winter of 1964, six or seven months before the season began, he held mini-rallies outside the dormitories on campus. This was way before spring football practice started. It was snowing then and it was freezing, but the kids turned out for the rallies. They'd never seen anything like them and neither had Ara. He got a bigger response than he was expecting. He grabbed the whole town that way. He liked golf and joined the South Bend Country Club. People there treated him like a regular person and he loved that. The guys would needle him about football and he would needle them right back. All the time he was stirring their interest.

"All great coaches have confidence in their ability, no matter what they say. Ara had that confidence and that charisma and he used it. One afternoon during a home game in his first year or two, it was fifteen degrees and snowing hard. The student body started chanting, 'Ara, stop the snow! Stop the snow!' He turned to one of his assistant coaches, Tom Pagna, and joked, 'Do you think I could?' A couple years later, it was raining during a game and the students began to shout, 'Ara, stop the rain! Stop the rain!' He turned to Pagna and said, 'Do you think I should?' "

When Moose talks about Parseghian, his tone is different from when discussing any other Irish coach. He speaks of Rockne as a son speaks of his father and he speaks of Leahy as a man talks about a friend. By the time Parseghian came to Notre Dame, Moose was in his fifties and he regarded Ara more as a father regards a son. He was more openly affectionate, obviously proud of the younger man. In 1964, Moose knew that it would take a particular kind of coach to resurrect the Irish football program from the mediocrity into which it had sunk, and without that coach, the tradition might fall into disrepair and never recover.

Football dynasties tend not to last more than a decade: the Green Bay Packers of the sixties, the Pittsburgh Steelers of the seventies, the San Francisco 49ers of the eighties. The college game has had a few longer-lasting reigns, but they've generally been tied to one coach: Bear Bryant's Alabama teams, Joe Paterno's Penn State Nittany Lions, Darrel Royal's old Texas powerhouses. There are a few exceptions—Oklahoma won big under Bud Wilkinson and Barry Switzer and the current Miami teams have triumphed with three different head coaches—but they are very rare.

Notre Dame's uniqueness has been its ability to rebuild the program and return to national championship form again and again, after some down years or even decades. One of the most well-worn clichés in sports is that no coach can successfully follow a legend, and the Irish experience seems to bear that out. The men who came immediately after Rockne and Leahy did not fare nearly as well as their predecessors, but when a little time was allowed to pass, a new figure has regularly appeared in South Bend, capable of rekindling the old tradition and starting a new one of his own.

In the mid-sixties, a handsome Armenian with black hair and burning eyes was exactly the man the Notre Dame athletic director wanted for his football team. Moose called him "Parmesan" and he had precisely the quality Leahy had once had and Rockne before him. No matter how often you try to analyze this characteristic or how deeply you try to penetrate it, it remains something of a mystery, like trying to understand fire by staring into the flames.

"Ara and Leahy were similar in many ways," Moose says. "They were very sensitive people, and when they lost, they couldn't sleep. They sat up all night and thought about it. One time after we lost a game to Louisiana State University, Ara was so upset he was wandering around the hotel. I found him in a restaurant eating spaghetti at six A.M. and I sat down at his table. 'What's the matter?' I said. 'We lost,' he told me. He was just looking at the wall, looking through it. It was something to see his eyes. You never forget them. I said, 'Look, we've lost before. Leahy lost a couple of games. We'll come back from this.' 'Yeah, sure,' he said.

"He didn't want to hear it. They're all like that. They hate losing."

11 A Time for Change

THE SAME THING THAT MOOSE HAD ONCE DONE FOR PARSEGHIAN after a loss, nearly three decades earlier, he now did for Lou Holtz after the Stanford game. On Monday morning he went into his office at nine A.M. and wrote the coach a note, telling Holtz that the worst was over and things were about to improve. Krause's longtime friend and assistant, Colonel Jack Stephens, also came in and wrote Holtz a few lines, echoing Moose's sentiments. They weren't the only ones scribbling that day.

If the tie against Michigan had brought forth an outcry from some Irish fans locally and around the nation, the Stanford debacle set loose an even greater response. More people wrote the *Blue & Gold Illustrated* praising Bill Walsh, asking for Holtz's head, and declaring that the Irish defense had become nonexistent. In the world of college football, one scribe said, "ND" now stood for "No Defense."

Holtz himself decided that change was in order and set about it that Monday afternoon, when he called a team meeting in one of the university auditoriums. Before it started, the

Knute Rockne traveled halfway across the nation to play football in New York and California—and to introduce Notre Dame to America.
(University of Notre Dame Sports Information Department)

Knute Rockne was always sidestepping the opposition. He put silk jerseys on his players so the other team had trouble holding on to them. (University of Notre Dame Sports Information Department)

Heartley "Hunk" Anderson (right) took over the Notre Dame football program after Rockne's death. (University of Notre Dame Sports Information Department)

Knute Rockne was at the height of his coaching powers, winning national titles in 1929 and '30, when he died in a plane crash in March of 1931. (University of Notre Dame Sports Information Department)

Frank Leahy (right) learned a lot about football when he and Rockne spent two weeks in side-by-side beds in the Mayo Clinic in 1930. Leahy never stopped questioning his mentor. (University of Notre Dame Sports Information Department)

Frank Leahy, the perfectionist's perfectionist, here shows his players the fine art of holding a football. (University of Notre Dame Sports Information Department)

Frank Leahy (left) insisted that his assistant coach, Moose Krause, block the players during practice, but Leahy never let Moose wear pads. (University of Notre Dame Sports Information Department)

Frank Leahy often looked nattily turned out, except after sleeping all night on the desk in his office. (University of Notre Dame Sports Information Department)

Between 1946 and 1949, Leahy's teams won three national championships and never lost a game. (University of Notre Dame Sports Information Department)

Ara Parseghian called his own plays from the sidelines by using an elaborate set of hand signals. (University of Notre Dame Sports Information Department)

As head coach at Northwestern, Ara Parseghian beat Notre Dame four straight times—so the Irish hired him. (University of Notre Dame Sports Information Department)

John Huarte (right) was a little-known player at Notre Dame until Ara Parseghian arrived in 1964. That year Huarte won the Heisman Trophy. (University of Notre Dame Sports Information Department)

The young men who played under Ara Parseghian never forgot the intensity of his dark eyes. (Br. Charles McBride, C.S.C.)

The 1992 football season gave Lou Holtz little to smile about, until his team won its last seven games and dominated the Cotton Bowl. (Steven Navratil)

Lou Holtz and the Fighting Irish take the field against the Miami Hurricanes in 1990. (John Dlugolecki)

In the opinion of many, Notre Dame has never had a faster or more exciting player than Raghib "Rocket" Ismail. (Greg Kohs)

Coach Holtz spent much of the 1992 season fending off controversial questions from the media. (Cheryl Ertelt)

In 1992, Irish quarterback Rick Mirer led one of the most powerful offenses in the nation. (Bill Panzica)

Chris Zorich, a two-time all-American, was the nose tackle on Notre Dame's 1988 undefeated national championship team. (Greg Kohs)

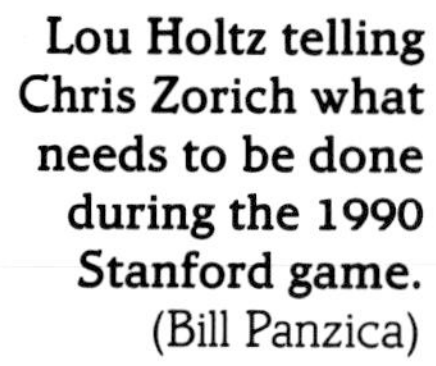

Lou Holtz telling Chris Zorich what needs to be done during the 1990 Stanford game. (Bill Panzica)

Col. Jack Stephens was Moose's assistant and sidekick for the last twenty-five years of Krause's life. (Bruce Harlan)

Flanker Tim Brown was the seventh and most recent Irish player to win the Heisman Trophy. (University of Notre Dame Sports Information Department)

In the first College All-Star game, held in Chicago in 1934, Moose played almost the entire game with a broken hand. (University of Notre Dame Sports Information Department)

Moose Krause is the only Notre Dame player ever inducted into the national Basketball Hall of Fame in Springfield, Massachusetts. (University of Notre Dame Sports Information Department)

The Krause family at home in South Bend in the 1950s. Left to right are Edward, Jr., Elise, Moose, and Philip. Not present is daughter Mary Elise. (University of Notre Dame Sports Information Department)

This billboard appeared in South Bend shortly after Moose's death on December 11, 1992. (Bruce Harlan)

Moose Krause never went anywhere without this Notre Dame ring and his cigars. (Gary Mills)

mood in the room was funereal: the Irish had lost at home, on national television, to a team ranked well below them, in a game that wasn't as close as the 33–16 score. They'd let down their fans and been kicked in public.

Holtz told the assembled young men that they'd come to Notre Dame to play in big games, and despite what had happened last Saturday and despite the fact that they could no longer win the national championship, plenty of significant games remained in the 1992 season. He took out a schedule and went through their upcoming opponents: Pittsburgh, BYU, Navy, Boston College, Penn State, Southern California, and perhaps—it was still possible—a major bowl game on New Year's Day.

Holtz talked about the caliber of their opposition, which has long been something of a sore point with Irish fans, who feel that Notre Dame often plays tougher foes than other top-ranked teams. Holtz pointed out that four future opponents—BYU, Boston College, Penn State, and Southern Cal—were in the Associated Press's Top 25, and the Irish would likely have the distinction of playing more ranked opponents this year than anyone else in the nation.

Time would prove him right. Notre Dame would compete in six games against Top 25 teams before the bowl bids were offered. By comparison, Miami would play four such teams (Florida State, Arizona, Penn State, and Syracuse), Alabama would play three (Tennessee, Mississippi State, and Mississippi) and Texas A&M one (Stanford). Holtz told the team that if they played the rest of the season as they were capable of playing, they could still finish in the top five.

"Everyone just kind of looked at him," says Art Monaghan, the team manager, who was in the auditorium that day. "The guys were way down and nobody really believed him."

In the future, Holtz went on, their routine before home games would be different and less distracting. Following the Friday-night pep rallies, the team would hold its relaxation sessions not in the new and comfortable Loftus Center, which had large meeting rooms and an indoor practice facility, but in a smaller, older space at the Joyce Athletic and Convocation

Center, a space that, says Monaghan, "has a musty smell and a nostalgic feel."

Before the Stanford loss, Holtz had not traveled with the team on Friday evenings to a motel outside South Bend, in Plymouth, Indiana, where the players slept before home games so they could escape the noise and excitement on the campus. From now on he would go with them and visit each of the twenty-nine motel rooms holding the fifty-eight players who had the best chance of seeing action the following day, (twenty-five to thirty other young men suited up for home games but did not make the trip to Plymouth). Before going to bed, Holtz would talk to every one of the fifty-eight individually, asking them questions about how they were feeling and telling them what to expect in the game. If his duties at Notre Dame already included making a vast number of speeches and giving countless inspirational talks, that number had suddenly shot up.

"Coach Holtz just felt," says Monaghan, "that he should be the last person to speak with the guys before they went to sleep."

On Saturday mornings, the team would no longer attend mass in Keenan Hall but move the service over to Sacred Heart Basilica, the old, tall, magnificent church in the middle of the campus. After the mass, which was conducted by Father James Riehle, C.S.C., the athletic department chaplain, the players would not disperse and go back to their dorms as in the past, breaking up the rhythm and the group feeling generated throughout the morning, but walk straight to the university dining hall and eat the pregame meal: pasta, pancakes, and ham, always the same menu, always a superload of carbohydrates. After consuming all they wanted, the young men would walk across the campus to the stadium as a unit.

"Coach Holtz decided that we'd been losing concentration on Saturday morning by not doing everything together," Monaghan says. "The players really like going places in droves. It gives them a certain feeling—a powerful feeling—and they loved the new routine."

In the past, all eighty players had suited up for the game

at the same time in the stadium locker room. Now Holtz wanted only the fifty-eight regulars in the dressing room on Saturday morning; the rest were assigned to a private locker room at another location. This left the main locker room less cramped and less hectic, so everyone felt there was more time to get dressed, to relax, to listen to music, or to read one of the game-day programs the assistants handed out.

Not everything would be different. Holtz would still send the various parts of the squad—the offense, the defense, the special teams—out for their pregame drills at exact times (12:00, 12:08, 12:15) and call them back into the locker room for their final instructions a few minutes before the kickoff. He would still stand before them for some last words, positioning himself right on top of the interlocking *ND* on the dressing-room gold-and-blue carpet. He would still give unpredictable speeches before and after the games.

"With him," says Monaghan, "you never know what's coming. Every time I try to guess what he'll say next, I'm wrong."

Holtz promised that from now on his team was going to pass the ball less and run the ball more, and in practice the first-team defense would regularly take on the first-team offense, so that both units would be sharper.

"Any time you lose and things don't go well," he said three days after the Stanford game, "there's usually a reason for it. You've got to look at it and say, 'Why?' I think our practices and our attitude about the game in general were starting to drift a little bit. So you just examine it, and as long as you believe there's a solution and don't give up, I don't think the players will. . . . There are times when players block out. You don't ever want them to block you out, but you especially don't want them to block you out after a loss. That is when you've lost a football team."

In a move evoking one of Rockne's old strategies, Holtz also promised one other thing: his second-team offense was going to play in the games more than in the past, just to shake things up.

* * *

After Moose and Colonel Stephens had answered their mail and made a few phone calls, they sat in Krause's office, drinking coffee and reminiscing. The Colonel, a diminutive, fiesty ex–military man, is the sort of guy who, at eighty, gives you funny looks for putting cream in your coffee. Sometimes you feel like saluting him and sometimes you don't. He has an explosive temper and an explosive heart.

For the past twenty-five years he's run interference for Krause, helping him when he was the AD and since Moose's retirement in 1980. Their offices are separated by a thin wall and a doorway. When the men want to communicate with each other or announce a visitor, they yell through the open door and it echoes out into the hallway. They yell at each other quite a bit. Moose's two greatest trademarks at Notre Dame are his cigars and his gruff-but-tender relationship with Col. Stephens.

Following his retirement as commander of the ROTC forces on the campus, the Colonel had been Ara Parseghian's assistant briefly before going to work for Moose in 1968. Moose was always the front man, the Colonel handling the details behind the scenes. Perhaps his major responsibility was keeping those who wanted more money off the athletic director's back. He's good at things like that. Stephens is about the only person at Notre Dame who calls his old boss Ed.

"People were always coming in and wanting Ed to increase their budget," the Colonel said, looking at his companion of the last quarter century with an expression that combined pride and protectiveness. "Give me this, give me that. Somebody always wanted something. You know how people are. I'd tell them that Moose was in a very very bad mood and if they went into his office, they were gonna catch holy hell."

Moose's shoulders bobbed in his chair. He was laughing again.

"That got rid of most of them," the Colonel said. "He never liked to get mad at people, but that didn't bother me at all. I had to keep the bastards away from his door."

Moose leaned back and blew smoke. Behind him, arrayed on the wall to his right and his left, were photos of Rockne,

Leahy, Terry Brennan, Ziggy Czarobski, a sketch of Parseghian, and a photo of Lou Holtz. Over part of his image, Holtz had scribbled a message to Krause. It began, "To my hero . . ."

A sign on the wall read, "The Lord is my shepherd but Lou Holtz is my coach."

Moose said to the Colonel, "Ara told me that hiring you was a big mistake."

The Colonel studied the sketch of Parseghian for a while and said, "That's a damn flattering portrait of him, if you ask me."

"Nobody did," Moose said.

"I'll tell you something about Ara," Stephens said. "The one guy who helped Ed the most through thick and thin was Ara Parseghian. He was like a son to him. When Ed was drinking and had some tough tough days . . ." He glanced at Moose and said, "Maybe you don't want to talk about that."

"That's all right," Krause said. "I do want to talk about it. I've talked about it to Alcoholics Anonymous groups all over the United States. In Cleveland, Detroit, Chicago. I don't mind doing it now. I'm not ashamed of it. Ara helped me, the Colonel helped me. I had a drinking problem but I don't anymore."

"AA helped you immeasurably," Stephens said. "You've been stone-cold sober for what—fifteen, twenty years now—and you've helped other people with their drinking. Back in the old days, the fifties and sixties, it was different, almost impossible not to drink. Moose had friends everywhere, every city we played in. They'd show up before the game with a bottle of scotch in one hand, a bottle of bourbon in the other, and the mix to go with it. They'd say, 'I wanna see Moose.' Everybody wanted to see Moose. They'd corner him and start pouring the booze and it was hard to say no. I tried to fight them off, but they all wanted to party."

"Everybody drank back then," Moose said. "It was a part of football, but that's pretty much gone now. Things are more businesslike these days."

The Colonel laughed. "Ed and I used to room together on the road. He snores real loud. One night he was over there making a lot of noise and I couldn't get to sleep. I walked over and bent down and kissed him on the cheek. He woke up and it scared him so much that he stayed up all night watching me. I got a good night's rest."

"You're the guy who snores," Moose said. "You wouldn't believe the sounds he makes."

"Ahhh." The Colonel waved a hand in Moose's direction. "Ara really stepped in for Ed in those days. You don't know how bad things were. Ed was drinking and got real big, two hundred and eighty pounds, fifty or sixty more pounds than now. Very unhealthy. One time he was pretty sick and I called his son, Father Ed, who was studying for his doctorate. I said I needed his help. He said, 'Colonel, I'm working on my degree.' I said, 'Do you want a doctorate or a dead father?' He said, 'If that's the way it is, I'll be there,' and he was."

Moose chewed on his cigar. "I started drinking heavily after my wife's car accident. That was in the late sixties. It was terrible. I just fell apart. She was in the hospital for a long time and then in a nursing home. I felt sorry for myself and was hittin' the bottle every day. I'd go to the nursing home with a bottle of scotch and sit there by myself and drink it. But I whipped it."

"You did," the Colonel said. "You won the battle, man. Our Lady and AA helped Moose make it through the most critical time of his life. The things that happened to him and to Elise. You wouldn't believe them. Ed was religious before this, but it was different after that."

The Colonel stood and went into another room for a fresh cup of coffee for himself and his boss. He came back, sat down across the desk from Krause, and watched him puff. The men were silent and appeared to be replaying scenes from their past together—good scenes and agonizing ones—things they couldn't forget if they wanted to. The old military commander was not much more than five feet tall and weighed less than 150 pounds, but he was solidly built and still did push-ups every day, a good person to have guarding the door. The men didn't look at each other and the silence went on for some time; it was very poignant.

After a while the Colonel left—he had a lot of work to do planning Moose's big eightieth birthday party in February of 1993—and a young man entered Krause's office, standing awkwardly before him and introducing himself. Moose said hello and told him to sit down.

"No," he said, looking a little awestruck. "I've only got a couple of moments. I'm a student here. I just wanted to meet you. My grandfather attended Notre Dame and he still talks about you. Do you remember him?"

"Yeah, sure I do. When you see him, tell him he's a pain in the butt."

"I know."

"You do?"

"I do."

"He was my classmate in 1931. He was gonna be a priest but then he discovered there were girls."

"I know."

"That's how you got here."

"I know."

"Say hello to your grandfather."

"I will."

"How old is he?"

"Eighty-one."

"Get him to South Bend for a game, will ya?"

"I will."

"He's runnin' out of time."

"I know."

"Ya promise?"

"Yeah."

"Okay."

"Good to meet you, Mr. Krause."

"Moose."

"Moose," he said, backpedaling toward the door. "Good-bye, Moose."

12 The Armenian Protestant

WHEN MOOSE GENUINELY LIKED A NOTRE DAME COACH, HE had complete faith in him. Others might carp at the man or question his gridiron judgment, but Moose did not. It was like a good working marriage: the relationship between the athletic director and his football coach was far more important than one incident or even one game, and Moose trusted that the decisions the coach made were for the good of the team and the school itself.

By far the most notorious and criticized event of Ara Parseghian's Notre Dame career was the famous 10–10 tie against Michigan State in 1966. Many people felt he should have gone for broke at the end of the game and attempted anything to win. Countless articles and an entire book entitled *The Biggest Game of Them All* by Mike Celizic have been written about this one contest, and yet, when people inside the Irish football program look back on those years, another game is mentioned more often.

It occurred in 1964, not only Parseghian's first year in South Bend but also the year that followed the 2-7 campaign under Hugh Devore. In the final game of that season, the undefeated Irish (9-0 and ranked number one) traveled to Los Angeles to play the USC Trojans. Notre Dame was leading 17–0 at halftime, and before sending the team back onto the field for the last two quarters, Parseghian asked the Irish to give him "just thirty more minutes of football," which would bring them a perfect year and the national title.

After USC scored to make it 17–7, the Irish answered with an apparent touchdown of their own early in the fourth quarter, on a one-yard plunge, but an official called "illegal use of the hands" on tackle Bob Meeker. The points were nullified and Notre Dame failed to score again. Southern Cal threw two passes for touchdowns, the last one coming with 1:33 left in the game, and the Irish's undefeated season and national championship dream were gone. Parseghian was named the American Football Coaches Association "co-coach of the year," along with Arkansas's Frank Broyles, and the NCAA statistical bureau designated Notre Dame's rebound from a 2-7 record to a 9-1 record as "the greatest comeback season in history." And yet . . . that 17–0 lead had gotten away.

Sometimes lost in the criticism surrounding the 1966 Michigan State tie is that the Irish went on to win the national championship that season. What people like Moose Krause recall first about that year is that the head coach's strategy worked and the title came back to South Bend after an absence of seventeen years. What hasn't been forgotten at the school—or in some cases forgiven—was the holding penalty against Bob Meeker in the 1964 USC game. According to many Irish supporters, this was a bad call because linemen are rarely flagged for such things in short-yardage situations, and the infraction remains a vivid memory around the Notre Dame athletic department, where one still hears grumblings about "those last damn ninety-three seconds."

"We had the championship won in Ara's very first year," says Moose, "except for a minute and a half. We were that close except for Meeker . . ."

In sports you tend to remember most deeply the game that broke your heart. And certain people's names inevitably become associated with one dismal event, regardless of how many good things they may have done over the years. Every baseball fan recalls the ground ball that went through Bill Buckner's legs in the last inning of the sixth game of the 1986 World Series, which cost Boston the game (most would say the Series) against the New York Mets. How many good plays did Buckner make for the Red Sox that year?

Bob Meeker's name rarely comes up in a discussion of Notre Dame football except for one moment in 1964. Nearly three decades later, that season isn't broached in Moose's office without the old athletic director frowning and shaking his head.

"I can't believe they called that on him," Moose says. "I used to teach guys how to block. See, his hands were up here near his chest, where they're supposed to be, and he was driving his man backwards and doing all the things you're supposed to do, and it was just a lousy . . .

"I knew this guy named Hughy Mulligan, the head of the Plastering Institute in Chicago. A big organization. After we hired Ara, he called me and said, 'Why didn't you get a Notre Dame man instead of a Protestant like that?' Ara won his first game and then his second and then his third. Toward the end of the '64 season, Hughy called me up and said, 'That Protestant is pretty good. The way he's goin', maybe we can convert him to Catholicism.' I said, 'The way he's goin', we might have to join his church.' "

Parseghian has white hair now, a little paunch, and he walks with something of a limp. Bad knees and hips seem to follow good football careers (he was a player before he coached). His eyes are still fierce and his head looks as if it were ready to be carved onto Mount Rushmore. His intensity remains palpable.

"Rockne could pace himself," Moose says. "Leahy and Ara never learned how to do that. They just couldn't."

When you sit across from his desk at Ara Parseghian Enterprises, a company in downtown South Bend that insures automobile, mortgage, or commercial loans, you feel something coming at you, a sort of electric buzz, and after a while you understand it's what the man radiates. He has a quick, rather shy smile and his voice retains its rusty edge. For some reason it's surprising to see that Parseghian has gotten older; you don't expect it of certain people.

When he arrived at Notre Dame, he was a relatively young coach and Moose was a middle-aged administrator, but by 1992 they seemed almost like contemporaries, two aging men with sore legs, men who no longer coach football or make a living at it but talk with fervor about the past. Watching the two of them together during one of Moose's visits to Parseghian's office, and listening to the competitiveness that still drives their language, you wonder what would have become of them without football. Where would the intensity have gone? The profound desire to win? The physical urges? The need to test themselves against other men? Through all of their words seems to float a sense of recognition and gratitude—that the game itself gave them a life nothing else could have.

Parseghian's office holds memorabilia: plaques outlining his achievements, including his entrance into the college football Hall of Fame; *Sports Illustrated* covers featuring Irish players; old pigskins with scores painted on them; a pair of longhorns, a memento of a Cotton Bowl victory over the University of Texas football team; an award for being the 1966 *Sporting News* Coach of the Year; and a desk weight that reads, "Coach Ara Parseghian." The man does not like to talk about individuals whom he coached, and when he doesn't want to do something, it doesn't get done. When Moose asks about his best offensive or defensive player in his eleven years at Notre Dame, he shrugs and says, "They were all good."

He isn't so reticent when talking about his former athletic director. "We had the finest relationship you could ever have," he says, looking at the older man and nodding. "We never fought about anything."

Moose interrupts to ask if he can smoke in Parseghian's

office, a formality he doesn't find necessary in restaurants or other public places.

"Sure, go ahead," Parseghian says. "I was very excitable when I was coaching, and Moose had a steadying hand. There was always a fire in the head coach's chair and Moose was there for me. The job had tremendous pressure. I would constantly get calls before games from New York and Los Angeles and Atlanta and Philadelphia. Holy moly. I couldn't believe it. The first day I came onto the campus and drove up the avenue that takes you to the Golden Dome, a charge went up my back. I remembered what Rockne had done and what Leahy had done, and I knew what I was responsible for.

"Coaching here, there were always so many criticisms against you and everything was black-and-white. A lot of it disturbed me. Moose helped me because he knew this would happen and prepared me for it a little."

"I loved the son of a gun," Moose says, exhaling a long feather of smoke.

"It was good for me to be able to talk to someone who represents the history of Notre Dame the way Moose does, someone who had seen the ups and downs and knew there was a tomorrow. Everything got harder the longer I was the head coach. Not easier. When Lou Holtz was hired at Notre Dame, I tried to tell him this would happen to him, but he didn't understand me. He will, he will.

"The pressure becomes more intense when you win than when you lose. My goal was to be perfect, and if you win a national championship and have a perfect season, you can't improve on that but you can sure as hell go down. Moose didn't criticize me. He never talked behind my back or was influenced by the alumni. He was at his most supportive when we lost. He'd come and eat breakfast with me the next day and try to calm me down."

"That was pretty hard to do," Moose says.

"He once asked me to take a leave of absence so I could get away from football for a year and rest, but I couldn't do that. I'd already made up my mind to retire. Then he said,

'Look, I want you to stay and I'll step aside as athletic director so you can have my job.' How many ADs would do that?"

"I didn't wanna lose ya," Moose says.

"Being a head coach was lonely. You don't want to share things with your staff or with your family. So I talked to Moose. I didn't tell him everything, but I told him some and I needed that."

"Yeah." Moose nods and blows another trail of smoke.

"When you're the coach, it's very important to recognize what you have on the team and to play people where they can do their best. I moved a number of guys around. I had personnel boards, and every day after practice my assistant coaches and I would go to these boards and study them and talk about every player and how they were doing and if they were at the right position.

"Our quarterback, John Huarte, didn't even expect to play in 1964 and he won the Heisman Trophy that year and took us within a minute and a half of the national championship. That's a great story. I told him before the first game, against Wisconsin, 'I don't care if you throw five interceptions. You're my quarterback.' I was a great believer in him. The worst thing you can do to some people is kick them in the ass."

Parseghian leans back in his chair, locks his fingers behind his head, and looks out the large window that gives onto a cold, blue, transparent October morning and the modest skyline of South Bend. He chuckles, as if to himself. "If Meeker hadn't gotten that call at the end of the game, we would have been champions."

The old athletic director grunts in agreement.

"How long have you been at Notre Dame now, Moose?"

"Oh, hell," Krause says. "I don't know. I'm almost eighty."

"Well, I'm sixty-nine," Parseghian says, pointing at Moose. "When I turned sixty, that SOB put a big sign out in that parking lot that said, 'Ara Is Sixty.' "

Moose laughs at the memory. "You playin' golf today?"

"No. My legs hurt."

"Yeah, mine, too."

Parseghian stands behind his desk and moves slowly across

the room. When he glances at you, you get the feeling that he's about to tell you to go block someone.

"Look at you," Moose says to his ex-coach. "You walk just like a duck."

"So do you."

They clap their hands on each other's shoulders and shuffle toward the hall.

Parseghian smiles and says, "You only made one mistake in your life."

"What's that?"

"You kept that little guy working for you."

Moose sighs deeply. "Oh, yeah," he says. "You mean the Colonel. You're right about that."

On any given morning ex-coaches or football players drift in and out of the two small athletic department offices occupied by Moose and Col. Stephens. One morning Joe Yonto came by and sat down in the chair opposite Moose's desk. Yonto had played and coached under Leahy before becoming an assistant under Parseghian.

"In terms of football knowledge Ara and Leahy were equal," Yonto said, "but Ara had it all over Leahy in terms of personality. He was much more outgoing, effervescent. Leahy was rigid. If I had to choose, it would be Ara. Both of them were highly organized, regimented perfectionists. Ara's seven A.M. meetings started at a quarter of seven. That was Ara's time, and being late was not possible.

"Both coaches worked on the little things. Things you wouldn't even think of. Fundamentals. Like a basic stance on the field or the proper way of holding a football or how to use your arms when tackling or how to carry the ball when you're running or the best way to fall down and maintain your leverage or how to recover a fumble. They worked on these things endlessly. Things you would think that college football players would know, but a lot of them don't."

Another day Wally Moore dropped in. Moore, who came to Notre Dame as Parseghian's freshmen coach in 1966, is short and round and does not at first strike you as being a football man—not until he jumps out of his chair in Moose's office and starts blocking the furniture.

Many things come to mind around Moore. For one, it's easy to get the impression, from watching football on television or even in person, that you know something about the game. TV commentators like to talk about "stunts" and "nickel packages" and "the red zone," and after a while you start to feel that you can keep up with them. It's only when you encounter people like Moore that you realize how much thinking, rethinking, planning, and refining has gone into the game over the years. It makes you wonder how Rockne and Leahy and other gridiron pioneers would look upon football today.

Another thing comes to mind when talking to Moore: the football-viewing public often seems upset or even shocked when there's a blowup on the sidelines and a coach yells at one of his players. The player might even scream back, especially if he's in the pros and has a long-term contract. What's surprising is not that this occurs but that it doesn't happen a lot more or doesn't occasionally get physical.

Few sports are more driven by emotion and violence than football, yet few of them demand more self-control; you must attack but at precisely the right time and in exactly the right way. Some of the emotions underlying football have fundamentally dark edges having to do with one man trying to dominate or punish another. That must be why this game, more than any other, has produced several great orators who could stir men's viscera before sending them into battle.

You can't ask people to make sacrifices in a whisper. You can't ask them to bang heads politely. You can't ask young players to walk out onto a field, sometimes in miserable weather, and give every ounce of strength and stamina they have without expecting a little conflict once in a while. We watch the game because it's harsh and because it shows us that some people have more physical skills and physical courage than others.

"As the freshmen coach," Moore said in Moose's office, "I was sent out to scout our varsity opponent two weeks down the road. My first year we were undefeated, but people always told me that if we lost, Ara would turn into a raving maniac and to stay out of his way. The next year we lost to Purdue, and when I returned from the scouting work, I was afraid of entering this madman situation back home. On Monday morning we always had to be in our chairs by seven A.M. for Ara's first meeting of the week.

"He was usually early, but this morning he was about five minutes late. No one says anything to him. We're all sitting there waiting, worried, keeping our eyes on him. He doesn't say anything. Total silence in the room. Everyone is really starting to get nervous. Then he looks at one of our defensive coaches and says, 'Why did we lose that game?' The coach gives his reasons for the defeat and Ara doesn't make any response. He goes around the room and asks all nine coaches for their explanations. Then it gets real quiet again and we're all waiting for the bomb.

"He tells us that he really appreciates our thoughts this morning, but here's why we lost the game. He writes very carefully on a blackboard seven reasons for the defeat. Boom, boom, boom, one right after the other. All very neat and orderly. He says we're going to correct each of these things starting now. He was totally analytical and organized, totally comfortable with what he was doing. No raving at all on his part. Never raised his voice during the entire meeting. When a coach is out of control and feels he's gonna get beat, the players pick up on that and they do get beat.

"Ara wanted to know everything that was going on. He always called the plays from the sidelines and did it by holding a card and moving it around to various parts of his body. At the Friday practices before games, the press would come out and interview him. He'd hold the card and look right at a reporter, and as he was answering his question, he'd announce what play the team was gonna run next. Then they would run it. The reporters were amazed. They had no idea what he was doing. 'How'd you do that?' they'd ask him. He would never tell them.

"He did all this to put himself in an artificial pressure situation, where he had to do several things at once, so he could make sure that he'd never choke during a game. He'd do the same thing with players. When Bob Thomas was being broken in as our kicker, Ara would stand beside him as he was practicing and throw a cap at his feet or walk right in front of him as he was attempting a field goal. Anything to distract him and prepare him for what was coming on Saturday.

"Ara devised the most unusual cadence system in football. Our quarterback was always taught to scan the defense before putting his hands under center to receive the ball. Then he never used numbers when calling the signals, just words. The word *ready* could mean go right or go left, or it could mean a certain blocking pattern or a specific pass route. The meaning of that one word depended on what play had just been called in the huddle. *Ready* told the line how to block, the receivers where to run, and the backs what to do. In practice we worked on these things thousands of times. Drove me up a tree. Ara wanted plays that could not be denied. He was always in a state of flux. Constantly changing things. Never satisfied.

"He was the greatest tactician I've ever seen. In 1974 we didn't have any defensive ends so we put Steve Niehaus there. He had a reputation as a great defensive player, but he wasn't an end. We spoofed the whole nation that year, and no one ran at Niehaus because they thought he was good.

"Ara always said don't worry about making touchdowns, make first downs. That sounds like a very simple thing, but it isn't. I've seen team after team go for long scores when all they need is a first down to keep the ball in their possession. Ara said, 'If you just make the first downs, the touchdowns will come.'

"At the 1973 Sugar Bowl, before we played Alabama for the national title, I was standing out on the field during one of our practices at Tulane Stadium. I'm five feet seven, and when I looked at one of the goalposts, my eye level was right in line with it. It was supposed to be ten feet tall. When I looked at the other goalpost, my whole head was over the crossbar.

"That night I walked all over New Orleans looking for a

string and a carpenter's level. I've always been a frustrated carpenter. When I found those things, I went back to the stadium in the dark and secured the string on the fifty-yard line. I walked down to the goalposts with it and discovered that one end zone was twelve inches lower than the other. A punter standing back there was four feet lower than some parts of the field and kicking uphill. I told Ara what I'd discovered, and we based our kicking strategy on this information. We won the game and the championship, twenty-four to twenty-three."

One other thing had come to mind while listening to Moore, something that had surfaced before when hearing other players talk about their experiences with Rockne or Leahy or Parseghian, experiences that went back decades yet were still extremely vivid to those telling the stories. This particular thing was much more subtle and elusive than the other thoughts Moore had evoked. It didn't even necessarily have a name and may have existed only in the realm of feeling or intuition.

It had to do with the sense that all of the ex-players had been speaking about something that included football but went a little beyond the game itself. It had to do with competitiveness and perhaps being male, and it touched upon the subject of violence. Why did some people enjoy playing football so much and why did so many others enjoy watching it? What need was it really fulfilling? Why was so much attention paid to athletes, and what was the envy that at least certain people felt for them?

These questions could have been stirred up while visiting any college with a major football program, but in fact they came from being at Notre Dame, a religious institution. You almost cannot visit the campus without being aware of its history as a Catholic school and without encountering a lot of Christian imagery. It's in the public sculpture, in the architecture, and it pervades the walls of Sacred Heart Basilica. The images conjure up the journey of Christ from the cradle to the crucifixion. The university, unlike so many other places in our society, can easily cause you to think about spiritual matters, regardless of your religious orientation. It provides a context for this activity.

Notre Dame feels surprisingly nondenominational, yet when you're there, you find yourself wondering about such things as good and evil, the nature of sin and redemption, the enormous suffering that has been, and remains, a part of the human experience. You think about what people have been and what they are and what they might become. You think about the light that surrounds Our Lady on the Golden Dome on sunny mornings and about the darkness that follows us everywhere.

And somehow at Notre Dame, all of these things become entwined, the football and the religion together. Of course, there are many jokes made about this entwining and many comments about "Touchdown Jesus," the huge mural on one of the campus administration buildings that depicts Christ with his arms upraised, as if someone has just plunged into the end zone and scored. "Touchdown Jesus" generates a lot of laughter, but not everything surrounding this subject is humorous.

The most striking thing about football is that young men choose to go out and punish themselves and one another, they choose the pain, the sacrifice, the hardships, and the risk of serious injury or even, in very rare cases, death. They might eventually earn big money from the sport and considerable fame, but if you've ever played football, you know that the distant promise of those things isn't enough to send you into the fray. The appeal is more mysterious. Young men enter the violence of the gridiron for vaguer reasons, and perhaps in time those things would reveal a little more of themselves and some of the questions could be answered.

Wally Moore, who went on to coach the varsity offensive line under Parseghian, was still talking:

"It was Ara who coined the phrase 'Hard work isn't easy.' Boy, did we work on blocking. You can count on your hands the number of times our quarterbacks were sacked. We taught our linemen not to block the defense but to—"

He leaped up and assumed a blocking stance near Moose's desk—knees bent, back stooped, eyes focused on an imaginary opponent. He looked twenty years younger. He looked mean. He pivoted one way and then the other, swinging his wide body around the small space, his forearms raised in front of him, elbows cocked, ready to take on all comers. Everyone else in the room leaned away from him.

"Now," he said, "whenever you try to block someone, you commit and then they react to your commitment. The secret is not to commit but to make them commit to you. Waltz with them. Usher them into your area."

He began a movement that looked like a heavyset man, who had started to pant, waltzing in a ballroom. Moose watched him, emitting a burst of laughter.

Colonel Stephens wandered into the room, having heard the shuffle of Moore's feet. The Colonel has excellent posture and exceedingly alert eyes for a man of eighty. He looks trim and fit and ready to start barking orders. He favors red-and-green plaid pants. After studying Moore for several moments, he shook his head and said, "What the hell is this?"

"A blocking demonstration," Moose said. "Go back to work."

"Yeah," Moore said, still pirouetting around the desk. "I'm showin' 'em how to lure your man into your area."

"Jeez," the Colonel said, "you ask some people what time it is and they make you a watch."

"Go on," Moose said, but Stephens didn't budge.

Moore had stopped dancing and everyone stared at him to see what he would do next.

"Okay," he said, "now once that man is in your area, give him a shot."

He lifted an elbow and jabbed it outward, driving home the point.

Moose drew on his cigar and applauded. The Colonel was rubbing his jaw.

Moore looked around and blushed, as if suddenly remembering where he was. "Well, that's the way I taught it," he said.

"You sure did," Colonel Stephens said.

"We were almost never sacked," Moore said, taking his seat and wiping his brow.

The room became quiet, except for Moore catching his breath, the color slowly leaving his cheeks.

"Ara was ambidextrous," he said. "He could play the piano by ear. He's the only guy I ever saw who wrote meticulous notes to himself, so he could improve himself in whatever he was doing. Every time he went out and jogged, he came back in and wrote down how far he'd run. He had to have a record of what he'd accomplished that day.

"Only once did I ever see him display emotion. He was a very strong man physically and mentally, but in our first home game of 1974—his last year at Notre Dame—he gave the players a little talk before they left the locker room. After he finished, he turned around and choked up. You could see how much leaving the school meant to him. A leader doesn't do these things in front of the people he's leading. There was always a tremendous amount of pressure on him and he finally showed it, but that's the only time I ever saw him cry."

13 The Tragedy

DURING THE PARSEGHIAN ERA AT NOTRE DAME, MOOSE CONfronted the most difficult and challenging time of his life. In early 1967, after his wife was in a near-fatal car accident, the aging ex-athlete and former coach was suddenly presented with a set of circumstances that he appeared to be totally unprepared for. As it turned out, he surprised everyone.

Moose's two youngest children, Mary and Philip, were in South Bend or the Chicago area for much of what followed the accident. If their father endured those years largely in silence, Mary and Philip, perhaps because they come from a different generation, have not always been as reticent. When they talk about the two decades, from the end of the sixties until their mother's death in March of 1990, they speak with great warmth, and with humor, as if laughter were necessary in the face of extreme pain and suffering.

Mary, a blond, pretty mother of four boys, resembles earlier pictures of Elise Krause. She and her husband, Sandy Carrigan, live in a Chicago suburb and go to many Irish home football games. In January of 1967, Mary was attending college in Chicago when circumstances caused her to transfer to St. Mary's in South Bend, so she could be near her parents.

"My mother had been invited to a cocktail party and it was a wintry evening," she says. "Dad was in Hammond, Indiana, that night on some business. He couldn't get home because the weather was bad, so Mother took a cab to the party. Cars had no seat belts back then. A young man ran a stop sign and rammed the rear of the taxi from the side. He'd been drinking. My mother's head was thrown very hard against the back of the seat. The cab spun around and hit a telephone pole, and her head was thrown just as hard the other way.

"They took her to the hospital and put her in intensive care. The doctor said she wouldn't make it through the night. Her lungs were punctured, her ribs were broken, and she was unconscious. A life-support system was keeping her alive. Daddy said she wasn't going to die. He just kept saying that. He wouldn't let her go. She made it through the first night and then she kept on living. She was in intensive care for months."

"It was Dad who brought her around," says Phil Krause, a tall, handsome man who lives in South Bend and is in the real estate appraising business. He's spent many nights at his father's apartment cooking him meals. "The doctor said it would be better if Mom died, but Dad wanted her there with him. He just kept praying and telling us that she was going to be all right. The problem wasn't her broken arms or her broken hands or fingers. It was the two hits to the head, apparently one to the memory bank and one to the emotional bank.

"That damage was permanent. The doctors tried to put shunts in her brain which would drain the fluid and relieve the pressure, but that didn't work. They tried everything. A doctor told us that Mom had basically died, but Dad never accepted that. He would sit for hours with her and just watch her.

"It was difficult for those of us in her family to see this woman who had been so active for so many years in this condition. When Dad became athletic director, she became the first lady of the Notre Dame athletic department, the one who entertained everyone, the one who took care of people and made everyone feel at home."

Mary and Philip speculate gingerly on why their father so adamantly refused to accept his wife's condition, and why he became so devoted to keeping her alive. They hint at traces of guilt in Moose because he'd been away from the family so much in earlier days. They hint at his denial of what had happened to Elise. But they also hint at a middle-aged man gradually discovering parts of himself in the midst of tragedy, loving and care-giving parts that he may never have known existed until then.

"We had to go see my mother in intensive care twice a day for a long time," Mary says. "One day it snowed hard all day long, and after we returned home from a trip to the hospital, I thought we were finished for the day. Daddy says, 'Get dressed, we're going to walk back and visit your mother.' I said, 'You're crazy. We'll die en route.' He said, 'My sweetheart knows when I'm there.' I said, 'We can go tomorrow.' He said. 'We're going now.' We put on our skis and skied into the emergency room at St. Joseph's hospital. The people there just stared at us. They let us stay extra long on our visit because we had to thaw out and then ski back home.

"Mom lost a lot of weight in intensive care on the life-support system. They moved her to a private room and she gradually regained consciousness. She weighed about eighty pounds then, after weighing one twenty-five normally. Dad put a picture of himself in the room and a picture of the pope. He tried to get her to say which one was which, but she couldn't for a long time.

"The mother that I knew had died. She was gone, replaced by almost a mentally retarded person. We had to retrain her in everything. Daddy would try to feed her, but she would get mad and throw the food on the floor. Then I tried to feed her, but she'd get mad at me. My husband also tried and my mother's sister, Dorothy, but she just wouldn't eat very much.

"The hospital said we should put her in a special-care facility but Dad said no. She still couldn't sit up. Her fingers didn't work. Dad said she was going home. She couldn't walk at all so he had to carry her up a full flight of stairs at home. Slowly, she began to eat, but she still only weighed about ninety pounds. My dad was real busy at the university and the burden fell on me. Over time Mother got stronger and was able to get out of bed. She became more aware of things. She could talk now. She took an instant dislike to some people and would start screaming at them. It didn't matter where she was. It was uncontrollable."

"She would blow up very easily," Phil says. "At totally unpredictable times. The part of the brain that holds the emotions in check was no longer there or no longer working. She would just explode at people, and most of them couldn't understand why. They couldn't get past these things and see them as part of her condition now."

"When we were growing up," Mary says, "my mother and dad were surrogate parents to so many kids on the campus, especially to the football players. They invited them to our home for Christmas and Thanksgiving and visited them in the hospital if they got injured. The players were always at our house playing with us, and they would carry me around on their backs.

"When the accident occurred, my parents were still very involved with the university, and that was part of the problem. After many months of convalescing, my mother began to get well, at least physically, but not in other ways. They still went to many Notre Dame social functions and it was a nightmare. You never knew which person she would attack, but it was usually another woman."

"Dad had been a social drinker before the accident," Phil says. "Both my parents had been. But now that she was gone from him emotionally, he drank more and his problems got worse. He'd had an uneven heartbeat for a long time—from the drinking and from stress—and it began giving him trouble. He'd had a ticker put in there in the early sixties, and that evened it out somewhat, but it was never quite right."

"My mother had so many phobias," Mary says. "In the

summertime we ate out on the porch and noise bothered her. If someone's fork accidentally hit the side of the table or a glass, she would get upset and start banging the table with her utensils. Then the rest of us would start pounding our utensils on the table, the whole family sitting there and banging away. We'd be laughing and crying and laughing some more. We didn't know what else to do. You had to laugh to get through it. It was like being in a prison.

"She also hated light. She'd make Dad and me sit in the dark and watch TV. We'd sit there and laugh in the darkness. My little boy, Rich, loved to slam down the toilet seat. Each time he did this, my mother would say, 'Oh, my God!' At school the teacher once asked Rich where God lived, and he said, 'In the toilet.' "

"Dad's heart kept getting worse," Phil says, "and Mother was just . . . after being home for several years, she began to deteriorate. She said outrageous things in public. I would bring a girlfriend home and she would corner her in the kitchen and try to kick her. It was unbelievable what we went through. Dad's drinking got really bad when he was trying to bring her back to life. Drinking and taking heart medication. That's a terrible combination. My sister finally got him to stop."

"In 1974," Mary says, "Dad had an arrhythmic heartbeat. Severe heart palpitations. He was frustrated at not being able to do anything about my mother's condition. He always felt that she would snap out of it and her memory would come back and there would be a miracle cure, but there wasn't.

"His heart got worse and he finally had to go into the hospital. He was in the operating room laid flat out on a table, where they were going to give him shock treatment. Before they did this, they explained to me that the shock they were about to give him was so great he might die, but they felt there was no other choice. The doctors said they'd never given such a shock to anyone before. When they did it, he jumped right off the table, right into the air.

"When all this was going on, I was pregnant with my first child. After the shock treatment was over, I told him, 'Look, if you don't turn things around in your life and stop the drinking, you'll never see your grandchild. I've got my hands full with Mother and I can't take care of you, too. We need your help.' He listened to me and started crying. Tears all over his face. He said, 'I'll never let you down again. I promise.' And that was it. He came out of the hospital and stopped drinking for good. I never had to say it again."

"As a family," Phil says, "we never expected my mother or father to live very long. The combination of everything that was going on was lethal. Colonel Stephens was around for the brunt of this, and he was extremely helpful. He was always the unsung hero. When Dad was drinking, I'd get calls from their office and he would say, 'You've got to come get your dad. He's no good.' And I'd go get him. After he came out of the hospital, he went back to work, but he spent a lot of his time taking care of Mother."

"My parents eventually moved out of their house," Mary says, "and into the apartment where Dad still lives. When we were growing up, Daddy often cooked dinner—he made ribs a lot—but after her accident he did more of the meal preparation. He made Mother all her meals. He'd cook her breakfast and lunch, go to work, come home at night, and make her dinner. He also began doing the laundry, which he'd never done before. That was very interesting."

"Near the end of the seventies he was thinking of retiring," Phil says, "but Father Joyce and Father Hesburgh wanted him to stay on at the athletic department. He decided to retire in 1981. We'd told him to keep working but he wanted to be with my mother, even after she fell down and broke her hip and had to go into a nursing home. She was there for eight years.

"He visited her every day, more than once, taking her food and feeding her because she couldn't feed herself. We told him that Mom was past helping now, but he didn't want to accept that. He still felt he could bring her around. He felt he'd traveled all his life and now he would be there for her. He would sit with her for hours. She could no longer talk but just make sounds. Dad said he was the only one who could understand what she was saying. He would reminisce with her, telling her about the good times they'd had in the past. He just wanted to be with her. He wouldn't go out with his friends, wouldn't play golf, wouldn't do anything. He'd stay there until she fell asleep."

"When Mother was in the nursing home," Mary says, "Daddy would try to get her to walk. When she couldn't walk, he would pick her up and carry her. I told him that he should take time off and go visit his friends in Florida, but he wouldn't budge. He said he had to be with his bride. They were married for fifty-two years. He took care of her for twenty-three of those. That's nearly half of their married life. They celebrated their fiftieth wedding anniversary at the nursing home. He wore a white tux and they held the wedding service all over again."

Joe O'Brien, the senior associate athletic director at Notre Dame, saw Moose and his family through many of those days. When he speaks about them, the memories cause him to wince.

"Elise was the sweetest woman you've ever known," he says. "She made a home, raised her children, and was very kind to people. After the accident her personality changed to such a degree that it was difficult for everyone. Moose was very gentle with her. To him she was never a problem. A lesser person couldn't have handled all of this and couldn't have beaten the drinking, but he did.

"As she became an invalid, he devoted his life to her. He became the darling of the Cardinal Nursing Home, where Elise lived for all those years. He would sit there and sing to her, the popular songs from the thirties and forties. He would try to get her to sing and she liked that. So did the staff. When Moose arrived at the home, he lit up their day."

Moose's oldest child, Father Ed Krause, is now a professor at Gannon University in Erie, Pennsylvania. "Father Hesburgh," he says, "once told me, 'Your father has had many public successes in life, but nothing is more important in God's eyes than how he cared for your mother for all of those years.' In a quiet way, Dad was faithful to her and to his family and to his Notre Dame education. The dome at Notre Dame is the sign of a love story, not just with the university or with football but with life itself. A love affair with the whole of life, with the energy of it and the mystery of it. That's what Dad's story is all about."

14 Ara's Men

MOOSE'S DIFFICULTIES AT HOME BROUGHT HIM AND PARSEGHIAN closer. When the older man talks about the younger one, you occasionally hear some of the same things that Parseghian's former players mention about him: Ara was strong for him, Ara listened, Ara was stern. In a way that sometimes happens in families, when Moose's life had begun to disintegrate into despair and alcohol, Ara temporarily became the parent and Moose the child. Things eventually straightened out and both men could return to their favorite subject: football.

Defensive tackle Mike McCoy played for Parseghian from 1967 to 1969. At six feet five and 275 pounds he was big by any standard, and his senior year he was voted an all-American.

"I was recruited by Penn State, Syracuse, and Indiana, but when I met Ara, I knew I wanted to come to Notre Dame," he says. "He didn't go out and recruit you, although he would make a telephone call. You came to him in South Bend. He felt if he left for one player, he'd have to leave for all of them and he didn't want to do that. He was very straightforward with me and didn't butter me up. He said I would be like every other student at the university, and I liked his forthrightness a lot. I was the first freshman to sign that year.

"His practices were very tough but we got a lot done. They were incredibly well organized, and when the horn blew, you went on to the next thing. At the end of training camp each year, we would do skits to lighten things up. I remember one of them that depicted Ara at home blowing his whistle for the members of his family—telling his wife and kids to get out of bed, do the dishes, clean up their rooms, or whatever had to be done around the house. It was pretty funny.

"He's a very emotional man, so emotional that sometimes during his halftime speeches his gum would fly out of his mouth. When I was a sophomore and starting my first game, I was scared out of my mind. Right before the kickoff he came up and touched my shoulder and said I was gonna be all right. It's amazing how a little thing like that can help you, but it did. Just that one moment and knowing when somebody needs something. That's the intangible part of coaching. Recognizing that kids get afraid.

"We had some great players on those teams—Alan Page, Bob Kuechenberg, Joe Theismann. When I came to Notre Dame, we couldn't go to bowl games. My senior year was the first time the university allowed us to, and Ara let us vote on whether or not we wanted to go to the Cotton Bowl. We all wanted to, but then we got beat by Texas. The strange thing about Ara was that he was better to us, as individuals, after the losses than after the wins. When we lost, he'd pay attention to you and tell you what you needed to do next time. But if we won, he didn't say much because he was worried about us becoming overconfident.

"He would motivate the team by calling upon the whole history and tradition of Notre Dame. What we were about to do that day on the field would be reflected for years and years to come, even though we might not realize it at the time. We weren't just playing our opponent but also against the previous Notre Dame teams and for our place in the history of the school's football program. Notre Dame itself was also very motivational. If you couldn't get up for playing there, forget it. The important thing was that the expectations were very high, and because of this a lot of people rose to that next level. That's what stayed with me. If those around you expect you to perform, it makes a difference."

In the late sixties Bob Kuechenberg started on the Irish defensive line, then went on to play for the Miami Dolphins in the early seventies, Super Bowl years for that franchise. His pro coach was Don Shula.

"When I remember Ara," Kuechenberg says, "I see that mane of dark hair flowing around him and that Notre Dame sweater he always wore. He had charisma, dynamism. He was big on speeches in the locker room and he could get you to listen. The first time I heard Don Shula give a pregame speech, I kept waiting for the crescendo and it never came. I just stood there anticipating something more while everybody else filed out of the locker room."

Over the past four decades sports columnist Joe Doyle has watched countless Irish practices before returning to his office at the *South Bend Tribune* to write about the team.

"Ara was always threatening to boot someone in the butt with his size-nine-and-a-half shoe," he says. "One day in 1968, his fullback, Ron Dushney, kept missing a block on an outside sweep. Ara watched this several times and finally called time-out. He came down from the tower where he watched the practices and walked up to Dushney. 'Turn around,' he said, 'and bend over.' The fullback did this and Ara administered a swift kick to the rear. Then he climbed back up on the tower. Dushney didn't miss that block again.

"The rest of the season, when anyone on the team made a bad mistake in practice, they would back up to the tower with their buttocks exposed, as if to say, 'Give me that kick, Coach. I screwed up.' Ara never had to come down again for that reason. The lesson had been learned."

In the early sixties Brian Boulac played offensive and defensive end at Notre Dame under Joe Kuharich, and in the seventies he coached those positions under Parseghian and Dan

Devine. Currently the assistant athletic director at the university, Boulac is a huge man with a broad chest and shoulders. He still looks ready to go.

"It was amazing to watch Ara call a game," he says. "He was way ahead of his time. In the midsixties, he used the spy in the sky: Notre Dame had its own TV monitor that moved along with him on the sidelines during a game and shot down onto the field. He would send in a play and then he would tell us to watch one part of the action on the TV screen—either one blocking assignment or maybe the pass coverage. So we could watch the coverage from this angle and see things that you couldn't see standing on the sidelines. The NCAA eventually outlawed this, but it helped a lot when it was legal.

"Every year Ara would start over and start anew with his strategy. New words, new plays, new options, new sequences of plays that he was calling, new patterns, new twists. During the season we'd work from seven A.M. till one in the morning. But near the end of the year, we might get to go home at nine."

Says Moose, "In the off-season, I'd always tell Ara to get out of here, go away, take a vacation, get some sun. Next week he'd be right back in his office studying film, planning for next year. I could never get him to rest."

"Ara was great at psyching people," says Joe Doyle, "motivating them even when they didn't realize he was doing it. In his first spring practices in 1964, he was determined that his offense would learn to use the clock wisely before halftime or the end of the game. The previous Notre Dame coach, Joe Kuharich, came out of pro football but he never taught the two-minute drill. At practice Ara would place the ball on the forty-yard line and tell the team, 'You've got two minutes left and three time-outs. Let's see you score.' He called for sideline passes, out-of-bounds runs, things like that. He controlled the clock with a stopwatch.

"One afternoon, after he'd told the defense not to hit very hard, the first-string offense scored seven times in two minutes. For the last score, he put the ball on the fifteen-yard line and said, 'There's one second left! Kick a field goal!' Then he kicked it himself through the uprights. Four touchdowns and three field goals in two minutes. Of course, what he didn't tell them was that he'd added two or three minutes to the clock while they were running the drill. He wanted the players to believe they could accomplish all this in two minutes, if they had to.

"Back then there were no injury time-outs and Ara made his players so aware of conserving time-outs that they would literally crawl to the sidelines when they got hurt rather than call time-out. He was a total fanatic about this. The team went all the way through the 1964 and '65 seasons without calling an injury time-out. Against Oklahoma in 1966, Jim Seymour went up for a pass in the end zone and came down wrong on his ankle. He sprained it so badly he couldn't get to the bench. Someone finally called for a time-out. The sprain was so severe that Seymour missed the next two games."

Says Brian Boulac, "We had some characters in the sixties. Ron Dushney and Bob Gladieux. Oh, boy. I had to make sure they were going to class. In the mornings, I'd go over to where they lived, wake them up, and walk them to their classrooms. They were probably back in their dorms sleeping before I got back to my office.

"Ara was the most intense competitor I've ever been around. You should have seen him play handball with Hank Stram. I've never seen such vicious games. Stram would come here to play him, and both men were pretty good and both hated to lose. At the end of the game, Stram's back would look like someone had taken a bullwhip to it.

"Ara was very approachable although he gave the illusion of being standoffish. The late sixties and early seventies was a tough time at colleges. There was a lot going on in terms of protests over Vietnam and other changes, and he had to evaluate how he was handling the kids. He was able to look at himself and make some adjustments. Not every coach could do that. The kids started wearing long hair and questioning authority, and Ara sensed that it was time to keep his door open for them to talk about things other than football.

"His morning meetings with his coaches started at seven A.M. sharp, and the first half of them might be devoted to what was happening in the world. By seven o'clock he'd read several newspapers and was ready to talk about the headlines. He expected you to be well-informed and able to discuss the issues with him.

"In 1969 he let the players vote on whether they wanted to start playing in bowl games again and they voted to do this. But in 1971 they voted not to go to the Gator Bowl. This hurt Ara tremendously because he'd pushed for it, but he accepted their vote. After the players rejected this, they went in and explained their decision to him. They respected him enough to do this, and he tried to understand their point of view. After that year, there was no more team voting. We went to bowl games if the university asked us to.

"The 1975 Orange Bowl was Ara's last game and the best one of all. He knew he was leaving and he was so relaxed. We went down to Florida and he let the kids go, gave them more free time. He was drawing plays in the sand on the beach and laughing and having fun. The kids responded to this and we beat Bear Bryant's number one ranked Alabama team, thirteen to eleven. Bear came to our locker room after the game and said to Ara, 'I want to live long enough to beat you.' He never did.

"Ara was a good recruiter but wouldn't leave his office to do it. He passed on a number of players because he didn't like the feeling of being with them. He could intimidate people. He had an aura. If a young man didn't respect his mother, Ara had a way of finding that out."

15 The Wake-up Call

LIKE MANY PEOPLE WHO'D WATCHED THE NOTRE DAME FOOTBALL program for a number of years or even decades, Moose was particularly intrigued with how the coaches motivated their young players, game after game and season after season. In 1992 he was given a perfect opportunity to see Lou Holtz at work in this area and to see how the coach would respond after his team opened the campaign with three wins, one loss, and one tie. Moose didn't let the opportunity pass.

On the first Tuesday after the Stanford loss the Irish held a full-contact practice, with an emphasis on the word *full*. Their next opponent was Pittsburgh, whose home field was artificial turf, so Coach Holtz had moved the team indoors to the Loftus Center, a new building on campus that houses, among other things, a running track, a weight room, and a covered football field with synthetic turf. On Tuesday afternoon, Moose decided to watch the practice and drove over to the center in his long blue Coupe de Ville. Notre Dame had just fallen to fourteenth in the AP poll, and he thought the workout might be interesting.

"Holtz has a great talent for raising hell with the guys when he needs to," Krause said, parking in front of Loftus. "I imagine he's pretty upset this week."

On his way into the center, Moose ran into the Irish quarterback, Rick Mirer, who stood before him in a clean football uniform, helmet in hand, looking as young, fresh, and handsome as a Hollywood gridiron hero.

"Don't worry, kid," Moose said, tapping him on the shoulder pad and blowing cigar smoke past his face, "you'll get 'em this week."

Mirer gave him a kind of stunned smile, as if Rockne himself had walked into the building and delivered a rousing pep talk.

After going through several levels of security—people don't just walk into Notre Dame football practices—Moose lumbered out toward the field, but then he veered away from the team and the coaches and slowly climbed the stairs up to some metal bleachers perched above one of the end zones.

The players at this end of the field were engaged in blocking drills. A number of them stood off to the side, helmets in hand, sweating and heaving from the workout. They watched as two huge linemen faced each other in a crouch, shoulder to shoulder and nose to nose, waiting to collide. "Go!" Joe Moore shouted, and the linemen went at one another with a ferocity that could be felt and heard thirty yards away.

In 1988 when Holtz was looking for a new offensive-line coach, he talked to a number of people about the best man to hire. Jackie Sherrill, who's coached at Pittsburgh, Texas A&M, and Mississippi State, said without hesitation, "Get Joe Moore." Moore had been one of Sherrill's assistants at Pitt. Others told Holtz similar things. He took their recommendations and offered the job to Moore. The sixty-year-old has a gruff voice, a weathered face, and sad eyes with bags under them. When he yells, he sounds twice as big as he is and half as old. Everything about him conjures up the Marines. Over the past half decade with the Irish, he's consistently produced one of the best offensive lines in the nation.

Moore had once been a running back at the University of

Tennessee but later decided—he spent seventeen years as a high school coach before moving on to college—that "the offensive line is one of the few areas where you can make a player better." He has only one inviolable rule with his linemen: "Don't ever ask me how well you've played or try to influence my opinion of your performance. You have no say in that. I'm the only one who makes that judgment." And he doesn't care much for questions from players during practice sessions. Questions are for team meetings. At practice he likes action.

"Go!" Moore shouted, and the same two young men went at it again, harder than before.

They grunted and drove straight into one another, each trying to move the other backward, each wheezing and gasping for air, neither giving an inch, two giants locked in combat, their arms pressed before them, their fingers digging into jerseys and flesh, their feet ripping at the carpet, trying to find purchase on the artificial turf, their toes curling in their shoes, their bodies sinking lower the harder they pushed, still lower until both of them were about to collapse onto the ground.

"Break!" Moore yelled, and they came unlocked.

The young men took a step backward, sucking air, hands on hips, circling each other warily, as if they weren't quite sure it was safe to relax.

"That was pretty good," Moose said, situating himself on one of the bleachers and puffing a new cigar. He chuckled and crossed his legs at the knee and bent over a little, intently eyeing the field below. Above him and to his left, a young man sat on a metal tower and operated a stationary camera, recording the movements of the players being tutored by Joe Moore.

Coaches used to work from memory and from notes—from what they could recall about last Saturday's game. But decades ago they began filming the contests so they could watch them over and over again, in slow motion or at regular speed or in reverse or on fast forward if necessary (there's an old football joke about a head coach who gets married and comes back to the campus after a week of travel with his bride.

"How was your honeymoon?" one of his assistants asks him. "I don't know," the coach says. "I haven't seen the films yet"). Nowadays, of course, even the practices are put on videotape and studied thoroughly by the coaching staff long after the players have left the field.

Twenty or thirty yards away from the blocking drills, off by himself, Lou Holtz was kneeling and watching two new players butt heads. His chin was in one hand. His other hand felt vaguely around on the turf, as if looking for a blade to chew. He wore a blue Notre Dame cap, which is constantly on his head indoors or out. He never smiled, not even partially. He was easily the frailest man on the field. He had no chest at all, no hips, his shoulders were without definition, and his glasses made him look like a weekend golfer with a bloated handicap. Years before he'd made a list of all the things he wanted to accomplish before his death. One item was to shoot a hole in one. So far he had shot two of them. He gazed at the blockers, said nothing, and didn't move from his spot.

As the linemen crashed into one another, Joe Moore leaned over them, right next to the earholes in their helmets.

"Elbows, Junior, elbows!" he screamed, his voice echoing around the Loftus Center and cutting through everyone within range. "Now hit! Hit! Hit!"

The blockers hit so hard they both fell down and rolled on the turf.

Moose laughed, causing the metal bleachers he was sitting on to vibrate.

"Good," he said. "This looks just like the old days. These kids need a good kick in the butt. I told you Lou might be a little upset today."

Holtz was still kneeling, frozen in thought and observation. One could only imagine the kind of pressure he was putting on himself since the previous weekend. He actually looked thinner than he had four days earlier at the pregame luncheon, as if by concentrating so hard he'd narrowed his face and body to a finer point.

Part of the appeal of sports is their peculiar kind of simplicity, of neatness. When coaches win, they get the credit. When they lose, everyone knows whom to blame. A thousand variables—injuries to key players, to name just one—go into the outcome of a game, but dwelling on such things after a loss doesn't play very well in this world. No one wants to hear excuses, and coaches strenuously avoid making them. Fans take a certain pleasure in all of this; it's the flip side of the fame and fortune that come to players and coaches with big-time athletic success. Fans like to praise lavishly when things are going well, and some enjoy cutting deeply when fortune turns.

The strain of his demanding and fickle profession was all over Holtz this week, in his movements, his voice, his eyes. It's what happens to you when you take everything as personally as he does. This was his team and Notre Dame was his school now, and it was his reputation that was being jabbed at by sportswriters in Chicago and elsewhere. They were calling him out.

One of the most intriguing aspects of superior football coaches is the difference between their media personalities and what you sense must be going on inside of them during the season. In front of TV cameras, they are, almost without exception, polite and soft-spoken, at times saccharine: "We've got a pretty good football team but they've got an awful good football team, too. They've also got a great coach and great tradition and they're just a great school and . . ." Once the game has started, you occasionally catch a glimpse of this same coach on the sidelines looking across the field at the enemy and his expression says, "I'd like to kill those guys."

You don't get to the top of the football chain without a little rabid dog somewhere within you. Holtz usually kept his quietly tucked away from public view, but this afternoon you could almost hear it growling.

"This kind of blocking is what I used to teach," Moose was saying. "For years and years. Back then the players weren't trying to block each other but me. We just beat the hell out of one another all day long. I'd block ten, twelve guys a practice. I never lifted weights but I was pretty strong. In those days we didn't even have a weight room."

Another pair of young men were lined up next to Moore. He walked around behind one of them, and as he yelled "Go!" he placed his shoe on the huge fellow's posterior and gave it a mighty shove. The blocker rushed headlong into his opponent, who was just as big as he was and just as determined and under just as much scrutiny. They smashed together and dug in, the grunting and the impact reverberating up from the field to where Moose was watching, reaching him and stirring something within the old man. He smiled and shook his head and tapped cigar ashes near his shoe.

"Oh, boy," he said. "Aren't you happy to be here and see this? This is just like when Leahy was coach."

Moore walked in front of all the linemen, now standing in a row before him, pacing back and forth. As he went by, he whacked each one on the helmet, not a bone-rattling blow but something more than an affectionate cuff. The players' heads moved but nothing else.

"I want more intensity," the coach said, and the young men nodded and shifted their feet.

"You understand?" Moore said.

For a moment or two there was the sensation in the air that you were not watching a football practice in 1992 but something else entirely, an ancient male ritual unfolding before you, the sort of thing that we often think of as having taken place in more primitive times. The elders of this particular tribe down on the field were instructing those who were on the threshold of adulthood, and the older men had been given complete authority to do so.

They could say whatever they wanted and do whatever they felt was appropriate with their charges, because it was understood that all of them were involved in something larger than their own individual lives. The younger ones weren't simply learning how to become members of their own group, they were being initiated into the duties and responsibilities of manhood. An implicit level of trust between the young and the old made all of this possible.

The sensation passed, but some part of it lingered, and with it came a peculiar glow of satisfaction, very unexpected and hard to account for at first. You had the feeling that what was taking place at the practice was not only connected to its own revered tradition—Notre Dame football—but to something much deeper and richer than that, something that went back further than anyone could possibly remember.

In "The Power of Myth," a show that ran on public television and was later published as a book, Joseph Campbell had said that what was missing from contemporary life, and what had become the underlying source of many of our troubles, was that modern society had lost its ability to turn boys into men through meaningful rituals. Long ago, he said, tribal elders had done this by putting their youths through intense physical hardships or by humiliating them in a group setting or even by cutting them and leaving a scar. Young men were given the chance to show their strength and courage, to prove they had the qualities to be adult males in the tribe. Some were weeded out.

The purpose of the rituals was not to harm anyone but to let the youths know that they were no longer children; they were members of a social order and had the obligation to exercise self-control toward themselves and others. Without these things, Campbell had said, young men can easily become lost in their impulses toward sexual chaos or violence. The rituals helped form the basis for what is perhaps the oldest known form of "male bonding." In our time that term has become a cliché, at times a joke, but it was important in certain ancient cultures, and there is still not much evidence that we've evolved a great distance away from what we once were.

"Civilization," it has been said, "is the thin veneer over what made us what we are."

As two more of the players lined up and rammed together, as they growled and strained and tried to beat one another down, Moose laughed again, and then something else happened that was fully unexpected. The game of football—and the exercises they were doing on the field—suddenly did not look like a sport but resembled a piece of heavy machinery whose metal facade had fallen away so you were now looking inside the thing itself, down into the levers and gears that made it run but were usually kept out of sight, down into the heart of the engine. There was steam and charge and combustion down there. There was heat escaping.

There was something so naked and powerful that you could sense, even if you'd never played much football yourself, how all of this could keep its hold on a man forty or fifty or sixty years after he'd walked off the field for the last time. There was a beauty in the midst of all this that was ugly, and by being ugly it was even more beautiful, and it hinted at why aging former football players genuinely like one another when they've become too old to suit up and knock heads.

Moose squirmed on his seat, grunting along with the linemen. "Wow," he said, "wouldn't you love to be down there practicing with them?"

The question slowly sunk in, and as it did, you were reminded of the former Irish assistant coach Wally Moore and of all of the thoughts that had been stirred on the morning of his recent visit to Moose's office. You realized that you'd long felt some envy of good athletes, not so much because they were well known or well paid (although you would certainly have enjoyed those things) but for other more complicated reasons.

Sports allow people to channel their aggression, to divert or release it. Down on the field this afternoon, the frightful thing itself—the violence that runs through all of us—was being released in a way that was oddly and surprisingly gratifying. It felt right. It felt very human. It felt joined to our past. Things weren't being denied down there, but unleashed and controlled, and maybe the players were releasing it not just for themselves, but, on some other level, for all of us.

You were struck anew by the notion that these observations could have occurred in many locales, but they were taking place at Notre Dame. No matter how one felt about Christianity or any other faith, part of the hold religion has on people is that it provides a framework in which to acknowledge the difficulties and challenges of being alive. It admits of sin and desire and of a whole welter of things that are often regarded as antisocial. It lets you know that part of you is still an animal, and it's all right to admit that.

Down on the field things were all right, too. It was all right in this setting for young men to attempt to dominate one another. It was all right to let out some of the rage that comes with our condition. It was all right to bring two good athletes face-to-face and see what happened at the extremes of competition.

Looking over at Moose, you realized that some men, if they're fortunate, could have it both ways. He was known for his rugged play on the gridiron, but he was also known, by those who were closest to him, as a tender person who had for years devoted himself to the most basic kinds of nurturing—to feeding, to dressing and undressing, to cleaning up after and putting to bed a very damaged woman. In a development that no one could have foreseen in his youth, the football player had become an example of sacrifice and servitude to others.

Part of the aura that moved around Moose was just that; you sensed that he'd managed to balance these forces within himself, the sweetness and the darkness alike. He still enjoyed doing good and unexpected things for other people, even for strangers, and he still enjoyed watching certain kinds of violence, but this came out in appropriate ways, at football games. He'd found his own balance and contentment.

You also sensed that he was very tired and that his work was done. This is by no means to suggest that he'd conquered every challenge or passed into sainthood. He would still tongue-lash anyone who criticized Notre Dame, and he said a few things that by today's standards would be considered politically incorrect. But if the man had his blind spots, the life felt rounded and complete.

You could not, of course, say this about every old football player—some were animals on and off the field—but it was part of the experience of knowing Moose. You felt that somehow, despite a life filled with harshness, he'd made not only himself but things in general better.

16 The End of Ara

WATCHING HOLTZ AT PRACTICE, THE INEVITABLE QUESTION arose: How many seasons could anyone possibly do this job? Ten? Twelve? Or was that too long at the helm without incurring a grave risk to your health? Mercifully, they don't even let modern American presidents govern for more than eight years, and most everyone has noticed how much better White House residents look soon after they've moved out. In 1992, Holtz was in his seventh campaign at Notre Dame, and you couldn't help wondering if he would last as long as Ara Parseghian.

Following the 1974 season—his eleventh as head coach of the Irish—Parseghian left football, deciding that he had to move on. He was fifty-one. Moose had tried to persuade him to stay, but the answer was always the same. Ara was not the sort of man who reached his conclusions quickly or lightly.

"After my last regular season game in 1974," he says, "Father Joyce picked up the phone and called my wife. He thought I was just being emotional and would change my mind after thinking about it. My wife said, 'No, he's been talking about it for some time.'

"After eleven years, it was like being on a treadmill. I could feel it getting to me. My blood pressure was high. I was taking medication. I was exhausted. I knew what was happening to me and what had to be done. You don't give up the Notre Dame coaching job impulsively. My wife made me promise that if I did leave, I'd stay away from football for a year, so I didn't even do color commentary for TV the first year I was gone. Compared to what I was back then, I'm very relaxed today."

As with Rockne and Leahy, when people talk about Parseghian now, they recall more than anything else his intangible qualities—his fervor and passion, his single-mindedness and intense focus and will, all the things that swirl around a person and can be felt but not directly seen. When the man himself is no longer present and all the games are over and his coaches and players have scattered across the nation, what lingers is the spirit he brought to the job.

"When Ara first drove to South Bend to speak at the annual Notre Dame football banquet," says Joe Doyle, "he ran out of gas on the Indiana Turnpike. That was Ara. He knew everything his guards and tackles were doing but not if he had gas in the car. You wouldn't believe how detailed he was in preparation for a football game. He would constantly be calling the local weather bureau and asking about the wind direction, the humidity, the chances for rain or snow, the temperature, the upcoming changes in these conditions. But that wasn't good enough. He'd call Chicago to find out what was going on there and farther west.

"One day during his first year as coach Ara had a player who came to practice drunk. The other guys saw this and hustled him out of there. Then the guy drank some more and staggered back onto the field. A week later I was in Ara's office and he said he'd had a talk with this player. I said, 'You mean he's in trouble again?' He said, 'Again? What do you mean?' I said, 'He was also in trouble under Kuharich.'

That was it. When Ara realized it was a second offense, he was gone. It didn't matter if it had happened under another coach.

"When Ara quit the game, he quit it completely, just like Leahy. He didn't want to collapse on the sidelines, he didn't want to die. He never slept on Saturdays after the games. He couldn't. He'd call me at two A.M. and say, 'You wanna come over and talk?' I'd go. We'd have Sunday-morning Bloody Marys and watch the replay of the game. If we were five and oh at that point in the season, he'd watch the replay and say we were now ten and oh. Ara's players liked him more than Leahy's players liked Frank because he didn't work you to death in practice. People only liked Leahy later on, sometimes much later on.

"Ara always wore a Notre Dame sweater for the games. When reporters asked him why, he said, 'I like the way it looks.' That wasn't the reason at all. He wore it so his players and especially his quarterback could pick him out on the sidelines. He flashed in the plays by using his card, and he needed to make sure that Joe Theismann or whoever was the quarterback could see him easily. It was illegal to do that at first but he got away with it for a couple of seasons.

"A few years ago he and I were talking and I said, 'They can't blame you for that tie with Michigan State in 1966 because you weren't calling the plays, right? Everybody knows that wasn't allowed back then.' He smiled and thought about it for minute and said, 'You're right. I'll have to tell my critics that. Maybe that'll help me.' Hell, he figured out ways to call the plays the whole time he was here."

George Kelly, the special assistant to the Notre Dame athletic director, is another man whose career at the university has spanned several eras. He graduated from Notre Dame in 1953, Leahy's final year as head coach, and became an assistant coach under both Parseghian and Holtz. Like Moose, Kelly is Lithuanian, and sometimes when the two men came together in the halls of the athletic department, they greeted each other in the mother tongue.

"When I came here from Nebraska in 1969 to be on Ara's staff, I was a yeller," says Kelly, who has a deep, rough-edged, commanding voice. "I yelled at players a lot. Ara took me aside and forewarned me about that. He said that when you lose your composure, you lose your ability to teach people. That advice made me a better coach. He said that you don't single out an individual and yell at him over and over again, you correct the whole team when it is breaking down. And when you lose, you don't let the kids read your emotions. They can see when you're not eating or sleeping or when you're down. So you don't show it.

"Ara had a lot of trust in those around him. He believed that the only friends you have are those who are working with you. So many people on the outside may seem to be your friends, but you often find out that they're not. That's why football teams and coaches become so close. That's why the players often have good memories of those times when they get older. That's where it becomes a family.

"The pressure Ara felt at Notre Dame was largely self-imposed. He never got it from Moose Krause or the administration. He beat himself up when they lost and took it very personally. He felt that the product on the field was an extension of himself. Lou Holtz is the same way. Every Saturday afternoon in the fall is a final exam, and you're responsible for the one hundred and twenty young men who play football for you. And those kids are eighteen, nineteen, and twenty years old and they are expected, under the national microscope, to be nothing less than excellent. That's the standard here. People don't come to Notre Dame to kill time.

"Ara's drivenness comes from his ethnic background. His family fought for survival in his childhood. They lived in Akron, Ohio, and came from the wrong side of the tracks. Sports won him fortune and fame at Miami of Ohio, where he played in college, and then with the Cleveland Browns, where he played in the pros, then coaching at Miami of Ohio, then at Northwestern, and then here at Notre Dame. Football was very important to this man."

* * *

Pete Duranko, one of many Irish players from Pennsylvania, was originally a fullback at Notre Dame. Under Parseghian he became a defensive tackle and was an all-American his senior year at that position on the 1966 national championship team.

"I played for Hugh Devore before Ara came to South Bend," Duranko says. "I loved Hughie but he didn't have control of things, so I saw good times and bad times in the football program. Everything changed when Ara showed up. His attitude commanded respect.

"When I was a senior, I had a strained ligament and I wasn't playing up to my potential. Ara called me into his office after the third game and showed me films of myself on the field. He said I was still babying my ankle. That was all it took. After our talk, I played fifty percent better. I didn't realize I could get more out of myself until he told me that. When you'd get slapped in the head by Ara, you knew it was for the good of the team. Nowadays coaches are afraid of touching a player for fear of being arrested."

Bob Gladieux, along with Ron Dushney, were known as the prime characters of the early Parseghian teams—the Ziggy Czarobskis of that era. Every squad has them: young men who act funny, say outrageous things, play practical jokes on others, and bring some levity to a game that over time has grown very serious. Many Notre Dame stories from those years begin with, "Gladieux and Dushney were always . . ."

Gladieux is middle-aged now, a curly-haired, mustachioed gentleman whose manner does not seem outlandish, although there is a hint of mischief in the wings of his eyes. In the mideighties he came back to Notre Dame as a graduate assistant coach, and the experience made a great impression on him.

"The time commitment of the coaches is truly amazing," he says, sounding relieved that he has moved on to other work, "and so are the sacrifices you have to make with your family. I wasn't aware of what it took."

When he played football, Gladieux felt responsible only for himself. The game was difficult and demanding but enjoyable for someone who was an excellent all-purpose running back for the Irish, gaining 2,575 yards total offense in his career and scoring 26 touchdowns. As an assistant under Lou Holtz, he suddenly felt responsible for every young man on the team, and when some of them did the kinds of things for fun that he used to do, it made him uncomfortable. That's part of the reason he found a new career and is now in the travel business in South Bend.

"Coming out of high school, I was either going to Ohio State or Notre Dame," Gladieux says. "My father had gone to Notre Dame and has known Moose since 1936, but I wasn't sure the team wanted me. I only weighed one sixty-five and they were worried about my size. Tom Pagna, an assistant coach, was in my corner. Before my on-campus interview with Ara, Tom told me to go in there and sell him on Notre Dame, not on my football ability. He said, 'Tell him that your dad went to school here and you always wanted to do that. Tell him you have a burning desire to come to Notre Dame. Tell him how bad you want it. Tell him what a great competitor you are and how great the competition is at the school.' When I saw Ara, I sort of left football out of it and it worked.

"What I remember most about Ara was his intensity. During practices and games, you tried to stay as far away from him as you could. We lost four games in the three years I was at Notre Dame.

"We ate our meals in a dining hall, and after a loss Ara would sit there near the door and not touch his food. He would stare every player in the eye as you came in to eat. Those big dark Armenian eyes coming right at you. We'd watch him and whisper, 'He still hasn't eaten. He's waiting for the next player to come in.' As you were sitting there trying to eat, he would come up to you and talk about the game we'd just lost. He'd talk about the stupid mistakes and the penalties. Some people take things harder than others.

"The only reason I got to play in the famous Michigan State game of 1966 was because the running back ahead of me, Nick Eddy, was injured and then re-injured right before the game. Ara wore wing tips, so naturally all the players thought we had to wear them. Coming down off the train that took us to the game, ol' Nick tripped in his new shoes and grabbed a railing and tore a shoulder. Ten minutes before the kickoff, Ara told me I was starting."

That afternoon Gladieux scored on a 34-yard pass from Coley O'Brien, the only Irish touchdown of the game.

Off the field, self-control didn't come naturally to Gladieux. "Our curfew was at ten-thirty, but one night I stayed out till about one A.M. I was downtown having a few beers. On the way home I picked up someone's bicycle and threw it as far as I could. Father Joyce was standing right behind me watching me. It was dark and he was all in black and I hadn't seen him. When I did see him, I jumped and thought, 'Oh, no!'

"He told me he was gonna let Ara handle this, and at first Ara told me he was gonna kick me off the team. Then he told me something that stayed with me all my life. He said, 'Anyone can make a mistake. But don't ever do it again.' It was very simple: learn from your screw-ups. No second offenses. If I ever made the same mistake, I was finished.

"In my four years at Notre Dame, only one person had what it took to talk back to Ara and that was Johnny Ray, one of our assistant coaches. And whenever he did this, it scared the hell out of all of us."

Johnny Ray would probably talk back to anyone, and the reason is obvious. He's a compulsive talker. Give him a question and forty-five minutes later he'll ask if you've got another one. He's a big man with thick shoulders, a square face, and a prominent stomach. He looks something like the old Soviet premier Leonid Brezhnev. He looks like a bear. After playing football at Notre Dame, he was simultaneously an assistant coach and a player at Olivet College in Michigan in the 1950s.

"At Olivet they called me the Iron Man," he says, "because I never substituted for myself."

He later coached at John Carroll University outside of Cleveland, where he became famous within girdiron circles for developing new and highly effective defensive strategies. In 1962, when Parseghian was voted the major-college coach of the year for his work at Northwestern, Ray won the small-college honor. He speaks faster than a high wind.

"After I got this award, Ara called in June of 1963 and asked me to speak at the national convention of football coaches," Ray says. "The convention was the following January. Seven, eight months away. They'd scheduled other speakers like Bob Devaney and Darrell Royal. Big names. I was the only one from a small college. Ara told me what was expected of me, and he wanted me to outline my speech for him. I said fine, I'd be happy to do that for him when I was ready.

"He calls me a month later and asks how I'm doin' on the speech. 'Fine,' I said. 'I'm doin' just fine.' I hadn't done anything yet. He calls me the next month and it's the same thing. Now he's startin' to piss me off. I said, 'Don't worry about it, all right? I'll make the speech. It'll be good.' He calls me a month later and I say, 'Get off may ass, will ya?' He said, 'I'm just following up.' I said, 'Bullshit you are. If you don't think I can do it, get someone else.' He backed off, just a little.

"In December of '63 he becomes head coach at Notre Dame. The SOB starts calling me again. Now I'm really pissed. He asks me what time I'm comin' to the convention and he wants to meet me there and I'm thinkin', 'Shit, he wants to talk to me about my damn speech.' In the meantime Wake Forest offers me a head coaching job while I'm at the convention, but before I accept it I have to go over and talk to Ara. I meet him and he looks at me and he's lookin' at his watch like, 'You're late!' 'Screw you,' I say to myself, 'I've got a job offer and I don't need you.' Then he said, 'Come up to my room tonight. Be there at eight P.M. sharp and don't forget.' I said, 'Ara, for chrissakes, I'm not gonna forget.'

"At eight o'clock I walk into his hotel room and he's sitting on his bed with his shoes off. I sit down and say, 'Don't worry. My speech is ready and it's good.' He says, 'That's not it. I want you to work with me at Notre Dame.' I say, 'I can't. I just got a job at Wake Forest.' He gets up and starts shakin' his head. 'Oh, no, no,' he says. 'That won't work.

Your goin' to Wake Forest as a Catholic is worse than me goin' to Notre Dame as a Presbyterian.'

"I tell him that I don't know if I can be an assistant coach anymore, after being a head coach. Well, Ara was a salesman. He tells me that if I go to Wake Forest down in Winston-Salem, North Carolina, my career will be buried.

"He goes to the phone and calls the coach who'd just been fired from Wake Forest: Jerry Hildebrant. You know Jerry isn't gonna say anything good about the place now. Ara gives me the receiver and Jerry tells me, 'There aren't any players down here' and 'Being a Catholic in this place isn't easy.' Ara hangs up the phone and looks at me. 'What'd I tell ya?' he says. 'You'd hate it down there.' Then he makes me call my wife and tell her we're moving to South Bend. She was really surprised. Then I had to go make my speech. That's the way Ara did everything—right now!"

Ray became the Irish defensive coordinator and an assistant head coach. Like many others who played or worked for Parseghian, he speaks with reverence about the man's ability not just to spot talent but to motivate players and to move them into positions where they could be more productive, even if they'd never played those positions before. Parseghian did that with Pete Duranko and with Jack Snow (a running back who became a wide receiver), but his most famous rehab project was quarterback John Huarte, who wasn't even expected to play much in 1964. Huarte won the Heisman Trophy that year—a few weeks before he won his first monogram at Notre Dame.

When discussing that season, Johnny Ray, in the time-honored tradition in South Bend, concludes his remarks by mentioning the heartrending loss to Southern Cal. "Hell," he says, "they called a lousy holding penalty on Meeker in the last ninety seconds. Without that, we would have won everything."

Soon after Ray came to Notre Dame, he and Parseghian and some other coaches were part of a football clinic held in South Carolina. The idea was to share with others some of the keys to your own success.

"As we're gettin' ready to do this," Ray says, "Ara comes over and tells me, 'Now, when you're talkin' to these people, tell 'em a few little things, but remember that there'll be a lot of college coaches sittin' out there, so don't tell 'em anything important.' I said, 'Okay, don't worry about me.' I'm the first one on. I give them all the bullshit about pride in the team and how we make a huddle and things like that. This takes me about an hour. I finish and start to come down off the platform, and the next speaker—Doc Urich, the offensive coordinator—whispers to me, 'Ara's really pissed at you for tellin' 'em too much.'

"I can't believe it. I say, 'What? I didn't tell 'em shit.' I walk over to Ara and say, 'Doc says you're upset with me.' He says, 'I don't want to discuss it.' Now that really pisses me off. I say, 'Ara—' but he cuts me off and says, 'Shut up. I don't want to talk about it.' There's a break in the clinic and the SOB leaves the room. I go find Doc. By now he could see that I was really upset. He says, 'Ara's just giggin' you.' I say, 'What?' He says, 'Yeah, he's just upsettin' you to see how you react to pressure. Don't let him get to you.' I thank Doc and walk away.

"When Ara's gettin' ready to go up and make his speech, I pull him aside and say, 'Look, I don't want you to embarrass us up there.' He stares right at me with those eyes, and for a second I thought I'd made a big mistake. Then he smiles and says, 'Doc told you, didn't he?' We were fine after that.

"Ara hired Wally Moore. Wally was a good coach but the most naive person I ever met. He told me he was afraid of flying, but he thought it was worth doing it for Notre Dame. A month later he had to fly somewhere for a recruiting trip.

"As he's leaving, I give him a dollar bill for air insurance. 'What's this?' he says. 'Well,' I tell him, 'as much as we fly in this job, the law of averages is gonna catch up with us. It might be your turn.' He started shakin' and sweatin'. Ara's in his office and he hears me doin' this and he calls Wally in. He gives him a five-dollar bill for insurance and tells him that it might just be his time. Wally went to the airport scared stiff.

"Ara would gig you for two or three days runnin'. When we'd win, he'd get all over the coaches. Always afraid of complacency. When we'd lose, he'd take all the blame himself. It was just the opposite of what you expected. He was super with us. He'd share the food and the booze that fans sent him. He shared his bonuses with us. A lot of head coaches resent their staff but he was always generous.

"His pep talks were prepared very carefully. He'd write it all down and study it, but when it came out, it sounded spontaneous. I was at Notre Dame briefly under Leahy and I coached against other men, including Bear Bryant, but Ara could adjust to things during the games better than anyone I ever saw. He would talk to the players and ask them questions and learn what they were doing out on the field and make the adjustments right then. Leahy would get so worked up at the games he couldn't do that.

"When I think back to Frank Leahy, I laugh. He had two things he always said to you when he saw you, no matter what—'How's your weight, lad?' and 'How's your family?' That was it. My answer to the first one was 'One hundred eighty-five pounds' and to the second one, 'Fine.' One day Leahy sees Johnny Lujack on the campus and he says, 'How's your weight, lad?' Lujack says, 'Two hundred eighty-four pounds, Coach.' Frank says, 'And how's your mother?' 'She's dying,' Johnny says. Leahy nodded and just kept walking. He was thinking about football and didn't hear a thing. He was the most concentrated man I ever saw."

Ray starts to laugh, the way many old coaches do as they go further into their memories. "One of my jobs on the sidelines was sending in defensive signals to Jim Lynch, our all-American linebacker. One signal called for me to scratch my nuts. Ara saw this and came over and said, 'What the hell are you doing?' 'Ah,' I told him, 'don't worry about it. It's natural.' Of course when television became more popular it got to be a problem."

Ray was eventually hired as the head coach at Kentucky and then as an assistant coach with the Buffalo Bills. After football he went to work for Ara Parseghian Enterprises and is now an executive vice president with the company. He knows his boss well.

"When Notre Dame traveled to games," he says, "I stayed in a suite with Ara. The other coaches got to go out the night before a game, but I was stuck with him. We'd sit in the room and he'd say, 'Are we ready?' 'Yeah,' I'd tell him, 'we're ready.' He'd ask me that twenty times.

"He left nothing to chance. Drove me crazy. He'd sit there and think up the most bizarre circumstance—if our three quarterbacks got hurt, for example—what would we do? He'd always have a 'disaster quarterback' around who could hand off the ball, and then we'd have a backup for him. He's the most thorough man I ever saw.

"One time I was late for one of his seven A.M. meetings. I had to pick up Doc Urich. I drove over to Doc's house and honked the horn. Nothin' happened. It was a little before seven and I knew Ara got there at six A.M. I was gettin' nervous. I honked again. Nothin'. Doc's wife looks through the window and calls out to me, 'Doc'll be right there!'

"I'm lookin' at my watch and squirmin' in my seat. I'm honkin' and tellin' Doc to get his ass out here now. He comes out runnin' and jumps in the car and I drive as fast as I can to the meeting, but we're a few minutes late. Ara's upset but he doesn't say anything for a while, just gives me that stare. Then he says, 'You SOB, you're gonna buy doughnuts for all of us for a week.' And I did, but I split the cost with Doc."

Rocky Bleier was a running back, blocker, and receiver on the 1966 Irish squad and the Notre Dame captain the following year. He also punted and returned kickoffs. After serving in Vietnam and rehabilitating himself from a serious war injury, a process that took two years, he played for the Pittsburgh Steeler team that dominated pro football in the late 1970s.

"Moose recruited me at my father's bar," he says. "I grew up in Appleton, Wisconsin, and we lived above a tavern. Moose was gracious enough to come in on a couple of occasions and speak to me. The year I was captain, 1967, I had to write a letter to my teammates before the season started. Ara wanted to see what I'd written.

"One afternoon I dropped in to talk to him about this and he told his secretary to make an appointment for me. He wasn't doing anything at the time, but he couldn't take five minutes off just then. Those five minutes were scheduled for something else. When we got together later and talked, everything was fine, but that was Ara. You needed an appointment with him and you kept it.

"To motivate you he would build up a theme for the whole week. After playing a game on Saturday, you were allowed to recover on Sunday, but on Monday he planted the seed of whatever the next theme would be. On Tuesday he brought out some articles that had just been written about how good our upcoming opponent was. He'd read them to us. He'd let you know that they were capable of kicking your ass up and down the field. He'd work on this idea the rest of the week and repeat certain things that had been written, so that by Saturday you could never take anyone lightly.

"If we won a game, he congratulated you as an individual, but if we lost, we lost as a team. People responded well to that. His emotions were powerful and they didn't come out so much in his words but in the course of the game itself. Players felt that and picked up on it.

"What Ara taught me about blocking allowed me to play in Pittsburgh for all those years. He showed me the right way to block and the Steelers needed a blocking back. I was the only player on their team who could block out of a right-handed or left-handed stance because he demanded that you learn this. It became second nature to me. This technique saved me a few steps and helped me not clip someone. I was explosive from either stance. Everything Ara taught you was for a reason."

Moose's assistant and sidekick, Colonel Stephens, had been stationed in the Philippines during World War II. He'd been awarded the Silver Star, the Purple Heart, the Legion of

Merit, and three Bronze Stars. When he went to work for Parseghian in 1968, he thought he was back in the military.

"Ara was a strict martinet," he says. "I loved the guy but whenever we lost a game, oh, boy, you had to walk on eggs in his office for a week. You didn't say a word. He had a sense of humor, but he could be an SOB when he had to."

Says Moose, "When Digger Phelps came to Notre Dame to coach the basketball team, Ara hid his office furniture in one of the bathrooms. Digger couldn't find it for a week."

Jim Lynch was the captain of the 1966 Fighting Irish championship team. As an inside linebacker he was an all-American, won the Maxwell Award—given to the top college player in the nation—and became an Academic all-American at Notre Dame. He was on the Kansas City Chiefs team that won the 1970 Super Bowl.

"A great coach," he says, "has two teams to coach—his players and his staff. Under Ara, if you didn't get your work done as a coach, it wasn't a reflection on your players but on you as a coach. His assistants understood that and worked very hard. In his locker-room speeches, Ara always let you know that when you took the field that day, you weren't going to be outcoached, and that gave you a lot of confidence.

"We lost three games in my three years. It's funny, but you remember the losses much better than the wins. After we'd lose, Ara would completely dissect the game and tell us why this had happened. I felt about winning exactly the same way he did. When Notre Dame wins now, I read the sports pages of three newspapers. When they lose, I don't read any of them. My time at Notre Dame was from 1964 to '66, and it was kind of magical because that was when the tradition came back."

Father James Riehle has been the Irish team chaplain from 1966 to the present. He performs the Saturday-morning pregame masses, blesses the players who kneel in front of him in the locker room just before they take the field, blesses them when they come in at halftime, and blesses them when they return at the end of the game.

"Ara went to the pregame masses with the players," Father Riehle says, "but he couldn't receive Communion because he wasn't a Catholic. So he just sat there by himself and watched. This was never an issue and he never talked to me about it. He felt that his presence at the ceremony was very important and another way for him to join with the team. He wanted to be a part of it.

"All of his children are married to Catholics and I think his grandchildren have been baptized in the Church, but he hasn't become a Catholic. Yet."

In his senior year at Notre Dame Dave Casper was a tight end on the 1973 national championship team. He was an all-American that season and went on to have an excellent career with the Oakland–Los Angeles Raiders. Many Raiders have been known as mavericks, so Casper fit in well with the franchise.

"I never wanted to talk to the head coach," he says. "My whole career, in high school and college and in the pros, I tried to avoid that. At Notre Dame, I showed up every day my last three years with my head shaved. Ara said I couldn't wear my hair long—I wanted to cut it once a year—so I decided to cut it all off.

"Ara understood his purpose. Fans want to be entertained, but players want to be coached. We thought he was impersonal but he was really just very organized and kept things simplified. I played for John Madden and Bud Grant and Tom Flores in the pros, but Ara was the most organized person I was ever around.

"He didn't try to get in your head and talk to you very much. I really liked that. How far can you get into the head of an eighteen-year-old? He didn't beat you up and he didn't overpractice you. His workouts were humanistic. He was the first person to understand that you don't get in better shape for the football season by hitting people in spring practice. You just get injured. So he brought in dummies and let us hit them.

"My senior year I was elected captain of the team. Ara said

no long hair and no facial hair. I went in to him and said we wanted to stay in touch with the student body and what they were involved in. He listened to me. He let us go out and socialize more and let us grow mustaches. He understood that the most important question was whether you played hard on Saturday and played with discipline. Over time he relaxed a little, and when something wasn't working, he could change his mind.

"He let me be me. I just wanted someone to tell me what to do and then leave me alone. He did that. I made only one mistake my senior year, when I jumped offside in the Sugar Bowl. When I came back to South Bend after the game, I went into the athletic department and saw him in there watching films of the game. His first words to me were, 'Why the hell were you offsides?' I just learned to stay away from him, and that was okay with Ara. He only made four or five comments to me the whole time I was at Notre Dame. He didn't mess with my mind. He knew what you went through as a football player.

"I've seen Ara in recent years and I always send him a Christmas card. When we get together, he's still the coach and I'm still the player. It's the same thing with John Madden and me. All good coaches maintain that relationship with you. It's very clear who's in control. I like that clarity. I think people need it."

17 Taking Charge

THERE WAS PLENTY OF CLARITY AT NOTRE DAME'S FIRST SERIOUS workout following the loss to Stanford, and as the afternoon wore on, things became even more clear. Watching the practice, you were struck by the notion that the world of sports is surrounded by paradoxes, and that is part of the appeal. The games themselves are contrived, played within artificial borders and boundaries of time, but in some ways they are "more real" and less muddled than many other things in life.

There is nothing artificial about being hit by a 250-pound linebacker or about facing a 98-mile-per-hour fastball thrown near your chin or about getting into a boxing ring with someone whose intention is to render you unconscious. The winning and losing in most athletic contests is clean and aesthetically pleasing, not unlike what you experience at a good play or movie. When the game or fight is over, you not only know what the outcome is, you have a decent idea of how and why things turned out as they did.

In more subtle ways, the games are also emotionally satisfying. They start from the premise that everyone agrees to play by the same rules and everyone will be punished to the same degree if those rules are broken. Everyone is treated equally, judged strictly according to his or her performance, and race, creed, sex, color, and the countless other things that divide people do not apply here. It is, you finally realize, the way you wish things were everywhere.

For a long time during the practice Holtz remained kneeling and watching the action, his fingers still touching the ground. He was the most important elder of this tribe, and what happened to his team the rest of the year would please or torment him for months to come, right up until the start of the next season.

Like many of the players around him on the field, Holtz had originally been led to football as an adolescent by an older man, a high school coach in Ohio named Wade Watts, who'd taken an interest in him and encouraged him to try hard at the sport, despite his small size and physical limitations. The youngster liked the game itself, but he enjoyed the togetherness of the teammates perhaps even more. Each year now, as the head coach at Notre Dame, he made Watts a guest of the Irish when they played USC, getting him tickets and letting him come into the locker room.

Kneeling and staring, Holtz seemed to be aware of nothing more than the linemen surging at one another in the blocking drills, but he was also watching other parts of the field where other drills were unfolding, and he was even aware of Moose Krause sitting up in the stands, taking in the practice. Once, he'd glanced up and nodded in Moose's direction and Moose had nodded back.

As with most good coaches, Holtz had antennae all over the place. He knew that several faculty members were present this afternoon, and he would later say that they were taken aback by the fierceness of the practice, which was by far the hardest of the season. (When asked in subsequent days if the players had responded positively to this session, he said, "I figured if they showed up on Wednesday, they'd responded well.")

What Holtz didn't say was that if you wanted to play football at Notre Dame or any other major university, there was a price to pay and this was how it was extracted. On the part of many people, including some football fans, there's a feeling that the young men who receive scholarships to play college sports are pampered and spoiled individuals, given special treatment from the time they enter school until the time they leave.

It's easy to feel this way about athletes—until you watch them at practice after an upset loss on national television. Then you realize they work for it, every bit of it, and you wonder how anyone could endure two or three hours of these demanding ordeals, go back to the dorm, and try to study for more than fifteen minutes without passing out.

"Break!" Joe Moore said, and gradually the two linemen who were stuck together in front of him came apart.

"Good, good," Moose said, watching the field. "He's teachin' 'em the right way to block. He's one of the best line coaches in the country. He's showin' 'em how to open a hole. This is the only way to coach football. You gotta make 'em hit and make 'em hit if you want perfection. You can't do this in dummy drills. These are the same kinds of practices that Ara had and Leahy had and Rockne had. It's amazing how all of this fits together and all these coaches are the same."

Moose was asked if he ever missed playing football.

He looked at the field and puffed his cigar and didn't say anything for a while, as if it were a question he hadn't thought about for a long time. A strange expression crossed his face. At the moment, except for his worn-out body, he didn't look like a man who'd hung up his pads half a century earlier but like a boy who still wanted a chance to make the team.

"Yeah," he finally said. "After I retired from the game, I was kind of lonesome. I liked being out there so much. I liked being with the players and going at it together. I liked makin' a good clean tackle. That was fun."

He was asked if he wanted to go down closer to the field.

"Oh, no," he said instantly. "I couldn't do that. It might distract Lou or the players and they're working real hard. They have to get things done right for Saturday."

He was quiet for several moments and then said, "My sons weren't football players. Philip was kind of skinny, but he played some rugby and that's a rough game. Ed tried out for the football team once, but he came home crying because they wouldn't let him play. I sat down with him and said, 'Don't worry about it, son. Find another sport. Just something you can do that you enjoy.' "

Coach Moore had changed the blocking drill from one-on-one and now had a single lineman blocking two defenders. The grunting and the digging intensified, and the lone blocker was swallowed up inside the arms and torsos of those he was trying to resist. His knees buckled beneath him, he wheezed and cursed, spit and coughed. He fell down but got up and tried again. Chugging and spewing, he went at the two behemoths, trying vainly to move them backward. They charged him harder. He fell down, got up, and tried again, all the while with Joe Moore bending over him and yelling in his ear. There were more shoes in the buttocks, more slaps to the helmet. He tried and fell again, and his place was taken by another young man.

Throughout all this, more waves of laughter rumbled up from Moose's chest, as always happened when he was in the presence of intense physicality. The noise came from down under, way down under, and it flowed outward, like a river rushing forward or sap moving through branches or a strong wind pushing the clouds ahead.

Coach Moore was again exhorting the linemen to go harder.

When one set of blockers was finished for the moment, they walked over to a tank with a hose attached to it, picked up the hose, and began pouring water down their throats. They threw back their heads and gargled, discharging the liquid and shooting it upward. They yelled at no one in particular, growled really, they paced and snarled. They rolled their fists and smacked each other on the shoulder pads. Taking off their helmets, they revealed big shaved heads and thick necks and missing teeth. They looked terrifying and you felt grateful that football had been invented.

Moore changed the drill again and this time it caused Moose to take the cigar out of his mouth and stare. Now it was three-on-one and the one man assigned to block the trio was quickly buried in the torn jerseys, bent knees, and the mass of flesh. Moose watched for a while without speaking, as if he couldn't quite believe what he was witnessing.

"I've never seen that before," he said. "We never did it when I coached. It's just to get their attention."

Moore called for the linemen to break and they did. He had four more of the young men go at it—three-on-one again—and then another set of four. When he called for this last group to stop the drill, two of the biggest blockers ignored him and kept going, grinding into each other, arms shooting forward and then hands. One of them threw a punch and a fight was under way.

Holtz shot up like a panther, running at full speed toward the brawl, as the pair of towering linemen flailed away and tried to wrestle each other to the turf. When the head coach reached the combatants, he leaped between them like a knife, pushing one to the side and grabbing the other by his facemask. Everything else on the field had stopped and everyone was watching Holtz.

He shook the facemask hard, shook it up and down, up and down, moving his face in very close to the young man's and talking in a high-pitched voice, saying that the other player was on his team and they were all involved in the practice together and this kind of behavior was unacceptable. When Holtz quit talking, the practice was utterly silent.

He let go of the lineman's helmet and took a step backward. The big fellow nodded at him, his shoulders slumped, and he looked smaller, humbled. Holtz told him to walk over and shake the hand of the man he'd been wrestling with, and the two of them came together and did as they were asked.

The coach made a brief speech about respecting your teammates and learning to control yourself under extreme pressure. Moments later the hitting resumed with the same intensity as before.

"Lou just took over, didn't he?" Moose said. "Leahy would never have jumped into something like that. He'd always say, 'Moose, go over there and break it up.' Or he'd have let them go at it for a while."

The first-string offense had begun scrimmaging against the first-string defense, executing the same plays over and over again, the running backs charging into the line or Rick Mirer dropping back in the pocket and throwing passes downfield. Holtz was again kneeling and watching from the sidelines, but each time he saw something disturbing, he came to his feet and scampered into the middle of things, waving his hands and raising his voice, getting into one face and then another.

When he spoke, nobody looked at the ground. They looked at him, as if they had no other choice. The strange thing was that his power so obviously wasn't physical. You couldn't see it yet he exuded it, like a scent. He paced and glared, paced and glared, walking in small childlike steps, then stopping cold and staring at the team.

Where, you asked yourself, did his power come from? One answer was that it came from his absolute confidence in his authority; he believed he had the right to lead. But then another answer, strangely enough, presented itself immediately, along with the remark Dave Casper had made about his old coach Ara Parseghian. People, Casper had said, need clarity.

What was being enacted on this field this afternoon was a set of perfectly clear agreements. The coaches had agreed to be beneficent teachers who worked extremely hard at their jobs, and the players had agreed to be taught, regardless of the difficulty of the lessons. When that kind of emotional tone has been set and remains consistent, people sense it and respond to it even if they don't exactly know why they're doing these things. And when that happens, extraordinary things can result. To put it in more scientific terms, there is little resistance to movement and to change.

Outside the sports arena, you see this phenomenon acted out most often when countries perceive an enemy and decide to go to war. Then they mobilize quickly. We're still trying to learn how to do this in peacetime.

Holtz was all over the field now, haranguing his linemen, scolding his quarterback, replacing one back with another, burning their ears, telling his coaches to run that play once more—a windmill of action. Then he wandered off and squatted by himself, twenty yards from everyone, gazing at his players with absolute focus, as if he were trying to penetrate to the essence of the game itself, find the secret so he could bring it back and share it with the Irish. He looked completely alone in his mission and transfixed. He didn't look happy but like something that went beyond happiness—like a man totally absorbed in his work.

Moose leaned back and exhaled smoke. He looked more relaxed than he had a short while earlier. The tension that had been building throughout the blocking drills had been released by the scuffle, and everyone appeared to be breathing more easily now. The players down there had settled into a rhythm and were running the same plays over and over again, repeating the same movements and efforts, maybe twenty or thirty or forty times today, a hundred times this week, a thousand or two during the course of a season.

They were doing essentially the same things that Parseghian's men had once done and Leahy's before that, the same things that Moose had learned in his youth when Knute Rockne was teaching the fledgling game on a field not far from the Loftus Center, nearly seven decades earlier.

"We never had an indoor facility to practice in when I was playing and coaching," Moose said. "We practiced outside no matter what. If it was raining and cold and miserable, Leahy would say, 'Gentlemen, it's a wonderful day for football because our next game might be in a storm.' "

Running back Reggie Brooks, who'd been suffering with a leg injury this season and was not dressed for the workout, looked up at Krause and waved.

"He's walking," Moose said, yawning and waving back. "Frank would have sent him into the line."

The old man began to stand, a process that took some time now. It was only late afternoon but he was ready to eat dinner. He said he wanted Italian food and he moved slowly toward the stairs, then gently made his way down to the field and stared out at the players.

"Look at the size of those monsters," he said. "I was two hundred and thirty pounds and the biggest lineman Rockne had ever seen, but those guys . . ."

He smiled and drew on the heater.

"Lou's really wakin' 'em up, isn't he?" he said, shaking his head and laughing again.

As he walked toward the Cadillac, his last words brought back something Joe Doyle had mentioned a few days earlier, while sitting in Moose's office and reminiscing.

"One afternoon I was at a Leahy practice and he was just killing them out there," Doyle had said. "One of his assistant coaches looked out at the players and then over at Frank and he said, 'What would happen if they turned on us?' For just a moment there was a flicker of doubt in Leahy's eyes. Then he shook his fist and said, 'They wouldn't dare.' "

The 1992 college season, as it turned out, became the year of rebellion on a number of football teams. After South Carolina lost its first five games, the players voted to ask for Coach Sparky Woods's resignation. Woods refused to quit and his Gamecocks defeated five of their last six opponents. When Memphis State opened its season with three losses, the squad protested by boycotting one practice, then won six of their last eight games and finished with the school's best record in the past half decade. At Morgan State, sixty-nine players signed a petition demanding the removal of head coach Ricky Diggs. When no action was taken, the team forfeited its final game of the season.

At Oklahoma the Sooners disrupted a practice after disagreeing with Coach Gary Gibbs's choice of a quarterback. And in the biggest rebellion of all, Earle Bruce, the head coach of the Colorado State Rams, was fired with two years left on his contract after several players alleged that he'd verbally and physically abused them.

In the autumn of 1992 all of those activities seemed very far away from Moose. As he'd put it more than once, he'd always felt lucky to be given the chance to attend college on an athletic scholarship, and he felt that today's football players should feel the same gratitude.

"I have several grandkids," he said one afternoon while driving around South Bend, "and they always ask me how come I had so much fun playing sports when I was young. I tell them that things were different when I was growing up. We had no money back then and we weren't thinking too much about the future. There wasn't much pressure on us, and we just went out and played whatever sport was in season, either baseball or football or basketball or track.

"You knew everybody at Notre Dame, the students and the teachers, and the campus was like a big family. You sat down with the guys in your dorm and had bull sessions, or you went out and watched movies together. People got along better and they didn't worry as much. My grandkids have a real hard time believing all of that was true.

"We didn't look at sports as a career, the way players do now. It was just a game. Sometimes I wish I'd done things differently, but in those days there wasn't much money in football or basketball. You never thought that athletics would support you for your whole life. When I see the money they make today . . . I just can't believe the owners of sports franchises are crazy enough to pay people like that, and I sure can't blame the players for taking the money. When I was young, I always wanted to play sports, whether they paid me or not. The most important thing to me was escaping the smell of those stockyards."

18 Recovering

LATE IN THE '92 SEASON, HOLTZ SAID THAT IT WAS DURING that Tuesday practice in the Loftus Center that Notre Dame "checked its hole card" for the football year. There must have been something there. Following this workout, there was an accelerated sense of purpose about the team, but despite this the Irish were surrounded by doubters. Disgruntled fans continued to carp at Holtz and compare him unfavorably to Stanford's Bill Walsh or to Miami's Dennis Erickson. They said he'd lost not only his coaching edge in terms of strategy—he was out of step with modern college football and its emphasis on the passing game—but his ability to motivate his team.

Holtz wasn't the only one under siege. Rick Mirer received hundreds of letters from people holding him responsible for ending their dreams of another Irish title. South Bend radio stations began playing a parody of "Achy Breaky Heart," the wildly popular recording by Billy Ray Cyrus that was then topping the country charts. The new tune went:

Don't break my heart, my Fighting Irish heart
I just don't think it'd understand
And if we lose again, that would be a sin
And we'd have no place to play on New Year's Day . . .

It was a rush job, but the message was clear.

On the Saturday after perhaps their toughest practice of the decade, Notre Dame traveled east to play the Pittsburgh Panthers in a night game. Just before the opening kickoff, a Pitt student flashed a large sign that spelled out the score of the Irish's last encounter: STANFORD 33, NOTRE DAME 16. It caught the eye of the visiting coach and he made certain that his team looked at the placard.

"I wanted to see it," Holtz said, "and I felt the players ought to see it, too. I thought it was great. I want to compliment the Pittsburgh student body."

With Notre Dame leading just 14–6, Holtz, fulfilling an earlier promise, sent his second unit into the game on the Irish's fourth possession of the evening. Led by sophomore quarterback Kevin McDougal, the team marched 65 yards in five plays and scored a touchdown. Holtz also began to substitute liberally on defense, another successful idea, as Notre Dame held the Panthers to 167 yards below their season's offensive average. The final score was Irish 52, Pitt 21, but there was more to the game than numbers. Holtz's men had not only come back from the Stanford debacle with a win on the road, they'd done it in a way their coach found especially pleasing.

"This was Notre Dame's style of football," he said, mostly referring to the 308 yards that his team had gained on the ground, although Rick Mirer had thrown two touchdown passes for a career total of 33, moving him ahead of Joe Theismann for the all-time Irish record. "It was nothing fancy, just good, hard-nosed football. . . . You can't always tell how players are going to respond after a loss, but they responded well today. We're going to give them some time off and then get back to work."

The Irish did not play the next Saturday, but the following

week they met the nationally ranked Brigham Young University Cougars in South Bend. At the Friday-night pep rally before the game, Holtz stunned the huge audience by vowing that his team would not lose at home again and then tossing the microphone he'd been holding into the air. It crashed to the floor of the basketball arena and bounced across the hardwood with a hiss. When questioned later about the vow, he smiled and said, "I don't think anyone should ever be held accountable for anything said at a pep rally."

For thirty minutes it was a close game, with Notre Dame leading BYU at halftime by 14–9. At the intermission some tremors were still floating through the stadium, some anxieties and fears that in the third quarter recent history would repeat itself, BYU's renowned passing attack would emerge, and the Irish would once again be buried.

History had other things in mind. In the second half, Notre Dame's defense dismantled the Cougars, and the offense, led by Jerome Bettis and Reggie Brooks—now called "Thunder" and "Lightning," respectively—ran over, under, around, and through the opposition. Bettis gained 113 yards and Brooks 112. Most football teams, even at the pro level, often do not have one good running back, let alone two of them who can complement each other with a mixture of speed and power. Throughout the season sportswriters had been saying that if the Irish ever got their offense uncorked, they would be nearly unstoppable; this game revealed hints of their full potential.

They defeated BYU 42–16, and late in the fourth quarter Holtz was penalized for throwing his hat and straying too far onto the field to protest the failure of the officials to call holding. After the penalty was called on Holtz, he demonstrated to one official, referee Tom Thumert, the headlock that had been put on Irish linebacker Pete Bercich by a BYU lineman. Holtz said afterward that he merely wanted to know from Thumert if the technique was legal, because "it's a heckuva lot more effective than what we're teaching."

He wanted to show everybody at home and in the national viewing audience what he believed one of the BYU linemen had just done to Pete Bercich, an Irish inside linebacker. Some people who analyzed the headlock said it resembled a sumo wrestling technique.

"It was just frustration," Holtz later explained. "I was completely wrong and that's the first fifteen-yard penalty I've gotten in a long time. I wanted to talk to the referee and I unconsciously got on the field farther than I thought. Then they threw the flag and I thought, 'Now who is he throwing that on?' I don't believe it should have been called because I threw my hat toward the bench. The game was over, but I guess it was the frustration built up over the last two weeks because this was a critical game for us."

The next Saturday the Irish went east again, this time to play Navy at Giants Stadium in New Jersey's Meadowlands. No one expected much of a game—it wasn't even being televised, except in South Bend. Navy had lost six in a row, sixteen of their last seventeen, and when the fourth quarter ran out, they'd lost once more, 38–7. Notre Dame scored on five of their first six possessions, and the second units played much of the last half. It was one of those contests where coaches are hard pressed to find anything to say in their postgame remarks.

"It was nice to win and get out of here without any serious injuries," Holtz said in the locker room. But then he added, "I was scared to death coming in here today because I was scared to death of the intangibles. We need to stay focused and we've got to get better against Boston College. Next week we're going to have the fight of our lives."

The three straight wins by the Irish had moved them up six notches in the Associated Press poll, to number eight. Notre Dame was definitely improving but had still not played exceptionally well against a first-rate opponent and had never looked like the squad that had been picked third in the preseason polls. Now they would get their chance, with their last three regular-season games all coming against teams rated in the Top 25 nationwide.

Before they went into their November 7 home game with the ninth-ranked and undefeated Boston College Eagles, Father James Riehle, in his pregame mass, told the players that "you could coast on your faith and not worry about the rest of the season and just try not to get hurt. Or you can make an example of your faith by not giving up and by showing people what kind of a team you really are."

If Notre Dame needed a little more incentive for this tilt, they found it on Friday night, when some BC fans had shown up at the Irish pep rally and repeatedly yelled, "Go, Eagles!" Then just before the opening kickoff, one of the BC players made a point of bumping into Rick Mirer on the field.

"All day long," the Eagle had muttered.

"I wasn't very happy when the game started," Mirer said later. "There had been a lot of talk about how we hadn't beaten a good team. We haven't had a lot of good fortune, but if we play the way we can, a lot of good things can happen to us."

What happened on this afternoon was that the Irish scored touchdowns on their first five possessions, while BC never ventured past their own 33-yard line. At the end of the day Mirer had moved within 6 yards of Notre Dame's all-time record in total offense, sprinting for one TD and completing 13 of 18 passes for 180 yards and three touchdowns (he would break the record the following week). Reggie Brooks, who'd been playing through an injury for more than a month, ran for 178 yards, including a 73-yard score. He became only the fourth Irish back to gain 1,000 yards in a season and the first such runner in the Holtz era.

"Reggie," the coach said after the game, "is finally healthy."

Overall, Notre Dame had 576 yards in total offense and held the Eagles to nearly 300 yards below their season average. The final score was 54–7, and around South Bend they were soon calling it the Boston College Massacre. Holtz, who has long been known for his postgame pessimism, was beaming in the locker room after this win. A sportswriter asked him if there was anything to feel bad about now.

"I was disappointed," he said deadpan, "in our punt returns."

Despite all the good cheer, the coach had managed once again to become ensnarled in something of a controversy by having his punter/placekicker, Craig Hentrich, run for a first down on fourth and one when the Irish were leading 37–0 with twenty-eight minutes left to play. The NBC broadcast team found much to chew on in this situation—what else was there to talk about during the blowout?—and suggested that perhaps Notre Dame was attempting to run up the score against the weary Eagles.

When presented with these charges, Holtz looked genuinely perplexed, as if the gulf between a successful football coach and an inquiring journalistic mind was, finally, unbridgeable. He tried to brush the questions aside by talking about the next game and the one after that.

"The thing we have to remember is that we're not the same team every week," he said. "We were at an emotional peak today, and that's the thing that scares me. Every time you're at an emotional peak, you have to come down off it."

He smiled again and momentarily relaxed. "I really do wish to praise our football players," he said, "and praise them in glowing terms for their performance today. This was a team victory."

On reflection you might have concluded that something in that infamous Tuesday practice had worked. Since the Stanford loss, Notre Dame had outscored its opponents 186–51.

In the days afterward, the great fourth-and-one debate refused to die, and the various points of view were argued with growing fervor. Holtz himself said, "We're allowed to run it. There wasn't anything illegal about it. Going into this game, we were going to run a fake punt. I just wanted people to know we have it. . . . Whatever we did in the first half, I thought Boston College was capable of doing in the second half. We were playing the number five offensive team in the country. They're a very explosive team with a quarterback who can get a very hot hand. Remember, we had Tennessee down thirty-one to seven last year and ended up losing."

There were other comments and countercomments, but the best line of all came from Lou Somogyi, the associate editor of *Blue & Gold Illustrated*.

"If Jesus Christ were to come back today and walk on water," he wrote, "the headlines would read, 'Christ Can't Swim!' "

19 Kudos for Krause

DURING THE LATE 1970S, MOOSE HAD BEGUN TO THINK ABOUT retiring but had never followed through. At the start of the new decade, he finally decided, because of his health and because he wanted to spend more time with his wife, who was now living in the Cardinal Nursing Home, to step down as athletic director.

On May 2, 1981, Notre Dame honored him at a dinner at the Joyce Athletic and Convocation Center. The master of ceremonies was ABC-TV sportscaster Keith Jackson, and the invocation was given by Father Edward Krause, C.S.C. The assembled "roasters" included *Chicago Sun-Times* sports columnist Bill Gleason, Johnny Lujack, De Paul basketball coach Ray Meyer, Ara Parseghian, NBC-TV sportscaster Don Criqui, former Air Force football coach Ben Martin, and the president of the university, the Reverend Theodore Hesburgh, C.S.C.

After Moose was singed by a number of nationally recognized figures, it was time for Colonel Stephens to present him with a bust of himself. Walking across the stage in front of the hushed, expectant crowd and carrying the sculpted head of his longtime companion, the Colonel tripped and dropped the work of art, smashing it into countless pieces. Two thousand people gasped, and under his breath Moose called the Colonel an SOB. Father Hesburgh, sitting near the disaster, rose slightly from his chair, stared at the broken likeness, and cried, "Oh, my God!"

Things became very quiet, and then the Colonel disappeared from the stage laughing to himself, returning a few moments later with the real bust.

In 1976, Moose was inducted into the Basketball Hall of Fame. He was later inducted into the Knights of Malta, the highest honor a Catholic layman can receive, and he oversaw the creation of the Edward Krause Medical Research Fellowship at the City of Hope National Medical Center in Duarte, California. He was the Man of the Year at the Walter Camp Football Hall of Fame, he was given the NFL's Most Outstanding Contribution to College Football award, and he was honored as the Distinguished American by the National Football Foundation.

Notre Dame named its five-thousand-seat multipurpose outdoor stadium after him. He became a member of the Indiana Citizens' Council on Alcoholism, and he was once, in a move that surprised even Moose, voted one of the best-dressed men in the state of Indiana.

Before departing the athletic director's job, he said, "Because I'm the last link so many of the old-timers have with the past, they don't want me to retire. When I'm gone, there'll be no one left to talk to."

He retired without leaving. If he was no longer hiring football coaches or laying out athletic department budgets, he was doing something equally important in the contemporary world of collegiate sports.

"Moose is," says Irish senior associate athletic director Joe O'Brien, "the greatest fund-raiser ever. All he has ever had to do was say, 'We need this,' and it would appear. When we needed money for one of our playing fields, the first person he asked gave us thirty-five thousand dollars. I daresay that he built the Athletic and Convocation Center. People donated simply because he was participating."

"Moose has the golden touch," Colonel Stephen says. "It's because he likes everyone. He walks with the poor as well as the rich. People recognize and speak to him more than they speak to our current university president, Father Edward Malloy, but you'd better not say that. You also shouldn't say that people write Moose all the time wanting things from him and I write back and sign his signature. I've signed it fifteen thousand times in this job. I can write his name better than he can."

As a going-away present at a retirement party for Moose in Chicago, the Colonel raised $100,000 for his boss.

"I swear to God," the Colonel says, "we got eighty-five thousand dollars in the first month. It was like pulling a slot machine. They gave him a hundred grand and a new Cadillac and a box of cigars every month for as long as he lived. He got sore with me because he wanted a new box every week. When the Cadillac wore out, they got him another one."

Says Moose, "I couldn't believe all these old players of mine treated me so well. I used to beat the hell out of them in practice."

The Colonel feels that Krause deserved everything that came with his retirement. "Ed could have made a lot more money by leaving Notre Dame and taking a job in pro football," he says, "but he was always loyal to the school. At Notre Dame we like to say that the priests take a vow of poverty but the university employees practice it."

Although Moose was now officially gone from the athletic director's chair, he lost none of his passion for his football team. He'd not been involved in the hiring of the new Irish coach, Gerry Faust, and he lived through Faust's five-year reign (1981–85) in South Bend—one of the low-water marks in Notre Dame gridiron history—about as gracefully as could be expected from a man who writhes in his seat each time the blue-and-gold make a bad play.

Faust, who'd been hired straight out of a high school in Cincinnati and had no college coaching experience, was not successful at Notre Dame, but he was also not quite the failure that many perceived him to be. His overall record with the Irish was 30-26-1, for a winning percentage of .535. Moose was never very harsh in his assessment of the man, and when asked about him in later years, he shrugged and said, "Gerry was a good kid and he tried hard, but he was in over his head."

Throughout Faust's tenure at Notre Dame, Moose had his eye on another coach. For years he'd been intrigued by Lou Holtz, after learning that Holtz, when he was head man at Arkansas, had dropped three players from his squad right before the 1978 Orange Bowl against Oklahoma because they'd violated his rules (despite being heavy underdogs, the Razorbacks beat the Sooners in the game).

As the outgoing athletic director, Moose had made a pitch for hiring Holtz in 1980, when Dan Devine, the Irish head coach following Ara Parseghian, left Notre Dame after that season. Nothing came of his efforts. After Faust had been given five years in which to prove himself, Holtz's name surfaced again, and this time the university was interested.

Holtz was hired before the 1986 season, and his first year on the job was not for the fainthearted—either for his players or the coach himself. The Irish opened that season by losing four of their first five games, the bottom of Holtz's career at Notre Dame. After the fourth loss Moose walked into Holtz's office one morning and told him that he was the right person for the job and things were going to work out.

"I'm not sure I believed him," the coach said later, "but it was encouraging that Moose believed it."

Holtz was born in Follansbee, West Virginia, and grew up in East Liverpool, Ohio, and when people talk about him, they convey that his background is very important—not just where he lived but his physical and psychological background, the way he looked and spoke and how he felt about himself. Most kids with his build would have stayed far away from football, but he always wanted to play. As a boy in the 1940s—a Catholic youngster with his ear stuck to the radio during Notre Dame football games—his heroes were Johnny Lujack and Frank Leahy.

If he soon learned that he would not be a Heisman Trophy winner like Lujack, he could still learn about coaching by studying the example of Leahy and others. After graduating from Kent State in 1959, he was an assistant coach for nine years, the last one at Ohio State under Woody Hayes; then head coach at William and Mary for three seasons; head coach at North Carolina State for four years; head coach with the New York Jets for one year; head coach at Arkansas for seven years; and head coach at Minnesota for two years before coming to Notre Dame.

When those who have been around the Irish football program for many years or even decades are asked to compare Holtz to his successful predecessors, the name mentioned most often is Frank Leahy. For one thing, it's impossible to imagine Leahy as a pro football coach, and Holtz's year with the Jets showed him where he was more comfortable. First-rate pro coaches—such as John Madden or Bill Parcells or Joe Gibbs—have the ability to focus their teams on the business of winning football games and treat their players like grown men. First-rate college coaches—such as Joe Paterno or Don James—are primarily teachers.

"I never try to motivate anyone as an individual," Holtz has said on numerous occasions. "I try to make people understand their role in the whole picture, and I try to relate this to everything that will be happening to them ten years from now. The future is my real concern, not next Saturday."

In a recent issue of the campus magazine, *The Scholastic,* he went further: "Our primary purpose is to educate people and I don't believe that learning can take place without discipline. It's very easy to have an anything-goes attitude but this doesn't work. There is a thin line, of course, between discipline and harassment. The players don't always agree with me but I tell them, 'This is a rule and if you abuse it, this is going to be the result.' Then I'm not making the decision to discipline them. They make that choice when they decide to violate the rule.

"At Notre Dame the standard has been set for us by Knute Rockne, Moose Krause, Frank Leahy, Ara Parseghian, Dan Devine and all the other great coaches and athletes who have been here. The standard is: We are going to play the best and be committed to being the best we can be. We are going to do it the right way, with honesty, class and togetherness—not only within the letter of the law but within the spirit of the law as well. Nothing is going to be more important than the individual student's future and academic work."

Holtz has other similarities to Leahy. If "Crying Frank" had his critics in the 1940s because he was forever downplaying his talent and minimizing the chances of Notre Dame's ever winning another game, Holtz has been known to employ some of the same methods with the media—and with the same results. There are papers in America that refer to him as "Boo Hoo Lou."

Moose dismisses that characterization with a wave of his cigar. "When Holtz talks to the press," he says, "it's just so the other team will read what they think he's gonna do next. He takes care of his players in the media and that's what's important. He never criticizes them in public, and when we lose, he immediately takes the responsibility for it."

Holtz's tendency toward pessimism—some would call it a simple terror of failure—is something he came by on his own, not by imitating Leahy. In the hundreds of interviews the coach has given over the years, Holtz has rarely talked in depth about his early years, but one thing he's said stands out. When he was a boy, his father made good money and then lost it. If the youngster learned nothing else, he learned that prosperity does not necessarily last and nothing can be taken for granted—not financial security, not good luck, not a healthy team or touchdowns or even first downs. Nothing.

Holtz isn't known as just an excellent gridiron motivator: he's now paid in five figures to speak to corporate or other groups who are looking for help. His techniques for grabbing people's attention are varied and highly developed. When he recruits young players in their homes, he's been known to engage in magic tricks, a maddening and totally effective way to get someone to watch you.

"Lou is very powerful when he goes to visit the kids," says Tony Yelovich, the recruiting coordinator for Notre Dame. "After we've narrowed the numbers down, he visits everyone we really want to come here. He wants to get to know the families and he wants them to know him. He understands the two most important things: how to listen and make you listen to him."

Before a crucial game, Holtz has been known to pose as a TV reporter and interview his players—asking them how they feel now that the game is over and they've won. Before bowl games, he's been known to have the Irish practice carrying the seniors off the field. He's been known to throw microphones at pep rallies. After winning the national championship in 1988, he prepared for the next season by reading the two-thousand-year-old Chinese classic *The Art of War* by Sun Tzu.

That's a long way from "win one for the Gipper," but somehow appropriate. While no one would suggest that Holtz, by ancient or contemporary Far Eastern standards, is a spiritual master (not every Irish player over the years has responded to him well), in the narrow discipline of college football he's learned how to wield power over young men who are twice his size.

20 A Very Complex Simple Man

MARK GREEN WAS A THREE-YEAR STARTER AT TAILBACK FOR THE Irish from 1986 to 1988 and a captain on the '88 national championship team. After leaving Notre Dame, he was drafted by the Chicago Bears and now plays for them in the NFL. He spent one year in South Bend under Gerry Faust before the new coach arrived in the winter of his sophomore season.

"Until Lou Holtz came," he says, "I didn't know what college football was all about. I thought Faust's way was the way you did things. We were all in for a surprise. Holtz showed up in February of 1986, and the first thing he did was schedule six A.M. workouts in the dead cold of winter. You had to get up at five-thirty just to get there on time. Guys were staggering across campus in the dark and the snow trying to find the right building.

"Holtz's conditioning drills were much more strenuous than anything we'd ever done under Faust. He let us know right away that there's a price to pay if you want to succeed, and we were going to pay it. His winter program was the toughest thing I've ever done in football, and I've played in the pros for four years. You can ask anyone who was there and they'll tell you the same thing.

"He broke everyone down into groups and put us through agility drills, where you ran from one station to another and rolled over on the ground and got up and ran again and changed directions fast and jumped over bags and went through some ropes and got down on your knees and bear-crawled and . . . just constant movement at six in the morning. Some of the players called it a pukefest.

"You were done by seven A.M. Then you had to go to class. I'm not a morning person, but even if you are one, you don't want to be doing this. Later in the day you worked on weights. Holtz brought in Scott Reardon from the University of Nebraska to develop a weight-lifting program, and he was really gung ho. He created a computerized system of lifting and you had to follow it and it was serious. All of these things served a purpose and showed you what you had to do to be a champion.

"Holtz had a list of seven principles—no mental errors, self-control, no turnovers, those kinds of things—that you needed to focus on in order to win. He told you to sit down and think about them and think about your goals. He told you to write out your goals and look at them if that helped you. It was all very organized. That's the thing you noticed that was different. Nothing was going on by accident. When I was captain my senior year, I got to know him some, but he was always kind of distant. He just wanted you to know your responsibility and to do it. You're close to your individual assistant coaches but not the head man.

"To motivate you he talked about the guys around you—the guys you lined up with—and he said that's who you play the game for. Not anyone else. He stressed doing things together with your teammates. Playing cards, playing basketball together, just being together and hanging out. In the pros, it's completely different. Under Coach [Mike] Ditka, it's very businesslike and individual. The issue is just 'Do your best' and 'Don't let your opponent beat you.' That's it. With Holtz, everything was for your teammates and Notre Dame."

Late in the 1988 season, in a situation reminiscent of Holtz's leaving three Arkansas players out of the Orange Bowl for breaking his rules, he sent two of the Irish's best players, Ricky Watters and Tony Brooks, back to South Bend from Los Angeles the day of the USC game. The young men had missed the start of a team meeting by forty-five minutes, after being warned against a repeat offense of this violation.

"We needed those two guys that day," Green says, "but we realized that what they had done was not respectful of the team. What Coach Holtz did with them brought the rest of us closer together. After it happened, Frank Stams, our defensive end, jumped up and said to all of us, 'I'm gonna kick someone's ass. Are you with me?' "

Notre Dame won the game 27–10.

"Leahy," says Moose, "would have done exactly the same thing with Brooks and Watters. Discipline was number one with him and with Holtz. People remember discipline when everything else is gone."

Dean Brown attended Notre Dame from 1986 to 1990 and was an offensive tackle on the '88 team. He now works for a holding company in Chicago.

"We were undefeated in 1988 and untied, and we won the Fiesta Bowl and the national title," Brown says. "That was our best season, but none of that is what I remember when I think back on Coach Holtz. What stands out for me is one night my senior year when he invited the offense to his home. He showed us a lot of trophies and things he'd collected during his career. Several players sat at his kitchen table and he talked about Woody Hayes and the other coaches he'd worked with.

"That night it wasn't like he was our coach but just a friend. When it was time for us to leave, he was like a little kid who didn't want us to go home. He stood at the door and had this expression on his face. I'll never forget it. He was more than a coach that night. He was a human being."

In 1989, Tim Grunhard was an all-American offensive lineman for the Irish, and he now plays for the Kansas City Chiefs. He was also on the '88 championship team.

"Holtz was a master of psychology," Grunhard says. "He knew within a month of arriving at Notre Dame exactly how to push your buttons to get you to perform better. He knew that I was an overachiever and was always looking for a pat on the back. I tried very hard to impress him because I wanted that.

"He would very rarely give it to me or say anything to me, but he would look at me with those squinty eyes of his behind those glasses he wears and I would know that I'd done well. After my senior year, he told me that I was one of the best guards Notre Dame had ever had, but he wouldn't say that until my college career was finished.

"He treated the '88 team the same way. He knew we were overachievers, and at the start of the season he said we were the worst recruiting class he'd ever had. Some of us who weren't even expected to play much became stars on that team. Everyone tried to prove to him that we belonged there and were part of the Notre Dame tradition. That's why we did so well.

"I still see Lou once or twice a year and I've invited him to my wedding, which will be in February of '93 at Sacred Heart Basilica on the campus. What I got from my college football experience helps me not just athletically but spiritually. When I get down and feel I can't do something, I think about what we accomplished at Notre Dame in 1988 and it pulls me out of the low spots."

Before coming to South Bend in 1986, Jim Russ was the trainer and physical therapist for the Tampa Bay Bandits of the expired United States Football League, and he once held the same job with the Florida Gators and Purdue Boilermakers. In South Bend his primary responsibility is the Irish football team. One of his most ticklish duties is examining injured players and telling Holtz if they're ready to play or not.

"Coach is a very complex man yet somewhat simple," Russ says. "He's very calculating but very fair. The pressures here are different from any other place I've been. Anybody would struggle with that and he does. There are days when he wants to go downtown and eat a sandwich and be Joe Blow, but he can't do that. Everybody wants to steal his time. Everybody's biting at him. Everybody's making demands on him, and if you work for him, he places demands on you.

"He demands that you be the very best at your job, but he has never put pressure on me to play someone when they're not ready to go. He understands that at times you have to protect people and not work them in practice, and he lets me make the final decision. I put pressure on myself because I want to do what's best for the team and the university.

"I have to say no to him sometimes about a player playing, after he's put together a game plan, and that can be disruptive to him. Sometimes he uses me as a sounding board for his feelings. I hear what others don't hear. Sometimes he fires me for about ten minutes, but I'm not afraid of him. My job is to keep him healthy. When he needs to lower his blood pressure by letting out his frustration, I get to listen to him. He uses people to help himself in this way. You have to learn to listen to his message and not how he delivers it.

"He has multiple personalities—one way with the outside world, another way with the team, another way when he's one-on-one with me. You have to see him as the head of a whole corporation who runs the entire operation, while the rest of us just see the pieces. He's complex because he manages to do all this and keep it pretty simple.

"Football isn't a simple game. You're trying to get eleven people to do eleven different things right at exactly the same time, and that's very difficult. Coach knows when to push people, when to coddle them. He knows how to turn adversity to your advantage. After we lost to Stanford, he didn't let the situation snowball. He changed things. We look to him to be calculating and to think several steps ahead of us and he does.

"Things bother him a little less than they used to, but I

don't think anyone could do this for twenty-five years. You just get spread too thin. For a man in his midfifties he's in good shape, but his job is . . . he could work at it three hundred and sixty-five days a year if he let himself, but he doesn't. He plays golf and gets some exercise, but he doesn't get the sleep he needs.

"The one thing he's taught me is patience. I know he doesn't look like a patient man to the outside world, but he is. He knows he's dealing with young people and unknown situations, and when you see how impatient he could be, you realize how patient he is. I've had to learn to be more patient with him. People ask me how I can put up with being his whipping boy. I tell them it's not me he's responding to, it's the information I'm giving him. When he's tired and crabby and you tell him someone can't play on Saturday, you have to understand his reality and what he's trying to accomplish."

Tom Clements was the Irish quarterback under Parseghian for three seasons and led Notre Dame to the national championship in 1973. He went on to play professional football in Canada for more than a decade before becoming an attorney and practicing law for several years. In 1992 he returned to South Bend to coach the quarterbacks under Holtz.

"When Lou hired me," he says, "he told me that he didn't know if I could coach. But he said he was doing society a favor by getting a lawyer off the streets."

Says Johnny Ray, who was an assistant to Parseghian at Notre Dame, "I've known Lou since the sixties. One day Jerry Burns, who went on to coach the Minnesota Vikings, called and wanted to meet with me and talk about a defense I invented. He brought along a little skinny kid in glasses from Kent State. Lou Holtz. Never heard of him. A graduate assistant. An eager beaver. He just sat there and listened and didn't say much and took everything in. I never gave him a thought. Can you believe what became of him?"

Says Colonel Stephens, "Lou likes to smoke a pipe sometimes. When he was an assistant at Ohio State, people told him that the one thing Woody Hayes hated was pipe-smoking. They said, 'Don't ever let him see you doing that.' Lou had what it took to go in and light up in front of Woody and smoke during the meetings."

Says Father Riehle, who conducts the pregame mass for the Irish football team, "I don't imagine he would like me saying this, but Lou is a better Catholic now than when he first came to Notre Dame. He's more involved. He attends mass every day. He does so many things with the team that revolve around practicing Catholicism. The kids and the place have an influence on you and it's been a good one on him."

21 One Great Comeback

BEFORE THE IRISH DEFEATED BOSTON COLLEGE IN SOUTH BEND, seven teams were in front of them in the Associated Press poll: Miami, Washington, Alabama, Texas A&M, Florida State, Michigan, and Nebraska. Of these seven the first four were undefeated, Florida State had one loss, Michigan two ties, and Nebraska one loss.

When Holtz was asked in early November if his team could still win the title, despite having a loss and a tie, he said that the thought had never crossed his mind. His only concern, he emphasized, was winning his last three games, against Boston College on the seventh, Penn State on the fourteenth, and USC on the twenty-eighth, all nationally ranked teams.

Anyone taking a clearheaded look at college football in mid-November might have concluded that for the Irish to finish anywhere above eighth in the country would be difficult, simply because they'd fallen too far too early in the season.

What an objective observer couldn't have known was that on the Saturday Notre Dame defeated Boston College, Washington would lose to Arizona and would soon lose again to Washington State. On November 12, a Thursday night, Texas A&M was nearly beaten by the Houston Cougars but won 38–30. On November 14, Illinois tied Michigan, 22–22, and Iowa State upset Nebraska, 19–10.

In one week, three teams ranked ahead of the Irish had suddenly descended, and if Notre Dame could just keep winning . . . the national championship was still out of the question, but Holtz's early-October claim that the Irish could finish in the top five didn't look so farfetched after all. Of course, if they lost to Penn State in their last home game of the season, none of that would matter.

The 1992 meeting between Penn State and Notre Dame was full of portents, surrounded by things that a desperate screenwriter would have thrown in for dramatic effect. (Appropriately enough, this was the weekend that the film crew of *Rudy* was shooting much of its footage on campus; the movie outlined the story of a young man who decides that nothing will stop him from attending Notre Dame, and then nothing will prevent him from making Ara Parseghian's football team and getting into a game. Ultimately, nothing kept him from going to Hollywood and banging on enough doors until they produced a film about his life).

The contract that Notre Dame and Penn State had once signed to play a series of games against each other would run out on Saturday, November 14, 1992. This date marked the final contest between two great football schools. Penn State was leading the series 8-7-1, and only a Notre Dame victory would give the team parity with Joe Paterno, one of the most successful coaches in college gridiron history.

This was the final South Bend appearance for all the Irish seniors and for two of them in particular, Rick Mirer and Reggie Brooks. For Mirer, a Heisman Trophy candidate at the start of the year, it had been a somewhat disappointing season, but perhaps something could be redeemed this afternoon, although he would be playing with a touch of the flu. For Brooks, 1992 had begun rather slowly, but he'd been gaining momentum for weeks and was lately showing signs of being a Heisman contender himself.

Also, if Holtz was to keep his recent promise of no more home losses, the Irish had to win, and finally, when the game commenced, it was snowing hard, big flakes twirling and spinning and filling the eyes, so that the overflow crowd could barely see the players, let alone the yard markers down on the field. There's nothing like a snowstorm to add confusion and tension to a football match, and this one would be fought to the very last second.

Up in his booth, Moose and his guests were warm and comfortable. At the start of the game, they yelled and clapped and tossed around a lot of questions, like: "Who was that? Who's got the ball? Did he catch it? Is he still running? Where did he land? Did you see him slide? Where is he? Where!"

Bishop Joseph Crowley, the retired auxiliary bishop of the Fort Wayne–South Bend Diocese, was in his regular chair in the right-hand corner of the booth, and former Irish running back Creighton Miller had come in for the weekend from Cleveland. He was sitting in the front row next to Moose, who had a cigar between his teeth, his elbows planted on the counter before him, his head in his hands, and his eyes fixed upon the blurry field. Despite the fact that he could see very little, he kept up a steady moan and a constant shifting in his chair. Whenever he thought something good was happening, he threw a shoulder in the direction of Miller, who would take off his hat and wave it above his head.

By late in the second quarter, the field was completely gone. Penn State had moved ahead 6–3, on a touchdown and a missed extra point, but just before the half the Irish kicked a field goal to tie it at the intermission. As the teams ran into their locker rooms, it looked probable that no more points would be scored this afternoon, and an air of resignation prevailed around Moose, as though a tie were better than a loss but not by much.

In the third quarter, the sky lifted and the snow began to

fade. A few rays of light shot through and patches of field reappeared. Holtz and Joe Paterno walked the sidelines, the former huddling inside his clothes and wrapping his arms around himself as though he needed more flesh to keep warm, the latter wearing his trademark sunglasses despite the bad weather. Holtz looked miserable and alone, as if everyone else in the stadium was merely watching the game but only he was trying to think five steps ahead, to peer into the future and see what would happen next. Paterno didn't even look chilly or was too worried to notice the temperature. Each coach stopped pacing and leaned this way or that, trying to affect with their body language the action on the field. Each resumed walking, muttering to himself.

The Irish gradually began to discover the heart of their offensive strategy—Jerome Bettis and Reggie Brooks running the ball straight ahead—and they took it right at Penn State, known for decades as a school that produces excellent linebackers whose job is to stop running backs. This was serious business. Notre Dame drove the ball nearly the length of the field but had to settle for another field goal and went into the final period leading 9–6.

In the last quarter both strands of weather had their way—it snowed again but the sun was shining, opening cracks of blue. Penn State began a drive of its own, moving the ball all the way down to the Irish 15-yard line. On the next play the Nittany Lion quarterback, Kerry Collins, was sacked for a 9-yard loss, and on the next one the Irish linebacker and cocaptain, Demetrius DuBose, batted away a pass attempt. On third and 19, Collins completed a 22-yard throw to the Notre Dame three. First down and goal to go.

Over on the Irish sidelines, Rick Minter, the team's defensive coordinator, looked stunned, while Holtz stared into the ground. Moose's booth had grown exceedingly quiet and was clogged with the feeling that this long football season, after false hopes had been raised again, was about to unravel for good.

Penn State failed to score on its first two tries, and on third down you could hear Moose inhaling smoke. When the Irish held once more, the booth exploded into applauding, back-pounding, and high fives, and even the Nittany Lion field goal that followed to tie the score did not stop the cheers and sense of relief. Everyone's expression said the same thing: maybe a tie wasn't so bad after all.

When Penn State kicked off, ten minutes remained in the game. The Irish started at their own 31, and on third down and 7, Mirer completed a pass to his tight end, Irv Smith, who ran for a dozen yards but then fumbled, and Penn State recovered on the Notre Dame 44. Holtz shivered and dropped his head, like a man already blaming himself for what had gone wrong. Moose looked out at the field and grimaced, as if he wanted to be down there playing.

Given this new scoring opportunity, Penn State now drove the ball with utter efficiency—to the Irish 30, the 20, the 15. Less than five minutes remained on the clock. Right before the next play began, Demetrius DuBose, instead of watching the snap of the ball, glanced at his wristband to see where he was supposed to be on the field. By the time he looked up, Nittany Lion running back Brian O'Neal had moved past him, carrying the ball 13 yards for a touchdown. The score was 16–9.

Holtz had once said that every team can expect three crises in a season. The first was the Michigan tie and the second was the Stanford loss. The third one had just arrived.

The Irish head coach paced faster, looking colder than before. When Notre Dame got the ball again, with just over four minutes left, Mirer ran onto the field and began driving the team one last time, throwing the ball and running it and handing it off to Bettis and Brooks. They made a first down and then another and then another. When they reached the Lions' 30-yard line, there were two minutes to go, but ahead of them lay a long stretch of confusing white flakes, the snow again falling hard.

A penalty sent the Irish back to the 40, but on the next play Mirer completed another pass for 20 yards, and on the next one Brooks ran to the 15. The stadium, the sidelines, and all of the private booths—including Moose's and the one holding Notre Dame athletic director Dick Rosenthal, and the other ones sheltering visiting guests and dignitaries—were filled with shrieks. The old ship was rocking.

With ninety seconds left, Mirer dropped back to pass, could find no one open, hesitated, and then ran downfield, veering to his right and leapfrogging a defender before rolling out of bounds at the 9. On first down Brooks carried to the 4, and with fifty-eight seconds on the clock Holtz, suddenly looking warmer, called time-out.

In the booth, Moose and Creighton Miller and Bishop Crowley were all standing and calling the next play, although each man had a different solution. The one thing they agreed on was that if the Irish scored, Holtz had to gamble and go for a two-point conversion, which would either win or lose the game—in order to obliterate the memory of the earlier 17–17 tie with Michigan.

On second down Mirer ran to the 3. With twenty-five seconds left he threw an incomplete pass, and Holtz called his last time-out of the game. It was fourth down and goal to go. The season hung on the next play. The booth had grown quiet again and the aging men looked at each other and seemed decades younger, just kids wanting to win a football game so they could feel good about their team and their school. Moose was still standing and leaning forward, against the window.

Mirer took the ball from center and backpedaled a few steps, searching the field and finding no one open, but then looking again. He flipped it over the middle to Jerome Bettis, who grabbed the ball near the goal line and rumbled into the end zone.

When he scored, the men upstairs began jumping like cheerleaders and windmilling their arms. Bishop Crowley, his face crimson, leaped up on his chair and yelled, while Miller pried open the window in front of him and flung his hat into a sea of hands. Moose raised his cigar over his head, as if simultaneously blessing everyone and signaling a touchdown.

"This is the greatest!" he roared. "One of the greatest comebacks ever at Notre Dame!"

In the booth next door, Dick Rosenthal, a former all-American basketball player at Notre Dame, sprang so high he nearly scraped his head on the ceiling. The other booths broke into applause and laughter. One floor below, some journalists covering the game momentarily violated their cardinal rule and began cheering and stamping their feet. Veteran stadium ushers who'd worked around the press box for years could not remember the last time that had happened. The student body was screaming.

Despite all this, nothing on the field had been settled and the Irish still trailed by a point.

When the referees were able to clear away the fans who'd rushed into the end zone to touch Jerome Bettis, the teams lined up again and the stadium became oddly and eerily silent, as if all the noise were hiding and waiting to emerge again. Mirer took the snap from center and dropped back to throw, fading to his left and seeing no one open, moving to his right and still not finding a receiver, taking a step forward as if he might try to run the ball, taking a step back. He stopped and threw toward the far-right corner of the end zone, where Reggie Brooks, not known for his pass-catching abilities, was crossing Mirer's line of vision, his hands outstretched, his body angling forward, his feet leaving the earth in an effort to reach the ball . . .

Because of the angle and his position in the end zone, he disappeared from the view of nearly everyone in the stadium, including those in Moose's booth, but was then seen lying flat on the ground in the snow.

The official nearest Brooks stood over him and peered down into the snow, as if trying to decipher a mystery, then slowly raised his arms, and this time the fans really stormed the field, scores of them, hundreds of them, many of them landing on the Irish players. Around Moose people were hugging, high-fiving, dancing, and wiping at their eyes.

Several minutes later, when order had been restored, the Irish were leading 17–16 but would be penalized fifteen yards on the ensuing kickoff for the disruption caused by their supporters.

The game was still not over, and when Penn State started its final drive from midfield with eighteen seconds left, they needed only twenty or twenty-five yards for a shot at a winning field goal. On the next two plays Kerry Collins threw incomplete passes, just missing his receivers downfield, and three seconds remained on the clock. No one in the stadium had sat down since Bettis had scored, and again the place grew still.

Collins took the ball once more and stepped backward, heaving it toward the sidelines but too far, and when it sailed out of bounds, the Irish had won and Lou Holtz smiled. For a moment Joe Paterno looked as if he were going to cry, but by the time he reached Holtz in the middle of the field for their postgame handshake, he was nodding and congratulating his rival.

The snow, mud, and ice on the gridiron were quickly covered with people darting in every direction, grabbing at the players, sliding into one another, and falling down. With their bare hands, fans began digging up the turf where Brooks had come down with the ball. The Notre Dame band played the victory march, Moose stared down at the scene and hummed along, the Irish teammates raised their helmets to salute the student body, and Dick Rosenthal left the upper level and ran out onto the field like a boy seeing his first great athletic triumph. Over in the NBC-TV broadcasting booth, analyst Cris Collinsworth said, "If that band keeps playing the fight song, these people will never go home."

In the locker room, after Father Riehle had blessed the team, Holtz began handing out game balls to those he felt were especially deserving this afternoon. He gave out a lot of them. In all his years of coaching, a team of his had never driven the length of the field on its last possession, scored a touchdown, and then a two-point conversion to win a game. Before he could finish passing out the balls, Demetrius DuBose grabbed a pigskin, carried it over to the coach, and put it in his hands.

"What's this for?" Holtz said.

"That's your game ball," DuBose said. "You earned it."

Later, when the noise had subsided above them in the stadium and the players were alone, DuBose said, "I can't describe this feeling. I can't say enough about the tradition here. I've heard about the Notre Dame spirit, but today it showed itself. It was out there. It was on the field with us and I'm now a part of that spirit with all the others who have played here before me."

The win over the Nittany Lions moved Notre Dame up to number seven in the AP poll. Two weeks later, in front of 91,000 people in the L.A. Coliseum, the Irish beat USC for the tenth straight time, 31–23. By most standards, the game was a thriller—not settled until Tommy Carter intercepted a Trojan pass in the Notre Dame end zone with just twenty-five seconds left—but in the wake of the Penn State victory, this was just another great finish.

Reggie Brooks, who went into the game battling influenza, ran for 227 yards, scored three touchdowns (of 12, 44, and 55 yards), and finished the regular season as only the second player in Notre Dame history to rush for more than 8 yards per carry over the course of a year. The other fellow was George Gipp.

"I was dead by the end of the game," Brooks said in the locker room. "Thank God I was able to come through before I was too sick to play. This whole season has been a blessing."

The win was the sixth in a row for the Irish, and they climbed to fifth in the nation, behind Miami, Alabama, Florida State, and Texas A&M. Number one ranked Miami and number two Alabama would meet in the Sugar Bowl for the national championship, but the fate of the other schools remained unknown until the very end of the regular college football season.

"I'm very proud of this team," Holtz said while waiting to learn of Notre Dame's fate on New Year's Day. "When we were three, one, and one, we were as low as we could be.

Everybody was down on us. What has happened since then says a lot for these young men."

In a move that surprised many people and again generated nationwide controversy, the Cotton Bowl bypassed what seemed liked a natural opportunity to match third-ranked Florida State against fourth-ranked Texas A&M and instead invited Notre Dame to play A&M in Dallas on New Year's Day of 1993.

In keeping with the rest of the '92 season, this decision unleashed one more argument about the Irish and their football program: Did they really belong in this bowl game or had they been invited simply because their presence guaranteed NBC a larger television audience? Why hadn't the newly created bowl coalition, which had been founded precisely to avoid this sort of conflict, picked the third and fourth teams to meet and settle which one was best? Wouldn't everyone involved look bad if Notre Dame went to Dallas and lost the game by a big score? Then the critics would really howl.

As soon as Moose received the bowl news, he took one of his ten-gallon hats out of the closet—he had a collection of them from previous Cotton Bowl trips—and began wearing it into the office. Colonel Stephens had one of the tall hats himself but refused to don it because of the way it looked on him.

The ten-gallon model fit perfectly on Moose, made him resemble a prosperous cattle rancher or Lyndon Baines Johnson. When people at Notre Dame saw him wearing it around the athletic department, they knew exactly what that meant: he was preparing to go to Texas.

22 Creative Tension

OVER THE PAST QUARTER CENTURY GEORGE KELLY HAS COACHED linebackers under both Parseghian and Holtz. In 1968, when he first came to Notre Dame from the University of Nebraska, he was struck by the lack of size on the Irish squad and the lack of speed; they weren't nearly as big or fast as the Cornhuskers. He often wondered what Parseghian could have done with more talented athletes. In recent years all that has changed, but Kelly believes that Holtz is still looking for something more in his players than just physical gifts.

"Football players aren't made, they're born," says Kelly, now the special assistant to the athletic director at Notre Dame. "But you can enhance their ability by teaching fundamentals and attitude, especially attitude. When Lou arrived at Notre Dame, he found athletes who weren't motivated and their self-image was not very good. He was looking for people he could teach, and in three years he turned them into champions.

"Lou uses humor to motivate and he works at his sense of humor much more than Ara ever did. He likes to tell people that he wasn't smart enough to get into Notre Dame but he is smart enough to be the university's football coach. He's proud of his ability to articulate things. He can move a team in two minutes. He knows how to hit the pride and the emotions. He has a demeanor that kids quickly grasp. He uses certain voice inflections that create tension around people, and he uses that tension to get results.

"Every night Lou goes home and spends hours planning the next day at his job. I think his appearance has a lot to do with why he's so driven. When I first met him, he had a speech impediment, but he's overcome that. He's what I call a little man who fights for recognition. He only got to play football when he was young because he understood the game. He didn't have the skills. Deep down he's just like Ara. He's a sentimentalist who's extremely involved with his family and with the family at Notre Dame.

"During his first year here I got lung cancer and had to stop coaching. Lou wanted me to stay around and figure out how we could recruit better and build a network of Notre Dame people again so we could bring in the best players. He wanted me to reorganize the Notre Dame family because at that time there was a lot of disenchantment. He feels better about that family now, but he was originally apprehensive about a non–Notre Dame guy being the head coach.

"He's a more sensitive person about his ability and his existence than most people. I constantly tell him to quit beating himself up. After the Stanford game, he was critical of himself for demanding too much of the players during their midterm exams, which come in early October. He felt he gave them too much mental ammunition before that game and it took away their aggressiveness."

"Anyone," says Holtz, "can coach when you're winning. It's when you lose that you see what you've got. After a loss, you say a prayer, ask for God's help, and go to work. And you never let the athletes lose faith in themselves. You say to yourself, 'What's important now?' We decided to go back to basics and back to tough-nosed football and back to practicing hard. People get their morale back when they feel they're getting better, and they feel they're getting better when they work hard.

"After we lost to Stanford, I decided to visit with the players the night before the games because I wanted to know what they were thinking and feeling. I wanted to hear about their families. I wanted to know what they like and what they don't like about Notre Dame. I wanted to know how they see their role here and what they think needs to be changed. I just wanted to listen to them. It was obvious to me that a lot of them were tired young men, so I got rid of some of our morning meetings and gave them more time for themselves.

"When you lose, the only friends you've got are those you eat with, sleep with, pray with, and cry with. You stick with those people and you go forward. I tell my players after a loss, 'You don't fingerpoint and you don't criticize each other. If you'll just ask yourself what you could have done better, you'll see so much to work on that you'll stay busy.' "

Former Irish quarterback Steve Beuerlein played his first three years in South Bend under Gerry Faust and his senior year for Holtz. He well remembers his first encounter with the new coach.

"It was the day after we lost to Miami down in Florida in our final game of the 1985 season, the last game Gerry Faust coached at Notre Dame," he says. "The score was fifty-eight to seven. We'd come home and were sitting in a meeting room. We were kicked back and feeling sorry for ourselves. Holtz walked in and said, 'I want you to sit up straight and look straight ahead and get ready to talk about winning football games.' From then on he had our attention. There was one person in charge now, and if we didn't do things his way, we weren't part of his plan."

Beuerlein was drafted by the L.A. Raiders but has since moved along to the Dallas Cowboys. "If there is one person I give credit to for where I am today," he says, "it's Holtz. I was hurt my junior year at Notre Dame, but when he came in, he stuck with me. When we first talked my senior year, he said, 'You have trouble with interceptions, but I guarantee you that you won't throw more than six this season.' I said, 'How can you guarantee that?' He said, 'After the sixth one, you'll be sitting behind me on the bench.' I threw seven interceptions that year, and the seventh one came in the last game against USC in the Coliseum. I'm from California and all my family and friends were there watching that day. After I threw it in the second quarter, Holtz took me out and said, 'Son, you're through for the year.' I thought, 'What a terrible way to end my career.' Two series later he came over and said, 'Son, are you ready to play some football?' I said, 'Are you serious?' I went in and threw four touchdowns and we won thirty-eight to thirty-seven.

"He believed in putting a lot of pressure on you in practice so you wouldn't be shocked when you got into a game in front of thousands of people. One time we were getting ready to play Penn State and they were number one in the nation. It was a Thursday, two days before the game. We were working on a drill and one of my offensive linemen was offsides. Holtz called me over and said, 'You're done. Go to the showers.' I said, 'Why? I didn't jump offsides.' He said, 'You're the quarterback and you're responsible for what your men do. You failed today. Go on in.' I played great against Penn State.

"He paid great attention to detail, physical details on the field. In the pros, you work much more on the mental part of football. And if you need someone rah-rahing to motivate you, you won't be around long. At this level, you've got to do it for yourself. Lou was very very emotional in the locker room. Very powerful. He could take you from laughing uncontrollably to crying uncontrollably in three minutes."

Tim Brown spent his last two years at Notre Dame under Holtz. As a senior in 1987, the flanker was an all-American and became the seventh and most recent Irish player awarded the Heisman Trophy. He's now a member of the Los Angeles Raiders.

"When Lou came to Notre Dame," Brown says, "everyone knew he knew how to win football games, but we had a few players who didn't believe in him and it took him a while to get over what he was trying to get over. By '87 he was getting the message across and we were starting to play better. We lost in the Cotton Bowl that year to Texas A&M, but afterwards he told us that we were responsible for bringing back the Notre Dame tradition, and we felt really good about that. I've been in his locker room in the years since then, and there isn't one 'me' person in there. It's all Notre Dame.

"When I think of him now, the most important thing is his way of motivating people. He's a great magician and on the field or in the locker room he does card tricks, rope tricks, or those tricks where you cut up newspapers and put them back together, and while he's doing these things, he throws some football at you. He's so good at getting your attention that he scares some people, but not me. If you aren't doing things right in practice, he comes up and grabs you by the helmet and talks right at you. He's smiling but you know he's serious.

"As a junior I was struggling and he called me into his office and told me that I didn't have to be the savior of the team. All I had to do was play my game. After that, my career really took off.

"To motivate you, he uses something called PMA—positive mental attitude. He has you lay down on the floor the night before a game and he pipes in the sound of waves, the ocean moving all around you. Then he talks to you about relaxing every part of your body and about visualizing yourself making a good catch or a good block or tackle the next day. I loved this. It took care of my nervousness and I use the same technique in the pros now. I go into the locker room before the other players arrive and lay down and spread out my arms and legs and see myself doing good things on the field. It still works for me.

"Last year I was real disappointed with my play and I called Holtz and talked to him about it. He said that I was making a lot of assumptions about what Al Davis [the owner of the Raiders] was thinking about me and I might be wrong. He told me to go in and see Al and find out what's really going on and don't make false assumptions. I did this and I caught five passes the next week. After this happened, I told Lou I was going to keep in touch with him more, if he didn't mind. He said that was fine."

From 1988 to 1990, Chris Zorich was a dominating nose tackle for the Irish. He could bench-press 455 pounds and run the 40-yard dash in 4.68 seconds. His last two years in South Bend he was an all-American, and as a senior he won the Lombardi Trophy as the outstanding lineman in college football. He now plays for the Chicago Bears.

"When I was being recruited by Coach Holtz, I had a meeting with him about my grades," says Zorich. "I wasn't the best student in high school and did not enjoy doing homework. He explained to me that in order to get a lot out of life I needed to be smart and think intelligently, regardless of anything that happened to me as an athlete.

"He said that if I were to bring the same work ethic I had on the football field into the classroom, I wouldn't have any limitations. He got me fired up about this—fired up about doing homework! Any coach who could do that—I just couldn't imagine how fired up he could get me about playing a game. I improved my grades and got a scholarship to Notre Dame.

"The first time I ever played at Notre Dame—it was against Michigan—he called me over to the sidelines and said I had to calm down or I was going to get thrown out of the game. He was an incredible motivator. He would take the smallest thing, like one remark that an opposing player had made about us, and use it to inspire us. He would say, 'What does this kid know about our football team? What does he know about Notre Dame or the tradition here or the academic standards?' After he finished, you were ready to go out and find that guy. I use this technique now in the pros. I'll use the slightest thing someone has done to me to get myself really fired up."

Raghib "Rocket" Ismail, who played for the Irish from 1988 to 1990, has been the most exciting athlete of the Holtz era at Notre Dame. The flanker and kickoff-and-punt returner is regarded as the fastest man ever to play football at the school, and an informal survey would tell you that he was also the most fun to watch. He scored 15 touchdowns for the Irish and averaged an incredible 61 yards per touchdown play for his college career. In 1990 he was a consensus all-American and the Walter Camp Outstanding Player of the Year. He now plays for the Toronto Argonauts of the Canadian Football League.

"Coach Holtz knew that when I came to Notre Dame, I didn't understand the pressures of big-time college football," Ismail says. "My freshman year he would get all over me in practice whenever I made a small mistake so that I could understand how serious it was. He yelled at you the most if you were expected to play a lot. Freshmen who couldn't take that were weeded out. The next year he didn't yell as much and would just come up to me and say, 'Rocket, you're better than that.' I watched how he did this with the other freshmen and sophomores each year so they would understand the urgency of the situation. By my junior year he rarely motivated me at all or he made a joke about my mistakes.

"After Notre Dame played against Miami, you would be tired and your body would be sore and the weather was cold and you didn't feel like practicing. Coach had a way of getting you to work when you didn't feel like working, and I still use that every day of my life in pro football.

"Sometimes in the locker before a game he would just tell us that the other team didn't belong on the field with us, and sometimes he was fire and brimstone. Once when we were warming up for the Miami game, we had a fight with their players in the tunnel that leads out to the field. That fired Holtz up. He told us, 'If they wanna take this up after the game, I'm right with you.' After that we knew he was there for us. His words set the tone for the game and the rest of the season. That was cool."

"I played for Ara and coached under Lou," says Bob Gladieux. "They're both like ghosts, always watching you. You kept looking over your shoulder and saying, 'Where is that

SOB? What's he doing now?' Players under Lou say he's the greatest—the same thing I said about Ara—but when you're an assistant coach, you're thinking, 'Jeez, that meeting's at seven A.M. and I'm not prepared and Lou wants excellence and I'm not sure. . . .' As a coach, your work is never finished.

"I'm in the travel business now with my wife. I got into that after working for Lou and it's been very educational. In my job now, I've noticed that people don't do what you ask them to do. This happens with the phone company, the insurance company, the printing company.

"When I went down to the newspaper to put in my first big ad for our business, they told me that all my troubles were solved. I called on Thursday to double-check my upcoming Sunday ad. No problem. I'm lying in bed on Sunday, waiting for the paper to arrive. Boom! There it is. I go out and pick it up and look at it, all of it. Nothing's in there. I look through it again and then again. Nothing. I said, 'How is this world operating?' Everybody I've been dealing with would have been fired under Lou. Everyone.

"I get to the office on Monday morning and I'm smokin'. I'm hot. I'm gonna find the person who's responsible for this. I find him and he says, 'It was an honest mistake.' Honest mistake my ass. I'd double-checked with them. A month later their sales rep calls and asks me how I'm doing. 'Not too well,' I say. He didn't understand.

"That's the difference between a place where people are committed to being number one and a place where they aren't. When I've got a problem, I think back to how Lou or Ara would have handled it, but it's frustrating because the business world is a different realm and there aren't many Lous or Aras out there."

From 1989 to 1991, Art Monaghan, an accounting major at Notre Dame, was the manager of the Irish football team, and in 1992 he became the head manager. When he talks about Holtz, he sounds like many of the players.

"When you're a freshman," Monaghan says, "he really gets in your face and you get a little nervous around him. He almost intimidates you, but it's not quite intimidation. If something isn't working, he wants it fixed. Now. If the buses are late, you hear about it in front of everyone. If his golf cart isn't working, you hear about that. Even his son, Skip, who's the offensive coordinator at Notre Dame, gets yelled at in practice. But as I've gotten older, he's backed off some. And if you do something well, he'll praise you, and that makes it worth it.

"Before the Boston College game, we hadn't played a really good game in all of 1992. In the locker room before this game started, he went through our whole team and said to the players, 'Would you trade Jerome Bettis for anyone else? Would you trade Demetrius DuBose? Would you trade Rick Mirer or Reggie Brooks? You guys are some of the best players in the country and it's time to start playing like it. All you have to do is trust your teammates and work together.' We went out and destroyed them. Trust is a very big thing with him. The biggest thing he's taught me is to trust the people I'm around. 'And if you can't trust them,' he says, 'get out of the situation.'

"Coach is very unpredictable. After we beat Penn State, you would have thought he would have been really excited, but he was worried that we were getting too high. He started talking to the team about academics and making their grades. The players looked at each other and said, 'Why is he focusing on this right now? We just won the game.' After a while I could see his point. He didn't want us any higher.

"When he wants something, he gets it. Two years ago, before the Navy game, we were trying to have our Friday-night relaxation session in our hotel. There was a band playing in one of the ballrooms and it wouldn't stop. Coach wasn't happy about that. He disappeared for a few minutes, and when he came back, the music wasn't playing. He was happy now. He'd given the bandleader twenty dollars to be quiet for twenty minutes.

"Sometimes when he gets upset, he flips things in the air. One day at practice someone missed a block and he took off his watch and flipped it and it fell into the grass. The field was getting dark and we had to line up some cars with their headlights on to search for it. We looked for two hours before finding it.

"As the head manager, I stand next to Coach on the sidelines during the games and carry a clipboard. I keep a log of the plays he calls. Last year I held the cord that was attached to his headset, and I had to follow him up and down the field, no matter where he went. It was exhausting. I never knew what was happening on the field. I couldn't watch any of the games. My mother would videotape them and send them to me by Federal Express. I'd watch them on Monday."

In the first week of December 1992, Holtz said, "Moose Krause is our connection with the past and with the spirit of Notre Dame. He was recruited by Rockne, coached with Leahy, hired Parseghian, and he's my good friend. People ask me all the time, 'What is the Notre Dame spirit?' I can tell you one thing: I've preached more about it in the last six weeks of this season than I have for a long time. I'll tell you something else. If you don't believe in it, you ain't gonna feel it. You can't describe the spirit but you can experience it.

"It's real and it's accurate. It's a sense of belonging to the past at Notre Dame and a sense of responsibility to the present and the future. It isn't a mystique or an abstraction. It's a feeling that you are part of something that has been excellent for a long time, and it's an understanding that many others have come before you who have sacrificed for this place to create this tradition. You have a responsibility to carry that on. The spirit doesn't mean that you're always gonna win. It means that you're always gonna try and you're always gonna expect a miracle."

23 Finale

ON THE NIGHT OF THURSDAY, DECEMBER 10, MOOSE ATTENDED the Notre Dame athletic department Christmas party. He was in good spirits, joking with his colleagues, kissing the women, and eating a full dinner, before driving home around nine-thirty and going to bed. Very early the next morning, he died in his sleep.

Colonel Stephens was informed of the death and, his work on Moose's eightieth birthday celebration finished, he drove to his friend's apartment to say good-bye. "Old soldiers aren't supposed to cry," the Colonel said later, "but I cried when I saw him lying there with a smile on his face." A huge memorial was planned, and for two days Moose lay in state at Sacred Heart Basilica, where hundreds of people came to pay their final respects. Near the open casket were his Knight of Malta medal, his cowboy hat, and a cigar.

His pallbearers were Dick Rosenthal, Lou Holtz, John MacLeod, Ara Parseghian, George Kelly, George Connor, Joe O'Brien, and Colonel Stephens. After looking this group over and considering their collection of bad knees, bad hearts, bad hips, and bad backs, Parseghian said, "This is the worst recruiting job in the history of the Notre Dame athletic department. Moose is in better shape than any of us."

At the service Father Edward Krause said the mass and delivered the homily. He called Moose a "gentle giant" and told the mourners, "My father lived the way he played ball. He never gave up, he never stopped trying. He was faithful and he was loyal. It wasn't important that he, like most of us, may not always have succeeded. What was important was that he, coach that he was, never stopped playing with all his heart and bulk, that he fought to the finish line, right up to the final whistle—a Notre Dame trait if there ever was one."

The memorial held clergymen, bishops, Hall of Fame football players, college waitresses and security guards, Heisman Trophy winners, personnel from the Cardinal Nursing Home, and university maintenance men. Following the service and a long procession down Notre Dame Avenue, which was conducted in an icy drizzle, Moose was buried at Cedar Grove Cemetery, next to his wife.

When all the prayers had been offered and all the speeches made, and when the last salute had been given by a Marine honor guard, the Notre Dame victory march was sung over his grave and then everyone left the cemetery and went to a reception, where they told stories about Moose and repeated his old jokes. Many people said it was the biggest reunion in the history of the school, and it reminded some old-timers of Knute Rockne's funeral, more than sixty years earlier.

"I think the true legend of Notre Dame just died," Gerry Faust said shortly after learning of Moose's death. "They talk about the Gipper, Rockne, the Four Horsemen, but I think he was the true legend. He cared for people, he cared for the university, and he always treated me first-class."

On the morning of Thursday, December 31, the temperature in Dallas was in the high seventies and the skies were clear. By late afternoon, the thermometer had fallen into the low twenties and the city was covered by a freezing rain. The wind was whipping and bitter, so that even the huge and cavernous lobby of the Loews Anatole Hotel, where President Bush had stayed when he'd visited Dallas, was chilly.

Swarms of Notre Dame fans, thousands of them arriving from every corner of America, had taken over the lobby, and by New Year's Eve evening it resembled the campus in South Bend on Parents' Weekend. Irish logos were everywhere—on the clothing, on the banners people were waving, on the books and programs and posters they carried in their hands (one of the posters featured a painting of Moose). Even a few Lou Holtz masks had made the trip to the Cotton Bowl.

The Loews Anatole lobby was almost overwhelming, in both its dimensions and its activity. With its high ceilings and terraced balconies, its arched skylights and sprouting plants, some people were moved to compare it to the hanging Gardens of Babylon. Others said it reminded them of being inside one of the great pyramids, and still others, who were more acclimated to the local environment, said that it was just a Texas-sized hotel and you might as well get used to it.

Whatever it was, it was bigger than some folks' hometowns, and when you stood on the ground floor and looked up, you had the strange impression that you were a foot tall. The lobby was teeming with little girls dressed as Notre Dame cheerleaders, with Irish grandmothers wearing Irish buttons and waving green pennants, with football players checking their parents in at the registration desk, with media types looking for stories or free meals, with hopeful fans looking to buy ducats to tomorrow's game, and with scalpers trying to unload some expensive seats at more than face value. It was a football carnival.

On the afternoon of the thirty-first, Irish rooters gathered in various meeting rooms, where they ate some excellent finger food—Texas-style salsa, chips, and barbecue—and renewed old acquaintances or made new friends. Some were getting bus passes to the game and some were shopping at the Notre Dame bazaar that had been set up on the second floor of one of the hotel's wings. Everything imaginable was on sale, and everything appeared to be moving. Several of the most popular items—wool scarves and wool caps and mittens—were in short supply. No one had expected the game to be played in arctic weather, and a few desperate bargain hunters were looking around for Irish long underwear.

Early that evening, in a meeting room right next to the bazaar, Father James Riehle held a mass, which he dedicated to Moose. The gathering was crowded with worshipers, who observed his passing with a few moments of silence.

At six P.M. hundreds of people went across the street to the last Irish pep rally of the season, which would be held in another vast building known as the apparel mart. The rally was also dedicated to Moose. For two hours, people sat at big round tables in a ballroom and ate dinner, chatting and listening to a country-and-western band deliver imitations of Hank Williams and Willie Nelson. Most of the crowd was casually attired, but some of the women wore evening gowns, as if they were determined, despite being at a football function on New Year's Eve, to show Dallas that they knew something about clothes. During the two hours leading up to the rally, there was a growing sense of excitement in the room, of anticipation, people waiting for something that would alter the pregame mood and shift it into a higher gear.

At eight o'clock, from one end of the ballroom came the sound of muffled thunder—the rhythm section of the Notre Dame marching band were hitting their skins, not too loudly at first, but then harder as they walked from one of the rear hallways up toward the second-floor balcony, which they would occupy for the first part of the rally. The beat grew in intensity and force, and the crowd looked up and cheered at the sight of a score or more of drummers appearing above them in row upon row. They played a driving cadence, played it again, the room more pumped with each rendition, more and more expectant.

Although every table in the ballroom was filled, hundreds more Irish fans or perhaps thousands of them had been standing out in the cold rain waiting to be let inside once the rally began. As the drummers reached a crescendo, the doors were opened and hordes rushed into the hall, scampering for a nook with a view, filling every corner and hanging over the balconies that surrounded the open room.

The Irish pom-pom squad ran onto the small stage at one end of the ballroom, and far above their heads a large fishnet opened and countless blue and gold balloons were released upon the crowd, many of whom took it upon themselves to pop the colorful balls, as the hall exploded and echoed with the sound of the fireworks, further arousing the fans.

People were asking questions: Would Holtz and the players come to the rally? Would the coach give a talk tonight? Could you imagine the frenzy he could instill in this gathering of holiday revelers?

The drummers came down from their perch and joined the rest of the large marching band, all of its members assembling near the stage. From a makeshift podium several people were introduced and the speeches began. Dick Rosenthal reminded the crowd of the recent death of the school's former star athlete and longtime athletic director, recalling a few anecdotes about the deceased man. His words were constantly interrupted with cries of "Moooose! Moooose! Moooose!"

Tim Brown, a Dallas native in town for the game, told everyone how much he'd enjoyed playing football in South Bend and how much he missed the enthusiasm of Notre Dame, now that he was a pro. A few local Irish supporters spoke, and one of them, in the time-honored tradition of pep rallies, interviewed a make-believe Texas A&M Aggie, who was portrayed as both inarticulate and corrupt. This drew a few laughs, but the crowd was ready for something more. The Notre Dame glee club sang four or five classic Irish ballads, and then the leprechaun made his entrance, shouting into the microphone and asking everyone to give it up—"one final time this season, for the Fighting Irish and their head coach, Lou Holtz!"

People leaned far out of the balconies looking for the team and its leader. They craned their necks and twisted their heads. They asked more questions. They called Holtz's name, beseeching him to appear, although most of them knew that he never showed up at pep rallies before bowl games and would most likely not make an exception this year. They waited and hoped, clapping in time as the band played the Notre Dame victory march, and when the song had ended and things had finally grown somewhat calm, an announcement was made that neither the coach nor the squad would be present this evening because they were sequestered in preparation for tomorrow's game. A palpable rush of disappointment shot through the crowd, but the announcement went on to say that Holtz had tape-recorded a short message, which would now be delivered over the public address system.

The hall became quiet and the coach began to speak, explaining in a businesslike tone of voice that he always stayed with the team on the night before a bowl game and he saw no reason to change his routine. People nodded along with his words, accepting his point of view, but they were clearly pent up and had been looking forward to a massive catharsis—a release of what had been building in the room for the past few hours. They'd wanted to see Holtz in the flesh, to cheer him in person—to chant "Louuu!"—to feel the excitement he created by his command of English, perhaps to touch his arm. But he was absent.

Holtz also missed what the crowd gave him. His words were brief and never gained momentum, so it was like listening to a gifted orator whose magic had temporarily deserted him. Without people in front of him, without his uncanny ability to pick up what was in the air and turn it into language and fervor, without that subtle and remarkable exchange of energy that takes place between a speaker and his audience, Holtz didn't seem that involved in what he was saying.

The rally ended on a curiously empty note, almost as if the Cotton Bowl had already been lost and it was time to go back home. People looked at each other with an expression of Is-that-all-there-is? and then wandered out into the biting Dallas night, wrapping their garments tight against their necks and shoulders, a look of anticipation still in their eyes, wanting more from the coach than he could ever give them.

The windchill on New Year's morning made it sixteen degrees and the sky was overcast, with more threats of a downpour. A caravan of buses took the team and various Notre Dame officials over to the stadium early, arriving around ten A.M. for a noon start. Most of these people went to a scheduled brunch, but others scoured the many concession booths that were set up around the Cotton Bowl in an attempt to find a stocking cap or an umbrella.

The cold air brought on earaches, and if the rains came, it would be miserable in the stands. The stadium was located in East Dallas, in the middle of an elaborate fairgrounds, which featured art deco architecture with some thoroughly unexpected Egyptian overtones. The effect was surreal, as if you'd slipped out of Texas altogether and landed on the Giza plateau. If you'd been imbibing the night before, it was enough to make you swear off.

Near the stadium was a small restaurant jammed with Irish and Aggie fans, some of whom were trying to get warm and some of whom were trying to get drunk. One tall cowboy with a pasty hung-over complexion was leaning against the bar, sipping beer and talking trash about Notre Dame with a friend and to anyone else who would listen. He spoke much louder than necessary and allowed as how Texas A&M was about to destroy its unworthy Northern opponent. As he talked, he looked around warily, as if expecting someone to throw a punch his way, but most of the crowd was ignoring him. When it became apparent that he couldn't stir anyone to action, he stared at his companion, another beer-drinking Aggie supporter, and smiled.

"We're gonna kick butt," he said.

Just before the game the Irish players attached decals to their helmets that read MOOSE. At the opening kickoff, some people in the stands were talking about his spirit and where he might have been this morning, but one thing was certain and irrevocable: Moose wasn't humanly present and he'd left behind a void. This wasn't just because the Irish had lost a great football fan—perhaps the greatest fan of their team ever—or because many of the school's alumni and subway alumni had lost a friend. His absence was more distinctive than that.

No longer was there that one person among the entire Notre Dame faction whom people could seek out and shake hands with or pay homage to, as if in speaking to Moose Krause they were honoring Notre Dame herself. The living symbol, the man who'd joined the old triumphs and old decades to the new ones, was gone, and that breathing connection could not be replaced. Moose himself had become a part of her history.

At the start of the game, the Aggie rooters—they filled nearly the entire Cotton Bowl, covering it with maroon and white—were extremely vocal. They repeatedly sang their fight song and constantly performed the A&M cheers. Their voices sounded sharp and determined, like gunfire on a cold day.

The team's fans from College Station, where the school is located, were highly optimistic and had good reason to feel that way. Their team was not only 12-0 and playing what amounted to a home game, but their opponent, in the eyes of many people across the nation, should not even have been at the Cotton Bowl because of their one loss and one tie during the 1992 campaign. Aggie fans began the game by rooting with an almost mantralike intensity.

For quite a while both teams played as if frozen. On the Irish's first long drive, when it looked as though they might find the end zone, Reggie Brooks fumbled and A&M recovered. Notre Dame made several more mistakes, and it seemed as if their will to win had run out or their luck had finally gone sour.

But the Aggies were having their own problems scoring, and it was 0–0 with just thirty-six seconds left in the half when Rick Mirer threw a 40-yard touchdown pass to Lake Dawson. The Irish had gone ahead, but in the season just past, A&M had outscored its opponents 216–66 in the second half and had had seven come-from-behind victories. When the Irish ran toward their locker room at intermission, there was no reason to believe that a 7–0 lead was safe.

In the final thirty minutes of its gridiron year, Notre Dame played old-fashioned, run-it-right-at-you football—Moose Krause football—and the Aggies simply could not stop Reggie Brooks or Jerome Bettis. By the fourth quarter Brooks had gained 107 yards on the ground while the A&M team had 45. (For the game, the Aggies had a total of 145 yards rushing and passing, a defensive bowl record for the Irish defense.) During one stretch Notre Dame ran the ball on twenty-eight straight plays, and when they threw it again, they were leading 21–0 and the affair had long since been settled.

With five minutes left in the game, Bettis scored his third touchdown of the afternoon, and moments later Rick Mirer walked off the field for the last time in a blue-and-gold uniform. Holtz sent in the second-stringers, then went up to Mirer and gave him a warm smile, touching his shoulder pad and patting him gently on the helmet. The coach looked about ten years old.

The action on the field now took a backseat to the sideline appearance of a megastar, the rap singer Hammer, who was joking with several of the Irish players and having his picture taken. He had an animated conversation with Reggie Brooks, and would later be engaged as Reggie's agent in the forthcoming NFL draft. Brooks and Mirer were not the only big names who would be leaving the squad. A few days after the Cotton Bowl, Jerome Bettis and cornerback Tom Carter, both juniors, announced they would not return to Notre Dame for the '93 season but would go into pro football. This team, the one that was defeating Texas A&M so convincingly, was about to disappear.

The Irish won the game 28–3—it was the Aggies' worst bowl loss ever—and just before the clock ran out, two big Notre Dame linemen grabbed a Gatorade bucket and sneaked up behind their head coach, preparing to douse him with the icy liquid (and to get even for that Tuesday practice back in October). They approached Holtz quickly and stealthily, and when they were within a foot or two, they raised the lip of the bucket up past his neck, past his football cap, but at the last moment he turned and saw them and sidestepped the stream as it shot past his chest; it was a pretty fair symbol for how the whole season had gone for the coach. When he'd first seen the Gatorade coming, he'd looked alarmed and frightened, but then he pointed at the culprits and gave them his biggest grin of the day.

Ten seconds later the gun sounded and the Irish had beaten their last seven opponents, five of whom had been ranked. The next morning the Associated Press voted Notre Dame the fourth-best team in the nation, behind national champion Alabama, Florida State, and Miami. When the final poll was released, Holtz, as is often his bent at year's end after downplaying his team's ability during the course of the season, said that he felt the Irish were "the best team in the country right now." He also said that he thought this was his best Notre Dame team ever, including the '88 champions. If he'd needed another controversy, he'd hatched one right there.

With the game over, the Irish fans returned to the Loews Anatole and the victory parties began. After a while the team showed up and went into a private banquet room where they ate dinner and listened to country and rock music. When Holtz arrived, little children followed him through the lobby, squealing and thrusting pens and paper at him in order to get an autograph. He stopped and scribbled furiously, but it was apparent that he was eager to be with his team in its hour of celebration.

Inside the banquet room he sat with his wife and family, and for the first time since August he looked relaxed, truly relaxed, the long frown that had dogged him for months now gone and replaced by an almost permanent look of happiness. When the meal was finished, a space was cleared near the front of the room and a few of the huge brave players got out of their chairs, took their female companions by the hand, and began to dance.

Out in the lobby the parties continued, but they were not rowdy. They were barely jubilant. Notre Dame had flown down to Texas and done a workmanlike job—they'd beaten A&M with what could just about be called ease. Their fans were every bit as competitive as their coaches and players, and in the back of many minds was the question that was lately being posed by a wider and wider segment of those who follow college football.

What would happen if the Irish could now enter a play-off system and go up against the teams that were still ranked ahead of them? How good were they? Who would survive a tournament and become the unmistakable champion? There are no answers, but there is an adage about football teams that goes: over the full course of a season, they will either get better or they will get worse. This Irish team, after a shaky start in 1992, the last year that Moose Krause would see his beloved Notre Dame on the gridiron, had absolutely improved.

The '92 season, if nothing else, had proven that college football is the most unforgiving game of all. In other sports, including pro football, a team can have a bad day early in the year and fully recover a month or two later, or win it all if they get into the play-offs, but in college football you may never have a second chance. The loss to Stanford changed everything for the Irish, and even seven straight victories against quality opponents could not erase that one grim afternoon. The craziness of college football coaches can perhaps be understood a little better when you realize what a single lapse by their players can mean.

On that Friday night in Dallas the fans at the Loews Anatole had to be content with sitting in the lobby and watching the Sugar Bowl over in New Orleans, where Alabama drubbed Miami, Notre Dame's greatest rival in recent years. Judging from the yelps of pleasure that came out of this viewing audience and echoed through the hotel every time the Crimson Tide did something well and every time the Hurricanes faltered, it was a most enjoyable way to begin the new year.

What comes back most strongly now was the way Moose walked in parts—the same way a lot of old football players walk—and his laughter and the smell of those big cigars. You could almost hear the rumble in Moose's throat down there in the Cotton Bowl when the Irish finally broke open the game in the second half and began to dominate. You could hear the joy it gave him.

And whenever you'd spent a few hours with him, riding in his Cadillac or sitting in his office listening to him talk about Notre Dame football, that powerful smoke got ingrained in your clothes and your hair, so that when you'd meet people in the Irish athletic department, they'd smile at you and say, "You've been spending time with the Moose." Something about the tobacco fragrance was perfect, because it touched you sharply and left behind a rich, pervasive residue, staying with you long after you and the man had parted. In Dallas you could still pick up the scent.

Remembering Moose

"He's a man!
"Who's a man?
"He's a NOTRE DAME man!"

HOW OFTEN I HAVE HEARD THAT CHANT ABOUT SO MANY ATHLETES, coaches, or Notre Dame people. It was reserved for special occasions and for very special persons.

No one was more deserving of this than Edward "Moose" Krause. For more than six decades, he was a part of the Notre Dame scene and his football memories included personal experiences with every coach from Knute Rockne to present coach Lou Holtz.

It was my privilege to work under his direction for 11 years as the football coach at Notre Dame. And our friendship continued from my resignation until Moose's death.

Not once in my coaching years or since did we ever have an argument or a heated confrontation about any subject. And be assured that this is highly unusual, considering the pressures that are constantly faced by athletic director and head coach.

Ed Krause was a big man physically and his body included a huge heart and the great sensitivity that allowed him to be the calming voice in any discussion. He was able to pour soothing oil over any troubled waters.

It was his patience and surprising gentleness that made his relationship with staff, faculty, administration, alumni, and the general public so favorable and successful.

His dedication to his faith and to his marriage vows are to be admired and emulated. No one could have been more devoted to his wife than Ed was in the long years after an unfortunate automobile accident robbed her of a normal life.

In those years, Moose was able to serve his wife and able to fulfill all her needs. There was no better demonstration of great devotion to family and his religion.

Anyone who ever traveled anywhere with Moose realized very quickly how many friends he had. People waited in airports, in hotel lobbies, and outside the stadium just to say hello to Moose. He was, without question, the greatest ambassador of Notre Dame good will.

The images of Moose from his years as an outstanding Notre Dame football and basketball player to the Cotton Bowl hat and ever-present cigar will be remembered fondly by all those who knew him, at Notre Dame and around the nation.

It was a stroke of good fortune that in the last year of his life he decided to do a book about his Notre Dame experiences. Many of his memories of his athletic and administrative tenure are recorded here.

Death may have taken Moose, but he has left behind some wonderful stories about the many people he was associated with in his more than sixty years around Notre Dame.

I am sure you will enjoy these recollections.

—Ara Parseghian

ONE OF THE FIRST PERSONS WITH WHOM I CAME IN CONTACT when I came to Notre Dame was Moose Krause. I could never thank him enough for the way he treated me, and now he'll never know how much his friendship and guidance meant to me. He went out of his way to make me feel at home, and he was always tremendously supportive. Moose was as positive and optimistic as anyone I've ever been around—I couldn't help but feel better whenever I spent any amount of time with him.

As a history major, I've always been intrigued with the past coaches here at Notre Dame, and I've tried to read and learn as much about people like Knute Rockne, Frank Leahy, Ara Parseghian, and Dan Devine as I possibly could. In that context, I found Moose to be a fascinating individual because of his knowledge of history at Notre Dame. I can't tell you how many conversations we had, usually with me quizzing him about Rockne and Leahy and how they went about their jobs as head football coach. We talked about how they did things and why they were successful, and I quickly found that Moose had great insight in that area.

He and I played golf many times and I listened to him speak on so many occasions. I don't think I ever heard him not be positive about the future or about any other subject. In my first seven years here at Notre Dame, we've had some great wins and some disappointing losses. Moose never once failed to stop by my office to see me after a loss and he always found the positives in the situation. He would compare what happened in a particular game to something he'd remember from a Notre Dame historical standpoint. I tend to get rather depressed after losses, but Moose always made me feel better about what had happened and where we were headed.

I'll never forget the sight of Moose driving onto Cartier Field in his Cadillac to watch us practice. I found him to be keenly observant about defense. He would evaluate what we were doing in practice anytime I asked him, and he generally was right on the mark with his comments.

We have a Quarterback Club luncheon every Friday before home football games and Moose always sat on the dais with me. I don't believe he ever missed one of those luncheons. He had been retired for more than a decade, yet he remained one of the most popular people connected with the athletic program at Notre Dame. I never tired of listening to him. He had a knack for putting an audience in the palm of his hand. He might use the same favorite story on more than one occasion, but even if you'd heard some of Moose's lines before, you couldn't help but laugh. He was always so sincere, and yet you didn't have to be around him long to understand his dedication to his family as well as what an inspiration he has been to so many people who have come in contact with him at some point.

I had the opportunity several times to speak to the group of former Notre Dame players who played for Leahy in the '40s. Those individuals seem to have a special bond among themselves—they have a particularly strong feeling for Notre Dame—and they constantly expressed genuine love and affection for Moose. In fact, that group on two different occasions raised enough money to present cars to Moose, and they did it simply out of the goodness of their hearts. That's how they felt about Moose, and that was their way of showing him how much he meant to them.

I never met anyone who was as concerned about other people as Moose was. He constantly gave of himself, and he was most appreciative of anything you did for him. I would be down and he would come to see me and make a point of trying to make me feel better. In fact, the day before he died, Moose came by my office with his cowboy hat on and he couldn't wait to tell me how excited he was about the Cotton Bowl. He couldn't have been happier that we were going to Dallas, and he was going with us.

The one thing I appreciated most about Moose Krause is that he constantly went out of his way to make me feel like I belonged at Notre Dame. When you come here to coach football as I did—and maybe particularly when I was not fortunate enough to have gone to school at Notre Dame, nor have any previous ties to the university—some people want to hold you at arm's length until you prove that you belong. There was never a question with Moose. He was an integral part of Notre Dame and what it's been about since he came to school here in 1930. He let me know right away that I was wanted here and that I was a part of the Notre Dame family, and that meant a great deal to me.

I looked upon Moose as a perfect example of why Notre Dame has meant what it has to so many people over the years. He taught me a great deal about this place and the people who have come before me at Notre Dame. He was a joy to be with, whether it was at one of our scrimmages or whether we were visiting in the office. I always had a smile on my face when Moose left. The university has lost a member of the Notre Dame family whose true value to the institution may never be measured.

—Lou Holtz